The Second Purpose
A Search for Life's Meaning

Sean Gabriel McDonald

PublishAmerica
Baltimore

© 2003 by Sean Gabriel McDonald.
All rights reserved. No part of this book may be reproduced in any form without written permission from the publishers, except by a reviewer who may quote brief passages in a review to be printed in a newspaper or magazine.

First printing

ISBN: 1-59286-094-X
PUBLISHED BY PUBLISHAMERICA BOOK PUBLISHERS
www.publishamerica.com
Baltimore

Printed in the United States of America

To my family

ACKNOWLEDGMENTS

The author wishes to extend his gratitude to friends and companions in bringing our experiences to the pages of this book. A big thank you to Kevin Heckendorn, Martha Mallory and Bill Manahan; and to Kathleen and Eric Abley for their suggestions and comments which were invaluable to the structuring of the story.

I wish also to extend my appreciation to Pamela Fraser of the Landon library in the Old South, London, Ontario, for her inspiration, humor and critical support.

A special thanks to Gerry Suelzle, a fellow writer, who painstakingly sand-blasted my unspeakable grammar, spelling and sentence run-on and on and on and . . .

To Bill Delaney my business teacher at the FAS educational center in Tallagh, Dublin. To be sure, if it was not for Bill's steadfast encouragement, it is highly probable the book would not have been written. Thanks for the generous servings of percentage marks on my exams Bill – you were far too kind.

And to Ron Hall and Ron Tench of Malakwa, B C, who were instrumental in my survival as a woodsman. Without their ongoing support, both financially and mechanically, as a lumberjack, I would not have survived.

Last but not least, to my nieces Blaithin (Little Flower) and Raelteen (Little Star) also known as Tressa, whose coming to our world gave me a special sense of purpose to write the story.

And to their cousins Senan and Laragh of the House of Geraldine and to the newcomers - babbie Molly and big babbie Cian - a happy mind, a healthy body and a song in the heart to one and all.

CONTENTS

Scrambled Eggs	11
Off To School	12
Growing Things	15
Land Of Milk And Misery	16
On A Wagon Bound For Market	18
Confirmation	21
Rejection	27
Twins Ahoy!!	29
Bodenstown	29
Swing High Sweet Chestnut	32
Tessy's Flight	34
Schooldays Over	36
The Making Of A Soldier	45
Madmen And Foxes	50
The Dublin Zoological Gardens	51
Field Of Champions	54
The Land Of William Tell	55
Flambo Shaunessy And The Chocolate Waltz	58
In The Trenches	60
Good Christian Soldiers And The Congo	62
The Rocky Road To Spain	66
It's A Long Way To London	71
The Spud Diggers	78
Oh, Canada	87
Rebellion	90
Desperate Times	94
Tony McRedmond	98
The Great Warfield	103
The Blue Canadian Rockies	105
The Kidnappers	110
Bill Dooker, The Lumberjack	114
The Making Of A Lumberjack	119
The Great Cat Skinner	124

CONTENTS

The Jerk That Tried To Murder Me	127
To Hypnotize A Hen	130
The Glass Dancers	131
Pains Of The First Nation	133
The Makings Of An Entertainer	142
Tom Byrne, The Bear And The Fish	147
Hanging On By A Thread	152
We Expected You	154
A Lost Soul At The Concentration Camp Farewell Nipigon	157
A Drunken Fiasco	159
Greener Pastures	165
There's Gold In Them Thar Hills	166
Wedding On Lonesome Mountain And The Wild Women of Soccer	179
Sailor To The Recue And The Dirty Dancers	184
Nanaimo Bound And Blackbeards Pub	187
Among The Gods Of Thunder	191
Walking Upon The Waters	193
Reaching Out	196
Refuge In The Forest	197
A Light From Heaven	203
Fire On The Columbia	205
Ghost In The Forest	208
It's Not Wise To Jump On A Bear's Meal While He Is Eating It	210
The Brazen Porcupine	212
Chainsaws Maim And Kill	213
Rubber Boots, Underwear, And A Grizzly Bear	214
The Fish River Country	215
A Man With A Vision	227
Invasion Of The Martens	232
It's Time To Go Home	241
Blaithin (Little Flower)	244

THE SECOND PURPOSE

I was ten years old when I entered our home that soft summer's afternoon - my heart and mind distraught. The man of the Cloth had snubbed my request for membership to his church choir. It was not the snub of an untrained or inadequate singing voice that pained me but the callousness of the cold rejection.

I came from what was deemed a poor corner of the world. The man of God with whom I had spoken favored those choir aspirants who exhibited a mark of affluence about them – I did not fit the bill. It was an unkind moment for me as I looked to the air to see the finger of the priest point towards the land from whence I came – Perrystown. However, my troubled heart soon found new interest in the strange but beautiful quietness beneath the roof of our cottage when I returned there. Such tranquility was not a common visitor to the house. Shrugging my shoulders, I walked to my bedroom and upon entering, I observed two dresser drawers open, and in each, a sleeping new born baby. Perceiving the entities hitherto unknown to our domain, I took to fright and ran from the house out the back door and into brother Gerrard who stood near by holding something that looked like a bicycle.

"What the hell's the matter with you John? Where are you rushing? Settle down a minute… I got you a new bike," Gerrard said in his calm but definite way.

"You got me a new bike!" I exclaimed. "That lump of rust looks like it was rejected at the scrap yard and you have the nerve to say you got it for me!" I blurted indignantly.

"Now hold on a sec, John. It just needs a little oil, a pedal, a wheel, a saddle and brakes and you're in business. I got it for you because I know you want to go to the mountains and the old bike, once it is fixed up will give you that freedom you're always talking about. Now say thank you and shut up with your bloody complaining or I'll fix it up for myself and then you'll be jealous," Gerrard fired at me.

"Okay, Ger," I said, accepting his rust ridden gift and, then almost as an after-thought, I asked him who owned the babies in the room.

"What babies?" He bellowed.

"They're in our room sleeping with lovely smiles on their faces and I don't know where they came from," I said as calmly as an excited octopus.

"You must have a bit of a fever John… maybe you need to take a few spoonfuls of cod liver oil," Gerrard said as he unburdened himself with the remains of the bike.

"I'm serious! There are two babies in our room… where's Dad and Mum?" I asked.

"They're in the garden, chatting," said Gerrard. Ignoring Gerrard and his lump of rust I took off to find my parents.

"Mum, Dad," I shouted as soon as I saw them. "There are two babies in the bedroom that I never saw before and I don't know whom they belong to. You better come and look," I shouted anxiously.

"John, John, John, its alright, everything is alright," said my mother, seemingly amused at my concerned behavior. "The babies are your new sister and brother." And so it was, the last born to our home were our twins, Marien and Joseph.

Such was life in our home at Perrystown. Surprises came in abundance and when the front door was jammed with a rush of them, the excess came in through the back entrance; our home was a busy place. I was the fourth eldest of eleven children – six boys and four girls. However, our first-born, sister Margaret, was not destined to be with us long, she died in infancy.

Fighting and arguing were a massive part of our family's make up and to find respite from the madness of it all, sister Tereasa often asked Mother to sing the song, "The Kerry Dances." That enchanting piece of music never failed to subdue the wildness of us children as Mum's exquisitely trained soprano's voice lulled the maddening banter to tranquil bliss.

> *O the days of the Kerry dance*
> *O the ring of the pipers tune*
> *O for one of those hours of gladness*
> *Gone alas like our youth to soon*
>
> *When the boys began to-gather*
> *In the glen on a summer's night*
> *And the Kerry piper's tuning*
> *Made us long with wild delight*

And all too soon the magic of the melodious moments gave way once again to wild activity. Such was life, life at its finest, inside the thick granite walls of our little fortress.

Our humble cottage was built around the turn of the twentieth century in the countryside southwest of Dublin city, not more than four miles from the foot of the Dublin Mountains. It consisted of two small bedrooms, a smaller living room, also used for sleeping quarters, a tiny kitchen and a wee concrete outhouse. At the rear of the house a quarter acre of rich fertile land gave rise to wholesome vegetables which Dad grew year around. Some of the produce was sold at the city market, some shared with the neighbors and the rest consumed with much delight around the kitchen table. He also raised hens, chickens, some turkeys, noisy geese, noisy us, ducks, pigs, and was never without a horse.

My father worked in general construction, which means he could have built palaces and cottages without the aid of architects, blueprints and helpers and, he worked hard. At times he had to cycle up to ten miles a day on a one speed Raleigh bicycle that by its robust design may well have been capable of taking its traveler safely over Mount Everest. That Raleigh came equipped with one speed only (fifteen to thirty speeds less than bikes have today) but it was as constant in its faithful delivery of Dad to the work site as it was maintenance free. Those times were grueling for my father; working ten to twelve hours a day, cycling home and then tackling the chores of garden and livestock. His was not an easy life but he never complained. He simply took what life threw at him and dealt with it, but there were times when the resilience and mettle of the man were tested to the fullest.

The hours had ticked by into the late of evening. Concern for his whereabouts gathered some measure when Mother threw a floating question to her offspring - "I wonder where he is? It's not like him to be home late for supper," Mum said in her quiet but inviting way. Such uneasy questions were usually followed with a perturbed silence, then a request to one of the family to throw a head or an eye out the window to scan the street for the one missing. It was brother Tommy who threw his eye out the window that particular night of long ago, and indeed, he did spot the chief strolling home without his faithful bicycle.

"Here he comes ma, but he doesn't have Bessie with him," Tommy shouted, his head stuck on the other side of the house roaring in the news. With that piece of welcome information we awaited Dad's presence expectantly.

As he always did, Dad entered the home in a quiet, unassuming way, removed his heavy Crombie coat while singing his unique, dissonant composition absent of the slightest rhythmic inflection, *di di di di di di di di,* then planked his weary frame upon a chair whose wholesome support of earlier times had diminished to a constancy of creaks and groans when engaged in a sitting. "Here's your dinner Lar and for heaven's sake, what kept you out so long? I was worried sick about you," said Mum as she placed a plateful of spuds, topped with a part of a cooked pig on the table in front of Dad's nose and continued with the question. "In the name of His Holy Mother, just what kept you Lar? You really did have me worried sick"

An answer never came too quickly from Dad and that evening the response was just as unhurried. A slow chewing of the spuds and bacon, followed by a deep breath, then a wiping of his chin with the back of his hardy hand gave some indication he might be considering an explanation. "You'll never believe this May," he eventually said to Mum and without another word attended his dining with the finesse and dignity a bricklayer might afford the mixing of his mortar.

"What would I not believe, Lar," Mum quietly but persistently prodded. After a repeat of the distinct dining characteristics peculiar to Dad, he at last gave account of his mysterious ordeal.

"Well, May,... as I was saying. You'll never believe what happened to me this evening," Dad's somber voice at last said. "You see, May, after I got off work I dropped into the chapel on Aungier St to say a few prayers and... be the hokey... when I came out, Bessie was missing," he said mournfully. "Can you imagine, May, some sleeveen (sly person) taking my Bessie while I was in communicating with our creator? Sure that's going beyond the beyonds altogether," he concluded with a slow shaking of his head, indicating that he could not fathom the act of an individual stealing a bike from outside a consecrated building, and his bike at that!

"Don't worry, God will work out something for you Lar," Mums said, injecting a little spiritual hope into the gloomy situation. "He's very good like that." She continued. "He will see to it that you're not without a bike for very long. Isn't that right, Tommy?" Mother said, drawing our eldest brother into a conversation he wanted no part of.

Tommy who was steeply absorbed in his school studies raised his head slowly locking his gaze onto the borders of the flowery patterned wallpaper and there his stare remained. Did he hear what he heard or did he not? It was easy to ascertain by the unflinching gravity of his focus, that what Mum had just said was the sole occupation of his mind. But if there was the slightest doubt about what was said to him, it was quickly put to rest, as Mum continued. "If there was ever a boy in the world with a heart of gold, it is you Tommy and I know you will be happy to lend your brand new bike to your Daddy until he gets another one." And to our brother's chagrin and Dad's surprise, that was how God found a replacement for Bessie.

Nevertheless, there was no doubt that Dad was close to being broken hearted over the loss of his bike but it was not just the theft of Bessie that brought him to dismay. It was the stealing of his transportation – his and the family's lifeline to food on the table. Mother, too, was not spared the harshness of poverty; her difficulties were many as they were varied.

When the gales of winter swept in from the Atlantic, they spared naught that stood against them. These were the pitiless winds that time and again snapped the clothesline, when after hours of exhausting labor - scrubbing laundry in cold water over an old washboard in a tin tub, send the wash into the muddy ground of the back yard. It saddened me to see the pained expression on mother's face as she picked the mud-ridden clothes from the syrupy mire to begin the back breaking chores over again. But mother's inner strength never surrendered to self-pity. She was courageous and gracious, accepting the torments of poverty with quiet dignity, sacrificing every breath for the love and care of her children. This lady with the golden voice, a smile that lit the world and a heart overflowing with laughter infused joy and hope into our meager world. This woman, my mother, had indeed come from the place of Angels.

And it had to be, that she indeed did come from the place of angels because any other mother would have had, I'm sure, difficulty in not strangling me. My nature as a child was as wild as a hurricane.

SCRAMBLED EGGS

The clucking of the hen caught my attention, an indication that perhaps an egg had been laid. I went to the shed where she did such things and ruffled her feathers while I eyed for shelled contents in her nest. I was not disappointed. Three warm, brown eggs dotted the cozy straw bowl. Without a thought for the creature that bore them, I tucked the eggs into the cuff of my arm and raced to the house. In the kitchen, I gazed up towards the corner of the wall, took aim and fired each egg in succession into its pit. As the yellow and white contents of the shell slid slowly down the pale, green colored wall, I was imbued with disappointment that I did not have many more eggs to smash. As my mind wandered with the slithering of the yellow yolk, I was quietly but firmly awakened to the fact that I was not a lone spectator.

"Jesus, Mary and Joseph, John! What have you done now? You've just gone and smashed your father's breakfast against the wall! Now he'll have to go to work without a bit in his stomach… shur it will be a wonder if he doesn't drop dead from the hunger! Now listen to me carefully, John. You are just going to have to leave the hens alone. You're going to worry them sick and they will not be able to lay another egg, and then we'll be in a worse situation all together. Now promise me that you won't go raiding the hen's nest in the future and I won't say a word about this to you're Daddy." Instead of getting a richly deserved clout on the behind, my mother just sighed as she had done so many times and searched for a cloth to wipe clean the shell flaked streams of yellowish slime from the kitchen wall.

OFF TO SCHOOL

Shortly after my fifth birthday Mum walked me to the school at the Presentation Convent – a day, long awaited by Mum. With my absence from the house, Mum could enjoy a few hours of well deserved peace and quiet. The time of learning had arrived for little John. I stood in the grayness of a long corridor of tall, dull-yellow walls as my mother soothed my uncertainties. Eventually, two Sisters appeared. "We'll take John from here, Mrs. McDonald," said one of the Sisters.

"Now be a good boy, John, and do what the Sisters ask of you," said Mum. With those words, I was released to the care and protection of the good nuns at the presentation Convent, Terenure.

However, as I watched my mother fade to the distance of the dark corridor I panicked; my wails, like long, forlorn howls of a timber wolf piercing the shadowy glares of my confines. But the good Sisters, having much experience with howling children, simply dragged me by my outstretched arms into the unknown. My yowls of despair diminished to sobs of sulking resignation, then to muffled sniffs as I was deposited beyond the threshold of a dreary windowless door. In the silence of the classroom, I stood gawking through fearful tears 'ore a flock of little heads into the light past the window. I wanted out, to be free again. But I was trapped and like wounded prey I slunk into a seat beside a little blond haired girl by the name of Carmel. Thus began my education.

I liked Carmel even though she spoke to me much of the time through a membrane of chewing gum. Often after much chewing of the gum, Carmel formed great balloons outside her lips and exploded them over her face. This she did with great regularity and expertise. To see her cute, innocent face disappear behind a pink balloon and reappear again after she detonated it was indeed entrancing. Although Carmel shared her spearmint gum with me, I could never get the hang of making balloons like Carmel did, no matter how hard I tried.

Trying to form a nice big bubble like Carmel generally resulted in my blowing spittle spray over Fiona Sullivan who unfortunately sat directly in front of me. Sometimes, the dear little darling got a belt of the whole piece of gum which flew out of my mouth at an impressive speed meshing solidly with her beautiful mop of blazing red curls. "Stop that John Mc or I will tell Sister Rafeal about you spiting at me," Fiona would say with an exasperated sigh, indicating that she really did not want to do such a thing but if I kept spitting at her she would have no choice but to report me. Then, one day, the eyes of Sister Rafeal locked on to a piece of gum as it flew through the air

It was not targeted for any particular mischief but the eventual resting place of the airborne missile was surprising. It found a home in Desmond D'Sleepon's ear. The landing of the misdirected missile did not go unnoticed. Sister Rafeal was a kind nun and as she sat looking at me, I could instinctively tell that she really wanted to burst out laughing but that would be improper behavior for our teacher to exhibit and add only to Desmond's disgruntlement. As I awaited the results of the silent judgment which was being calculated by my teacher with the help of a massive intake of air and there held immovable by her lungs, so too, became immovable all parts of me; even my thoughts were held from rambling prior to the moment of sentencing.

"What did I see you doing, John McDonald? Did I see you throw something across the room at one of the boys?" Sister Rafeal said in her lovely soft voice as though she would rather treat me to a bowl of ice cream instead of throwing me through the window. As I sat in my seat awaiting the worst, Carmel, quietly but firmly slipped her hand into mine and held it in a lovely innocent show of support only children can effect. "Say you're sorry for what you have done and I will let it pass this time but if I catch you again John McDonald I shall have to deal with you a little differently. Do you understand, John McDonald?" Sister Rafeal said as she crossed her arms and lay back comfortably in her chair sporting a slight but indulgent smile.

Looking across the room, my eyes fell upon Desmond D'Sleepon who poked intensely with his index finger into the great yawn in the side of his head, digging for the slightest remains of the gum that might have insisted on staying in its new home. He seemed satisfied with the final effort of his search as he plucked a teeny, weeny bit of gum from somewhere in his ear and added it to the lump in his hand which he was exhibiting to the class as though it was something of immense value, worthy to be sold at the auction block.

"We're waiting John Mc," said Sister Rafeal as I hummed and hawed about the apology I was to present, not because he didn't deserve an apology but because I never told anyone as far as I could remember that I was sorry for something out of line that I did and I wondered why Desmond D' Sleepon should have that honor. "Today would be a good time to say your sorry, John Mc, as we really do not have the whole day for you to say your sorry for your little misdeed," Sister Rafeal urged, her lovely voice growing softer by the word but exhibiting within its tone, the urgency of her request. But saying sorry for lobbing a bit of chewing gum into Desmond's ear was proving difficult for me. No matter how hard I tried, the word sorry refused to budge from the vocal controls. I began to act as though I had a case of elephant hiccups and this proved embarrassing for me as all eyes turned to lock on to the little frame of John Mc as he blurted and blurted but blurted nothing of a distinguishable apology. I felt, to be sure, my end had come as the good Sister rose from her seat and moved swiftly towards me.

Above my little frame appeared a long arm veiled in black and at the end of the arm, a graceful hand that descended with lightening speed stopping abruptly between my shoulder blades. Sister Rafeal was no slouch in the department of timidity as her thundering thump brought my elephant hiccups to an end. "It's proving difficult for you John Mc, to say your sorry but I'll keep it in mind and let it go this time. Perhaps you can tell Desmond another time that you are sorry for planting chewing gum in his ear," and with that comment the good Sister dismissed the class for recess. In the freedom of the convent playground, I searched out Desmond and apologized to him. He just laughed, clapped me on the back and said, "great shot Macker, don't worry, I'll get you another time," and with that exchange of words we became good friends.

Slowly the time passed to that day when the lads continued their education at the boys-school - St. Joseph's, Terenure. That day came when I was seven years old, the day I would say good-bye to my Carmel and Fiona forever. According to the teachings of the Catholic Church, seven is the age of reason and the age when boys and girls start giving each other the eye. It is time for the opposite sexes to be removed from the seeds of temptation.

There were two things I liked about St. Joseph's; the school had the namesake of one of my brothers and I loved looking at the picturesque scenes of the countryside on the Esso calendars, which hung on the walls of the classrooms. Such beauty beyond the cities mesmerized me. I wanted so much to be free - to get up from my seat and walk into the picture of the luscious countryside depicted on the calendar but a slap across the back of the head from my teacher snapped me back to reality. Still, I would drift back to the lure of the lands without buildings and smoke stacks. The molding of the wanderer was taking shape right in my classroom and I longed for the day I would be free, to see and experience the openness of the natural world far from the congestion of urban life.

GROWING THINGS

Helping Dad work the garden was something I loved and it gave me some respite from my yearning for the hills, particularly when the seeds were sown in the springtime. In the morning, before setting out for school, I would visit the garden to see if the seeds had sprouted their little green faces above the ground. This was the magic of my childhood - lost in wonderment by the neat rows of tiny seedlings peering through their blanket of dewy, cloaked earth. This was my Eden, my sanctuary. All that was lovely and natural in my world was here. However, a seed of another nature in that same garden would take root in the deep recesses of my young mind, left there to lie contentedly dormant, then to chip away in its own good time at the natural goodness of my life, physically and psychologically scarring every decent fiber within my soul, eventually; drawing me into the very pits of hell.

Busy at my weeding chores in my patch of earthy plants, I was not surprised to see Jiggs, a man who had helped Dad prepare the garden on numerous occasions make his way along the garden path towards me, an assortment of garden tools resting across his shoulder. Jiggs was by all accounts a good and pleasant person and while we chatted about the nature of things, from his back pocket, he removed a flat bottle of amber liquid, whereupon he pulled the cork from its neck, placed the bottle to his lips and swallowed a mouthful of its contents. I watched in amazement as his cheeks appeared to wobble around the back of his neck and slip quickly back to there proper resting places only to repeat the process several times until his lips made an enormous sucking motion, followed by a great churning and protrusion of the Adam's apple, then, finishing the unusual ritual with a massive burp; a huge discharge of foul smelling breath and finally, the long, flat sounding haaaaaaaaaa.

"Ah be the lord Harry, that was a fine belt indeed," he declared, followed with a dirty big belch that apparently indicated the purity and quality of the drink. I asked him what was in the bottle and he answered in a hushed voice as one might confess their greatest sins to a Jesuit, hoping that the priest was hard at hearing – that it was a "drop of the pure," John Powers whiskey and, that it did him the world of good. "Here," he said. "Don't tell your mother or dad that I let ye have a little sniff of the bottle," as he placed it under my nose. Immediately I pulled back from the foul smelling odor and asked him how could he possible drink something that smelled so revolting? "Give it time and it will make a real man out of ye," he said as he corked the bottle and placed it back in his pocket.

They were the words that stuck in my mind. "Give it time and it will make a real man out of you". No doubt, I wanted to be a real man and I reasoned that it would indeed take a real man - a very brave one to accustom their senses to the revolting smell I had just experienced and, then, to drink the stuff? That would indeed take a real man and a real man I wanted to be. I would ponder the words the gardener had imparted to me and keep them safe in the far reaches of my mind until I was old enough to embark on my career of being a real man. In the meantime, help was needed in paying the endless bills at home. It was time to find a part time paying job.

LAND OF MILK AND MISERY

I stood knee high below the big boss man's intimidating frame. He asked me if our family was a good and faithful customer of his Dairy Company. I told him our family was and went on to embellish the lie ten-fold. I expressed our family's devotion to his moo, moo and that my dear mother bought loads and loads of milk and everyone in the family loved drinking it, including our visitors who came from all over Ireland and even one or two from Russia. He eyed me with that suspicious look which only a Dubliner can give and then asked me how large a family I belonged too. I told him at least twenty-five and Ma and Dad promised new members would be coming soon. The great overweight giant intensified his look of suspicion, and then cast his eyes to the sky as though he was asking someone for forgiveness in case he made error in judgment by hiring me. He then wiped his forehead with an arm that resembled the leg of a hippopotamus and continued asking me questions about the validity and honesty of my family.

"Twenty five in yer family?" he eventually said.

"Yes sir, and more will be coming and that's a promise," I answered enthusiastically.

"And how much does your mother spend every week on milk," he asked.

"At least forty shillings," I replied, which was a dirty big lie because I knew Dad earned only thirty shillings per week.

He eyed me with that look with which only the face of a dead haddock can effect and said. "Ye say your name is McDonald?"

"Yes sir," I answered.

"O. K, be down here at four in the morning and ask for Pat and if there's an outstanding balance on your family's account, we'll deduct it from your wages."

Four a.m. came far too early for me. It was off to dairy land to meet with Pat, the driver of the horse drawn wagon filled with crates of milk for delivery. I hated the job. Bitterly cold winter mornings, half asleep, I moved as only the miserable do in their hopelessness and desperation - reaching, grasping and clinging to each step of mystical pain. It seemed I moved through the land of the frozen dead, placing sickly white icy bottles of nourishment by doors of well - kept secrets. Those who dwelled within were the chosen, the gifted, the blessed; I should be so honored to serve my fellowman. But ungloved hands, chilled claws retreating into long sleeves, hiding from winter's harshness gave rise to great discontent within my heart. If this was my song of life, the lyrics were going to be changed.

Still, as miserable as the job was, without Ned, it would have been more difficult. I always viewed Ned as an elephant without trunk and tusks; he was so massive. This magnificent Clydesdale, as gentle in nature as a soft summer breeze, was thoroughly devoted to hauling our wagonload of moo. Indeed, Ned seemed to feel and understand the extent of his helper's discontent as my mind limped against fate's miseries, particularly on Friday morning when a three fold delivery was made to supply our customers for the weekend. Ned's head never failed to follow my movements, waiting and watching patiently while his helper coursed the darkness searching for gate latches and door steps, where upon I would deposit bottles of nourishment for sleeping people. Upon my return, he would nod his massive head, indicating he was pleased with my efforts as he clomped on to the gateway of the next customer, the piercing echo of his steel shoed hooves clip-clopping to the rhythmic swing of a grandfather's clock, interrupted occasionally by the melodious warble of the songbirds as the strength of darkness slowly gave way to a new dawn. When deliveries were finished, it was home for breakfast and then to school. I arrived in class tired. Great yawns were frequent, followed by slaps across the back of the skull, compliments of my teacher who found my oral statements unwelcome and disturbing. It was hard for me to concentrate on the teachings of my masters. It was hard to listen and learn while being tired and fearful. It didn't have to be that way but it was.

ON A WAGON BOUND FOR MARKET

Father's devotion to gardening rewarded him with healthy vegetables and greens, particularly cabbages, which he seemed to hold favor for and winter was just as cooperative as summer in producing his leafy favorites. When the crop was abundant, Dad and Tessy delivered the excess to the central market but when Dad was called to construction work weekends, other arrangements were made for their delivery.

Sleep was hard to ignore as father's voice broke the little snores of the early morning. "Come on lads... time to get up to pull the cabbages. Come on boys... Tommy, Larry, John, Liam... time to get up and wring the necks of the Savoies (name of the cabbages). There's a bit of a frost on the ground, so throw your coats on and put some socks on your hands to keep them warm (we couldn't afford gloves). I've got to be at work this morning, so Tommy, you will have to drive Tessy to the market, and you, Larry and John, might as well go with him," he said almost as an after thought. At that moment I wanted to be in Liam's shoes because Liam was going back to a nice cozy bed after he pulled his cabbages while his brothers three were going on a winter survival mission.

"Come on now, up yis get... I'll get Tessy ready while yis are pulling yourselves together. Now I want yis to listen carefully! I don't want to come back from the yard and find yis are all back sleeping... de yis hear me?" Dad said in a quiet but determined tone.

"O Godddeee Almighteeeeee! Alright, we'll be along in a few seconds daaa," Tommy said with as much enthusiasm as one might display when walking to their own execution. And with those miserable words ringing in our ears, we reluctantly crawled out from under our toasty blankets to face the chill of a bitter winter's morning, to pull cabbages from the frozen ground

THE SECOND PURPOSE

Plucking cabbages in the dark while sleep walking in a frost bitten land is difficult. Not a word was uttered as our little group stumbled around the garden, wringing the necks of cabbages and stacking them pyramid shaped on top of the cart, their spiral shaped hearts, protruding like petite, green, frosted warheads. "I'll give you sixpence, Larry, if you pluck my cabbages," I eventually said, my mind dabbing at the notion that it should send its body back to bed.

"And where did you get sixpence, John? Did you rob the bank last night?" Larry said fully aware that all I wanted to do was sneak back to bed and leave the cabbage plucking to my brothers.

"No but I'll get it for you and that's a promise. Really I will," I blustered, my words falling limp to the cold darkness. But Larry was having nothing to do with my buy and sell pitch because he knew, as I did, that I just wanted to go back to bed and to hell with the hardy, frosted cabbages. Still it was worth a try, even though it was a pathetic one. Two hours of miserable, bitter labor at four o' clock in the dark of the morning did nothing to stimulate my love for life and it broke my heart to see my brother Liam wave good bye to us as he made his way back to his cozy bed after the wringing and stacking was completed.

Out through the heavy steel gates, Tessy hauled our cart of cabbages to the voice of Larry singing the words of Molly Malone while Tommy and I joined in the chorus.

> *In Dublin's fair city where the girls are so pretty*
> *I first set my eyes on sweet Molly Malone*
> *As she wheeled her wheel barrow through*
> *Streets broad and narrow, crying cockles*
> *And muscles, alive, alive o*
> *Chorus*
> *Alive, alive o- alive, alive o*
> *Crying cockles and muscles Alive, alive o*

A fine cart load of the green darlings could fetch up to thirty shillings (three dollars) and that amount of money, although small, would help aid the family in paying the bills. Although it was a tough go, the effort of getting the cabbages to the market was worth the effort. Still, traveling by horse and cart through the busy morning traffic to the Central market was a dangerous task. It took courage to tackle such an undertaking - steel nerves when the roads harbored black frost.

Above the city on the high banks of the south west side, Christ Church cathedral, built by the Normans, dominated the landscape as it had done for a thousand years. Huddled together on the front seat of the cabbage cart, overlooking Tessy's rear end, we thought it suicidal to descend the icy slopes by Christ Church cathedral and, no doubt, so did Tessy. But it had to be done. To circumvent this route would have meant going through the horrible traffic congestion in the heart of Dublin. Undertaking the treacherous descent of Christ Church hill seemed a more attractive alternative route to the market, which lay, not far to the north side of the Liffey River.

"Go on now, Tessy, love," The voice of Tommy urged as he gently shook the reins across our Tessy's back. And as Tessy pulled the cart forward, she gently shook her thick coated main, an indication, that she did not want to be blamed for the harebrained venture if things went wrong but she was prepared to engage the impossible.

It took raw courage to tackle the slippery slopes of that ice bound hill but that is something Tommy had and it was to be tested to the fullest that frost ridden Saturday morning. He was eleven years old, two years between him and Larry and four from me. "Hold on for all you're worth, this is going to be a rough ride," Tommy warned as he encouraged our noble Tessy beyond the safety of the hill's crest. Obediently, Tessy went forth and as she did, she hunched on her hind legs bringing most of her weight to bear on them, simultaneously angling her front ones slightly forward, pressing her steel spiked shoes into the veil of snowy ice and slowly but deliberately descended the perilous grade, foot by fearful foot until she had us delivered safely to the flat streets by the market place on the north side of the Liffey river.

Life for Tessy was not easy either. It was rare for her to have a day off. Her chores were continuous; hauling pig feed, hay feed, cabbages, spuds and the plough. And if that was not enough to drain her energy, she also hauled the family each Sunday during summer to the beach at Mount Merrion, a sea resort, some eight miles from our home. Here, in the allure of it all, Dad rode Tessy bare back across the silvery beach, galloping through the lapping waves of the ebb tide; the squawk of the seagull high on the wind, like some jeering portent stabbing the void between the earth and heavens. This wonderment of nature gripped me to the very core and I knew in my heart that the openness of the world was the essence that would nurture my spirit. Even at the age of seven, the smell of the ocean and what lay beyond the hues of its horizon beckoned to my curiosities and, to be sure, there would be no true peace in my heart until the roadways to the world lay open to me; the seeds of the wanderer were taking root. At school, in my classroom, such cultivation did not go unnoticed.

"And is Mr. McDonald with us today or is he lost at some crossroads in Sweden?" the teacher said as a grubby cigarette butt peered out from the corner of his lips like a little mouse viewing its last moments on earth from the jaws of a cat. My teacher, Mr. G, was truly an advertising icon for the tobacco companies. I often felt that it was not possible for Mr. G to see the pupils in his classroom because of the smoke screen he set up in front of his face when he exhaled the mists of Hades from the bowels of his lungs. But he did see through the fog and when I got his attention it was not for my academic brilliance. I always ignored the call of my teacher when his sights bore down on me but an elbow from my seatmate confirmed my worst fears; my little frame was the subject of the lord of the class.

A switch to my Gaelic name followed when my whereabouts was demanded. "Sean Mc Domnaill from the land of lostness, it's the strap ye'll be getting if ye continue your insolence," he'd say, with a look of exasperated determination. Then with that air of great authority, he'd continue from behind the smoky veils. "I've been watching ye for the past half hour staring at the calendar on the wall and if it is not too much trouble, would ye redirect your focus on your text book and at least pretend you're part of the class," he'd conclude. It was wonderful to hear him make such a comment because now I felt that I could just pretend to learn and all would be well but I was mistaken, badly mistaken.

CONFIRMATION

I was now ten years old and being of the Catholic faith, the time came for me to make my confirmation - the sacred act of being confirmed into the Catholic folds. My mother managed to scrape enough money together to buy a new blazer, new pants, shoes, socks and cap. I wasn't used to the feel of new clothes and felt uncomfortable wearing them. Mum said that I looked like the cheese. Looking like the cheese is a term of endearment, meaning one is gifted in deceiving themselves. A big white rosette with cute little ribbons dangling from the lapel of my burgundy blazer seemed to imply I was something very special – to be presented to the Angels that watched over me. Beneath the rim of my cap, my snowy colored fringe of hair danced in the light summer breeze as Mum and I walked to St Joseph's Church that day.

Outside the church, my classmates, like me, seemed to have been transformed from rags to riches. We had some difficulty identifying each other because none of us had ever seen the other dressed up to the nines. There we were, all nice, clean and tidy, refraining from beating each other (common behavior during regular school hours) while our mums chatted about this and that and the other, each mum seemingly very proud of her boy's ascendancy to the tenets of higher spiritual values. Looks are indeed deceiving, because, although we, the ones to be confirmed, looked everything that may have been intellectually primed at the finest Irish colleges, the outcome of the special event was to prove disastrous and this statement was given proof by the look of murder so eminently displayed on the face of our teacher, Mr. G, after we had taken our seats in the church and the ceremony began.

Before the act of Confirmation takes place, it's the practice of the Church to question the pupils on the knowledge of their Catechism – Christian teachings. Months of religious instruction prepared us for all and any questions that may be asked of us by his eminence, the Archbishop of Dublin. As we took our seats in the pews, we did so with the comfort and confidence that we knew more about religious matters than the Great God. Our mums, church and country would indeed be very proud of our group of theosophical elite.

"And who is responsible for the death of Jesus on the Cross," the Archbishop asked Patrick O' Flynn who sat beside me in the long pew. Patrick took to muteness as he gawked into somewhere. The Archbishop looked as though he was a veteran of such answers and smiled the smile that suited the answer. "Anyone else like to attempt answering my question?" the Archbishop asked politely. Flannery Daley, who hardly said a word in class, extended his hand to the air, indicating he would like to share his knowledge on such historical religious matters. "Yes, please do answer my son," the Archbishop said, pointing to Flannery.

"The soldier with the steel helmet and a long spear killed our Lord Jesus Christ," Flannery said confidently.

It was at this moment the look of murder was most eminently displayed upon the face of our teacher, and unfortunately for him he could not sink down through the marble tiles upon which he stood. Intuitively, I felt he wanted to call us a bunch of elite morons but it was not the time or place to express the truth in the matter. However, the good Archbishop was undeterred by our exceptional performance of stupidity. "You there my son, can you tell me who killed Jesus our Savior," he said, pointing at Desmond Slaney who sat near the far end of the pew. I was hoping Desmond would get it right because it seemed our teacher was not doing well concealing his fury towards us.

"Pontius Pilot killed our Lord at the desire of the Jews, your Eminence," Desmond said with a touch of authority.

"Excellent, excellent indeed," said the Archbishop as he walked away, ending the humiliation for our teacher

However, it seemed ambiguity was the only element of religious learning that clawed its way into my mind and took firm root there. I was truly left to wonder if the Jews were right in believing that the man who claimed to be the Son of God was indeed an impostor. Was the true Jesus Christ crucified or was the man who died on the cross a false prophet? It was a good question. After all, I could not see the necessity for the Master of the Universe to subject Himself to such agonizing humiliation as was demanded by those who supposedly condemned Him. What reason would it serve? Who was telling the truth and who was lying? I had no idea. To subject a young mind to the contemplation of the figure of a man nailed, bloodied and dead on a cross is a form of mental torture in itself, serving no purpose other than causing confusion and revulsion to the innocent mind.

Why such a preoccupation with the ritual of blood sacrifice – that murder which seems to fascinate much of mankind? It all seems so wrong, so very, very wrong and counterproductive to the development of man as a spiritual being. However, what was beginning to emerge from the confusion brought about by religious dogmas and fear based teachings was the forming of my own ideas on the life and times of Jesus Christ but they were never allowed to ripen, at least not as a child. Nevertheless, it was hard to believe why a Man would sacrifice Himself for such a worthless cause, when two thousand years later, very few seemed to have gotten the message of what the Son of God was all about. In His Name, we are still murdering, butchering, plundering and raping all that is within the realms of mankind and it seems it is not about to stop. The very act of Jesus casting the salesmen from the Temple; those who would defile His sacred halls has come to stay with us down through the ages as we may well bear witness to those who manipulate His name for greed and power's sake. To be sure, I found the teachings of my church difficult to understand and frightening in the extreme.

Fear of burning in Hell for all eternity was something I just could not comprehend and I felt that if God meted out such unspeakable punishment to people, no matter what rotten thing they did, He could not possibly be a loving, forgiving and caring God. What could an individual do so wrong that he or she would be sent to burn for a never-ending life-time? This was a tough revelation for my mind to absorb and as much as I tried to comprehend such a God fearing sentence, the psychological implication of such barbaric religious dogmas served only to confuse me and fill my mind with fear, a fear that has never released its ugly grip from my mind.

Attending mass was less enjoyable than going to school and I did it from the dread of the Great God beating me up or my parents laying a licking on me. Psychological scars were seared into my mind by the pious lectures delivered in flaming spit from the pulpits by the gods of Rome. Still, I would remain loyal to the Church, not because of its claimed faultlessness but like all religious denominations, within its realms, there were great men and women who truly cared for humanity – saints living among us and, one of these good people was Father Union.

Father Union was the parish priest of Terenure. His church adjoined our school. We were always happy to see him. He was a gentle person and when it was known he was visiting our school, the teachers hid away their tools of painful expression. Father Union was loved and respected. Death came to him and he was sadly missed. Nobody felt happy about having a day off for the funeral. He had been an understanding friend to the children of the school and we were going to miss him.

I often times wondered in my young mind why my denomination had priests as kind and understanding as Father Union and others who mentally tortured their flocks. Indeed I wondered why people in long robes who purported to be representatives of all that is Heavenly would inflict such terror into the hearts and minds of those who sought nothing more than a kind word from their spiritual advisors. It was indeed a church divided unto its self. Mad men, ranting raving lunatics in long black robes, preaching fear to their flock - their victims, while the others, the decent ones who put aside religious elitism, communicating through kindness, advocated patience, understanding and love. These were the giants of life, individuals the Church and humanity needed - people like Father Union.

Still, today was special. I was being confirmed into the folds of the Church and even though I was confused with the message of life, death, hell and resurrection, there was something beautiful in the ritual of confirmation - something safe and decent about this day in the journey of the innocents; a feeling I could not define, but certainly, one imbued with spiritual essence.

When one is confirmed into the folds of the Catholic Church through the ritual of confirmation, it is a time for celebration. Hand in hand, my sister Tereasa escorted me to meet my neighbors and to share the sacredness of the occasion with all. Small gifts were bestowed upon me with many blessings and compliments. It was, in the truest sense, a special day for me. Still, I felt uncomfortable in my new clothes and a little shy about meeting our neighbors. It was a shyness that would persist throughout most of my adult life. Here on this lovely day of sunshine and smiles, my pockets jangling with treasure and my heart brimming with delight, I was preoccupied with what shyness really meant. Many years were to pass before I fully comprehended the meaning of such a small word but one of powerful consequences.

"We have just a few more friends to visit, John, and then we must return home. The men from the gas company are coming to install a new stove and we must be there to help Mother," said my older sister Tereasa.

A wonderful contraption called a gas stove was introduced to our tiny kitchen. This wonder of the ages performed remarkable feats. At last some of the hardships Mum suffered gave way to modern conveniences. With the advent of electricity, the old 'heat over the fire' clothes iron was discarded and the new plug in the socket type introduced. Our family moved slowly but surely into the affluence of the twentieth century. A cooking stove, a clothes iron, electric light and a socket in which Tereasa could plug in some miracle device that created waves and curls in her hair more numerous than those on a flock of sheep gave credence to mans ingenuity. And while electricity seemed to be working miracles in our lives, so too, did sister Tereasa.

Each year during my childhood as winter bit into the late December landscape, my mind endlessly wandered into the magical world of Christmas, Santa Claus and reindeer.

One morning, as I sat on an upturned rusting bucket outside the hog pen talking through the patched wooden door to Jerehmiah, the pig, my sister Tereasa, three years my elder, came and spoke to me. "Why are you talking to the pig, John," Tereasa said, a concerned look showing on her face.

"I don't want him to die," I blurted out, then, remained silent.

"Is he not well, John," Tereasa responded.

"Yes he is well but he won't be too well when Christmas time comes. He's going to end up on the table in front of our noses and we'll be calling him 'Lovely Bacon' instead of Jeremiah," I said, my voice full with anguish.

"Oh don't worry John, I'll talk to Daddy and make sure Jeremiah enjoys

Christmas with us and not on the table, okay. I came out to talk to you about something else! I need to know what you would like from Santa because I am sending a list to him tomorrow!"

"I want two elephants from Africa and a buffalo from America… that's all I want and Gerrard and Brendan told me they each want a herring because the fish look so much alike," I said with excited delight.

"And why does Brendan and Gerrard want herrings for Christmas, John," Tereasa asked, a bemused look lighting her face.

"I'm not too sure but I think after they eat the fish they count the bones of the skeleton," I answered.

"And why would your brothers want to count the bones of a herring's skeleton, John?" asked Tereasa.

"Because they play some kind of 'a count the herring bones game' and when all the bones are counted, that is as many as they want in the herring bone design of their three piece suits when they become millionaires," I explained with the solemnity of a hungry man who might ask kindly for a measure of charity to preserve the essence of his being. With a light sigh of disbelief, sister Tereasa decided not to pursue the topic further.

"O. K, John, just leave that to me. I'll talk to Brendan and Gerrard about it later and maybe they can request something easier for Santa to bring for them… he just does not have time to go ice fishing for herrings. As for you, John… Santa has no room on his sleigh to bring you two elephants from Africa and a buffalo from America. It is just too, tooo, toooo much to ask of him but he will bring you something nice like he's always done," sister Tereasa reminded me. "Now before I send the list off, do you know what your other brothers and sisters want for Christmas, John?" Tereasa said, her voice mingling with the snorts of Jeremiah the pig, who seemed to understand that Tereasa was going to see he was spared a visitation to the Christmas table.

"I think Ann wants a Merceedees Buns because it will go lovely with her beautiful blond hair," I said with a feeling that if Ann got a Merceedees Buns she go to Hollywood and make lots of money and save us all from the difficulties of life."

"Dear God, John, just what is a Merceedees Buns?… I never heard the likes in my life! Is it a loaf of bread of some kind?" Tereasa asked in her characteristic quizzical manner. Larry, who had quietly joined our gathering, volunteered his input on the subject.

"It's nothing to do with a loaf of bread or anything from the bakery. It's called a Mercedes Benz, a motorcar made in Germany that has the most advanced electrical and mechanical systems in the world. It is very expensive and Santa can't afford one for himself, let alone, give them away for presents," he casually said, then rose from the long seat and continued on his way somewhere.

"Well, isn't that a revelation," said Tereasa. "I suppose it won't do any good asking Santa for a Merceee Bunny or whatever kind of car it is? Perhaps a nice box of Jacob's biscuits will do the trick... Ann just loves those Mikados," sister Tereasa said enthusiasticaly, while my mouth watered for the taste of the just mentioned. I, too, was a lover of Mikados and would have gladly traded Ann, my elephants and buffalo for her Mikados but Tereasa would have none of it. "I think I have everyone on the list, John, so there should be no disappointment for anybody. I'll be off now and you can carry on talking to your little piggy." And with the Christmas wish list wrapped safely in her hand, Tereasa set off to mail the letter to St. Nicolas.

And when Christmas arrived, so too, did the presents sister Tereasa asked Santa for. And every Christmas too, without fail, when aunts and uncles and neighbors gathered beneath our roof, the golden voice of Mother graced our ears with the beautiful strains of her melodic voice, particularly when Mum sang 'Silent Night'. Such were the Christmas seasons in our house. Nevertheless, as soon as a semblance of religious comfort crawled into my mind, a hard slap across my soul often replaced such sentiment.

REJECTION

A new church was built in our area, not far from Kimmage Manor. I had heard through the grapevine that prospective candidates were being interviewed to form a choir. I wanted nothing more in the world than to be a member of a choir, to sing and be a part of something I knew I would love. I dressed my self up to the nines in my tattered clothes and set off to meet the good Father of the new church, a church that our parents had donated generously towards its construction from the little money they had. I felt proud that I had a bit of a voice and now I could put it to use singing songs for God.

As the evening's summer sun arched towards the Dublin Mountains, I walked to meet with the good priest that would no doubt open the door to the sanctuary of singing for the little boy from Perrystown.

Self assured and smiling, I greeted the man of God. "I hear you are looking for singers for the choir and I was wondering if you might like to try me out, Father," I said with a feeling that everything I wanted in life was about to be presented to me on a silver platter.

"And just where are you from," the priest replied with that lordly look that was seen only on the faces of people like Napoleon and Mussolini.

"I'm from just over there Father," I replied enthusiastically, as I pointed towards the land of Perrystown.

"Perrystown! Ye mean the cottages where ye people keep pigs and the like," the man in the long black robe said, displaying a contemptuous quiver across his reddening face. "And who said you could sing," he continued.

"My teacher, Mr. Coughlan said I had a bit of a good voice and that I would do well in a choir," I responded, my enthusiasm being sapped by each of the lord's demeaning questions. It was now beginning to dawn on me that this priest was a man who did not like people who kept pigs in their back yards. Here, I was standing in front of an elitist priest that made it clear who would be welcome to his sparkling new church and the people who raised pigs, chickens and worked a garden were not really overly welcome to the folds of his nice new house of worship.

His look of cynical contempt towards me cut deep into my mind as he pointed his finger to the distance and said. "In a year or two drop back and I might be able to squeeze ye in, but not before." His finger was still pointing to the yonder as I distanced myself from the House where God dwelled. I was not wanted, and the silence of the directive chilled my soul through as though I was some vile thing that not even the Great God might spare a moment of pity for. It is hard to forget that demeaning treatment I received from Father god that faithful day but it put me in my place - that place on the lower rung of the ladder.

It was slowly dawning on me, that this great institution of Rome was reeking with class distinction. Fear of school, afraid and unwanted by the church, a guilt-ridden confused mind hardly distanced from the cradle slowly began to develop unhealthy defense mechanisms. I had no idea what to do about the religious confusion gripping my mind, no idea who to ask about it and no idea how to ask about it. And from all this, the picture of Jesus that hung on the wall in the kitchen of our home chased me in my dreams. The picture had wheels, which it stood upright on and followed me as I tried to hide from it. Jesus was angry with me and no matter how fast I ran I could not get away from Him. The religious zealots had done their job.

Where could a young child go to express his fears of burning in hell for eternity? I did not know. I did nothing wrong to be sent to that place but I was made feel that I had. I was not supposed to be afraid of anything because Jesus would take care of me and watch over me. After all, He died to save all humanity from being tossed into Hell and, as far as I knew, I was human so I should be O. K. But the guilt took hold. I was afraid. I was afraid of many things. I was afraid of going to school in case I received a beating. I was afraid of the powers of Heaven. I was afraid of the powers of Hell. I was afraid of the darkness. I was afraid of death. I was afraid of life. I was confused. But no matter the uncertainty of it all - a sense of humor; a spiritual value in its own right often came to the rescue removing the religious torments from the mind that served only to scourge it, perpetuating the decline of the souls creative expressions while its body was still in its infancy.

TWINS AHOY!!

I left the grounds of the church determined that I would never set foot on them again and slowly walked home, my spirit drowning in the full mire of rejection. "Just keep going son," my inner voice said. "Just keep going and to hell with it all." It was good advice I got from my inner source. It seemed to know what the truth was and if I listened to it I would be just fine. So I listened while it dug deep to help remove the muck of guilt and rejection from my spirit and I went home to find two newborn babies in my bed room - our twins, Joseph and Marien.

In time, the necessary parts were added to the pathetic, rusted frame Gerrard had presented to me, and a bicycle was resurrected. I could now travel to those far away mountains. There I could feel the magic in the wind, the call of curiosity from the hills beyond the hills and breath the life of the universe, unhindered, uncluttered into my being. But traveling by roadway can be dangerous.

BODENSTOWN

I heard the sweet strains of music carry on the wind. Alas! I knew not from whence they came. Through a haze, I watched as many black shoes shuffled around the pavement and voices echoed through the deepest recesses of my mind. The voices grew louder – the leather shoes mirroring the sun. Somewhere to the distance a band played the national anthem. I wanted to sing, to stand to attention but I was between two worlds. My head lay on its left side, resting on a gray, blackish, deep red cloth. I felt very much at peace as a voice whispered. "It's all right, everything is going to be all right."

Suddenly, my mind cleared its haziness and the reality of my situation flooded my mind. My shoulder stabbed with pain and my head felt heavy and numb. The scene before my eyes unveiled its mistiness and beyond the black shoes were many other shoes. I must have moved as I heard a voice telling me to lie still. I asked the voice where the music was coming from and it answered, "From the cemetery." I asked if I was dead and the voice replied, "No." I then asked the voice where I was and it told me I was outside the cemetery. The voice went on to tell me I had been in an accident and I was going to be fine. I asked him who he was and the voice told me he was a priest and he asked me if I wanted to make a confession, to which I complied. I was given the last rites and told an ambulance was on the way.

"How come I hear the national anthem ringing through my head, Father?" I asked the priest. "Am I imagining things?"

"No my son," came the answer. "You are outside Bodenstown Cemetery, the place where Wolf Tone was laid to rest and this day, the nineteenth day of November, (my birthday being on the twentieth of November) marked the anniversary of his execution by the British back in 1798 and that is why you are hearing the national anthem," said the priest. So that's what it's all about, I mumbled - the anniversary of one of our great patriotic heroes being celebrated on one side of the wall of the cemetery and me out by a ditch on the other side bleeding to death being given the last rites as I drifted back into unconsciousness.

As I cycled past the cemetery that fateful day I was struck by a car driven by a drunk driver. I was lucky to be alive. In time I recovered with the help of the good doctors and nurses at the Meath hospital, but a turn for the worse was happening at home.

My father became ill with tuberculosis and it was feared he would not recover. He spent three months in a sanitarium during which time our neighbors helped our family through such difficulties associated with his illness and absence. To add to the ominous strains, my lovely and dear sister Ann was struck by a car. How she survived without a scratch can only be attributed to a miracle. The car had screeched to a halt but not before my sister was beneath it.

THE SECOND PURPOSE

I had entered the house to an unusual silence unaware that my sister had been involved in a serious accident. Mother had said something to me in regards to the accident but I was too preoccupied with something very disturbing that had happened in my garden and I casually replied that Ann should be more careful when walking across the street.

I do not know how far I ran. It was a good distance to be sure. Pain now replaced the numbness at the back of my head where Mum's hand slapped me. I was certain I barely escaped with my life. I decided to visit my school friend Michael O Tool. Apparently, throughout the land, Michael had the reputation of being the finest fisherman. It was said that he was able to catch the largest rainbow trout on unbaited hooks. I figured I would spend some time with Michael, help him net his fish and perhaps take one or two home with me as a peace offering.

"Now pay attention, John," said the great fisherman. I'm not only going to show you how you can hook a fish in a few seconds but how you can play them safely into the net." And I paid attention to Michael. "This lure is my favorite, John. It is called a Blue Devon and it works miracles for me," said Michael as he secured the lure to the two lb test line. Then raising the fishing pole in his right hand, he brought it back across his shoulder and with the finesse and skill of a true angler he cast the lure across the tumbling, glinting stream and into its under-bank. And true enough, just as the great fisherman said, the line was struck within a few seconds and into the air rose a beautiful rainbow trout. And that is how Michael became the greatest angler in all of Ireland! He simply knew what he was doing. Within twenty minutes he had caught enough fish to feed his family and mine. It was a good day. "Here you are John, take these fish with you to your family and have a nice feast," said Michael and with those words I bid my friend farewell.

However, I was a wanted man at home and as darkness descended I did not relish going back to the house to subject myself to a woman's wrath. I decided to climb a tree and spend the night in it with my fish tucked safely behind my shirt against my belly. Sleeping in a tree was something I enjoyed and had done it on numerous occasions. I knew my mother would not be too concerned about my whereabouts because I had at times spent the night away from home with friends on occasion and this occasion, under the circumstances would hold no mystery to it. This evasive action was more favorable than returning home and being subjected to a woman's wrath.

Next morning, I arrived home hungry, thirsty and cold. I was apprehensive about my standing but felt that with a nice catch of fish being presented to

Mum from behind my shirt I would be received favorably. But things other than John and his belly fish occupied the family's concern on my arrival home. Brother Liam had disappeared.

The search had moved from house, to garden, to fields afar; to schools, police, neighbors, anywhere and everywhere but no sign of Liam. Morning turned to afternoon, and then to evening and much was the concern for our missing brother. He was lost! Mother decided to visit our aunts. It was possible that he went to visit them. As the kitchen door swung back from the wall and Mother reached for her coat, which hung behind it, she grew silently still. We thought perhaps she had had a vision and gone into a trance. The words Mum uttered were hardly discernible but her uncharacteristic behavior indicated something profound had taken place. It most certainly had. Mother's eyes were fixed firmly upon her sleeping son. Quite oblivious to the concern he had caused to his family, Liam simply rubbed his eyes, sat up and announced he was hungry. Mum cried openly tears of joy. It seemed Liam enjoyed a little quiet in his life and took to napping behind doors. We nicknamed him the "quiet man." He was a genius in the art of hideology. There was much merriment in the discovery of our brother and soon after Liam's sleeping episode Dad was released from the sanitarium, fully recovered. He had spent three months in recovery during which time the whole family had truly gelled but when Dad returned all the chores we had taken over during his absence were delightfully handed back to him as we escaped to those places where children swing from trees.

SWING HIGH SWEET CHESTNUT

"Anyone want to come pick chestnuts?" Larry asked the assembly of brothers three: Liam, Brendan and me. These chestnuts were not the edible type, they were for playing conkers with; that art of drilling a knitting needle sized hole through the center of the walnut sized conker, then sliding a two foot length of cord through the hole. A knot tied at one end kept the chestnut from slipping off. The nature of the sport was to see two competitors face each other, their chestnuts dangling from a string, which was held firmly in the hand. Each competitor took turns striking the other's chestnut until one of the nuts was smashed from its string. It was by all accounts an exciting game, nevertheless; collecting chestnuts had its moments of terror.

The afternoon had slipped into the early evening of autumn. Liam and

Brendan had ambled home, pockets filled with the miniature spiky orbs as Larry and I pressed on felling and collecting more. High above, from the outer reaches of the tree, Larry stood upon a long, slender branch weighted with clusters of chestnuts while above him, his hands gripped a sturdier branch to secure his balance while vigorously shaking the branch on which he stood by rapid jabs of his feet.

"Are any coming down John?" Larry roared to me, his voice failing on the slight evening breeze.

"There are some nice ones coming down but their not very big. Give the branch a good shaking… I can still see some real big ones dangling from the branch," I hollered back, encouraging Larry to knock every last one from the branch.

"OK, let me know when they're all shook off," Larry roared back. As the grayness of the evening gathered across the land, chestnuts rained from the sky. Larry had indeed put a lot of vigor into the shaking of the branch – so much so, that the branch snapped. I did not see it happen, I heard only the shouts of desperation as my brother hung sixty feet from the end of a limb that reached into the coming night. The last words I heard were, *'John, I'm going to die,'* and then there was silence. Twilight was upon us now and as I gazed up into the darkness of the trees canopy, my eyes fell upon my brother's form, silently swaying in the grip of death.

Somewhere in the far reaches of my mind the primordial call to survival awakened, and driven by fear for my brother's life, the long lost instincts of far distant times when our ancestors were but dwellers of the jungle, burst like a searing flame in the centers of my mind. I cannot remember the desperate climb, I remember only holding my brother's wrist. He was going to live. "I've got you, I've got you, I've got you," I screamed so many times that Larry in his humorous way told me to shut up or we were going to be the next two nuts to fall out of the tree. And so I was quiet. Ever so carefully, while holding on to him, he brought his right foot up and locked it into the juncture on the branch that was now supporting both of us. Our situation was far from safe and as the saying goes; our lives did hang in the balance. It seemed like an eternity as Larry inched his frame up on to the precarious offerings of safety our branch afforded, but he did and we retreated carefully to the safety in the broad crooks of the tree's trunk. Such an ordeal was never mentioned but from it grew a closeness that silently endured through the years; that brotherly attachment that naught can break.

TESSY'S FLIGHT

The late autumn was upon the land, giving little daylight to complete the family farm chores but the pigs had to be fed and it was my turn to travel with Dad to collect the pig feed from those good people around the city who saved waste food for the feasting of our hogs.

"John," said my father. "I've got Tessy hitched and ready to go. Get your coat on. We should be out for only an hour or so." I knew that 'an hour or so' meant about five hours and if he stopped to quench his thirst at one of his favorite watering holes, it may well be more than five hours.

"O K Dad," I answered in a tone that exhibited my full displeasure to his request.

"Giddy up now, Tessy," Dad said to the horse as he gently shuck the reins across her back as she pulled the cart out through the gates into the fading light of a winter's evening and headed towards those houses around the city that donated left over food scraps for the good of our pigs. As Tessy plodded along the road an ominous mist began to descend quickly sliding the evening into full darkness, the red glow of the cart lamps flickering against the black of night. As I huddled against the chill of the evening on the long seat-board beside my father, an eerie screech split the night.

"What's that noise John, I wonder," said Dad as the devilish scream swept in upon us. I had not the time to answer my father as the noise and the contents of its origin slapped into the back of our cart. It happened in a flash. Dad and I were thrown out over the back of the cart into the bright lights of a swerving vehicle. Inches away from the wheels of the now stationary vehicle, I lay on the ground beside my father, whom I thought was dead as Tessy bolted at full speed into the busy home coming traffic of the evening. Tessy was a beautiful chestnut filly that possessed as much grace and elegance as any thoroughbred and to see her race into the bright lights of the evening traffic towards her death, was horrifying. I stood in the middle of the road watching as a double decker bus moved rapidly towards her. Tessy had moved over into the lane of the oncoming traffic and it would be only a few seconds before she would collided with the mighty bus. On she bolted full speed into the glare of death.

In the cab of the bus, the driver observing the oncoming tragedy steered his big machine up onto the sidewalk and there, brought it to a stop and waited for the inevitable. Traffic all along Kimmage Rd. East had come to a virtual stop as the horrifying drama played itself out. I was now running, screaming

– crying and screaming with everything in my frame at Tessy to stop but it was not to be. In the moment before the looming impact, the driver with one more last ditch effort shuddered his bus as far up on the pavement as was possible and in the moment of certain death he dimmed his lights and prayed for a miracle. And that flick of the switch by that wonderful man brought about a miracle as our beautiful Tessy wheeled out from underneath the dimmed lights and proceeded to career on down Kimmage Rd East towards the traffic lights of the Kimmage Cross Roads. It was certain she would not survive the busy six o'clock traffic as she disappeared into the distance. I walked back to where my father had been laying on the road but he was up and calling for me as he had been knocked unconscious from the force of the blow and when he came too he was not sure what had happened to me. He had been badly scared into thinking that I may have been killed or was still in the cart as Tessy bolted towards the traffic lights of the KCR.

"Stay here son, I will go after Tessy and when I find her I will come back and get you," my father said. I just stood there on the road shaking like a leaf as Dad moved on towards that place where our Tessy might be. As I stood there, I could see my dad talking momentarily to the busman, then shake the drivers hand and then hurry on towards the cross roads to see what happened to Tessy. I was now feeling very cold and shaking uncontrollably. I did not know it then but shock was setting in. However, I did not budge from the spot from where I stood, as my eyes remained glued toward the place where Tessy had bolted. The traffic was now moving at its normal pace and the man who was responsible for the accident was sitting in his little Morris Minor, which had come to rest in some good person's driveway, was smoking cigarettes as though he was just about to be banned from smoking for life. Still, my thoughts were on Tessy and if she was safe. I waited and waited for my father to return which seemed like an eternity. Then through that dark mistiness of the evening fog and the shimmering lights of the traffic, a man, a horse and a cart emerged from a picture of surrealism into shades of reality and I cried and cried that Tessy was alright and Dad was alright and I was alright and the man who belted the hell out of us was alright and that he wouldn't die from cancer within the next few minutes the way he was hauling cigarette smoke into his lungs.

Tessy had all her angels working overtime for her that evening. She had kept up her galloping pace, never slowing as she approached the red reflection of the traffic lights. The station attendant was surprised to see a horse and cart bolt out of the night without a driver and more surprised when

Tessy paid no attention to the ominous color of the traffic lights. She just bolted right through them, crossing the road at an impossible diagonal angle and into the driveway of the KCR gas station and there stopped outside the little convenience store that Dad had so many times before stopped at to pick up a packet of smokes. Tessy was familiar with the KCR surroundings and there remained until Dad arrived.

"You go on home John, it has been a bad night for you. I will collect the feed myself and I'll see you when I get home," Dad told me when he returned with Tessy. But I was not going anywhere unless it was with my Dad, and I said so. So we all went together to collect the pig feed, as the man who walloped us apologized profusely to my father and promised he would drop around to the house to talk things over. That is the way it was then. Dad just sorted out things in the spirit of the moment and left it at that.

SCHOOLDAYS OVER

The end of my school days were drawing to a close and soon the countryside pictures of the school calendars were but a memory; the one thing about school I truly loved – the beckoning of the wilderness. I was thirteen years old, ill prepared to venture into the world of the workman but prepared to give it a try.

Searching the newspapers for advertised jobs, I was drawn to an ad. that required a messenger boy to deliver false teeth. I did not care much for the product I was to deliver but I liked the idea of the freedom of cycling around the city. Delivering false teeth for a living was something one kept to one's self. Although I was notorious for sharing the most sacred and most secret with anyone who cared to listen, this business I was in was top secret. Nobody was going to know the real truth of what I did for a living. I figured since the area of my deliveries were centered around the upper class districts of Bray and Black Rock, it would not be too big a lie if I told family and friends I was a deliverer of precious jewelry. This misinformation seemed to have a nice bite to it.

Said Mr. Forger, as I stood in his little brown box office, "John, you have a very special delivery to make to one of our very special customers. Mr. Rosebud, the dentist, has a patient in the chair at this moment and she was fitted for a front partial last week. However, due to extenuating circumstances, we were not able to have the denture ready for her before she arrived to have her three front upper teeth removed this morning. I am counting on you to get the denture there without delay. I'll make sure there's a doughnut or two left over for you when you get back." A doughnut or two! I mused. I pretended I knew what a doughnut was and told Mr. Forger that he was not to worry - the job was as good as done. I tied the precious box of false teeth securely to the handlebar of my bike and speedily made my way to the lady in waiting.

    I made pretty good time getting to the dentists place of practice, which was located in a laneway somewhere off the main drag. Whistling a merry little tune as I most often did, I reached to untie my package of importance. It was not in the hanging place. I looked to the other side of the handlebars. It was not there either. I did, I think, what most people may do in a situation like mine. I kept looking in that empty space expecting the package of false teeth to materialize at any moment but it was not happening. I looked in the direction from which I had come, scanned the pavement but did not see my lost treasure. To make matters worse I noticed someone peering through the window of the dentist's office. I had no doubt it was the dentist and I was sure he had no doubt who I was. I decided to ignore the spy in the window and set off through the laneway on my bike in search of the missing teeth. It was a good move. A sharp bend in the laneway put me out of the window watcher's view. I felt more comfortable being unobserved – on the other hand, I had lost his false teeth and I was worried.

    The Irish setter was set in field position, its left paw firmly planted on the ground, the right one bent back at the knee, its tail stretched back into space and its nose pointed towards a little brown packet which lay on the ground with that lost look that only a false teeth box can exhibit. I had no doubt that the package was my lost mouthpiece but in a moment, the setter had it in its chops and was trotting off to its private picnic grounds. I did the only thing a man can do at a time like this. I called to the red creature as it sauntered down the laneway looking nice and smug as though it had a nice fresh hunk of fried chicken in its chops. "Here boy,... here boy," I called politely, but it paid no attention to me. Then I thought it might be a girl, so I said, "here girl," but the response was the same. I then called it names that may befit Irish setters, some nice, some not so nice but the name-calling proved useless. The red setter, uncaring about my plight, kept sauntering down the laneway and then out into the main action of city life. I knew now I had a very large problem on my hands.

    At this point I parked my bike and started a hurried skip and dart maneuver in an effort not to lose the thief. I even took on the side run that one observes in some purebred animals, where one is not sure if its the head or the behind of the animal that's leading the way. I was now dying for a pee and running after the dog wasn't helping my pain. I had to do something quickly to corral the dog. I called to the faithful citizens to stop the animal, explaining to them that the dog stole my teeth but my calls fell on deaf ears. Just as I was about to give up, I heard the voice of a little girl calling the dog. Her pet's name was Princess.

"What you got there in you mouth?" said the little girl to her Princess as her pet sat in front of her with its tongue hanging over the side of its chops and its tail sweeping the ground behind its behind.

I called to the little girl. "Hello little girl, is that your dog?" She answered, she was not a little girl and she was not allowed to talk to strangers. I told her she had nothing to worry about, that I just wanted my teeth back because her Princess had stolen them, otherwise I would lose my job. The little girl gave me one of those non-believing looks and told me I was a liar, that I had teeth and she could see them. "No!" I said, "I'm not talking about my own teeth but the teeth of a woman down the lane in the dentist's chair," and for sure she knew I was nuts. With one last desperate plea I asked the little girl to take a look in the package her princess was drooling all over and if there were no teeth in it I would go away.

And prettily the little girl said to Princess, "Let me have a peek and see what's in your mouth Prinny sweetheart." Prinny would not cooperate

Now I am not a vicious man but I wanted to ring Prinny's neck. By now, the paper was dripping from Prinny's chops and the thoughts of Prinny chewing on the lady's teeth like Carmel chewed on gum back at the Presentation Convent became a nightmare. But, the little girl kept coaxing her Prinny and soon Prinny surrendered her prize. The little girl knew by now I was telling the truth because the teeth were now wrap less, box less and washed all to hell with Prinny's saliva. I didn't hang around. I grabbed the teeth and headed for the nearest grocery shop, told the person that there was an accident and I needed some brown paper to put some teeth into. I was given the down the nose look as I stood there waiting, dying to have a pee. The man who had just given me the 'down the nose look' passed me a piece of brown paper as though he were passing me a plate of Black Sea caviar. I thanked him as much as a man in much bladder pain could and raced back to the dentist's place.

Back in the laneway I picked up my bike and raced as quickly as I could to the dentist's office. The pressure within my bladder became unbearable and I had to have a pee. I just could not go another inch and so, I didn't. I proceeded to do my most private of rituals against the flatness of a wall without pillars or corners and indeed I truly felt exposed. I had just about finished the business of personal relief when a voice addressed me from behind. "Are you the fellow from the denture company?" I knew I was in big trouble because for sure I was the fellow from the denture company and the fellow behind me was the dentist looking for his false teeth to put in the mouth of the lady who was waiting in his dentist's chair. I told him I was indeed the man from the denture company as I passed his teeth back to him while I completed my business. I never did see the face of the man who had spoken to me and I hoped he did not see mine. For obvious reasons, I did not bother with the doughnuts and decided to try my hand at something less demanding in the line of work.

The Gresham Hotel, one of Ireland's finest hotel's, located on O' Connell Street in the city center required a bellboy and I saw no reason why I should not be working in such a lovely place - a step up from cycling around Dublin delivering false teeth. I decided to apply in person, as the advertisement in the *Dublin Mail* suggested. However, I did not have a decent pair of shoes, at least two that looked alike, so I borrowed Dad's rubber boots. Rubber boots are handy because they can be cleaned with a little water and pant legs can be comfortably tucked away in them, giving one the appearance of being a member of the gentry – the only noticeable difference between the gentry and me being, that I traveled by bike and the gentry by Rolls Royce.

Having this look was in fact a good idea because it was to the Gresham I was going for the interview and the look of importance was essential to a positive outcome of the meeting. I felt I was fully prepared both intellectually and dress-wise for the occasion, apart from the odd streak of hairdressing oil inching down my forehead.

Oily hair to match my oil boots, coat collar in the stand-to-attention position, Windsor knot executed on the tie; one last check on the pressure of the bicycle tires and it was off to the fateful meeting. Visions of grandiosity flooded my mind as I pushed off from my home in Perrystown. Working at the Greshham would put me in touch with the great stars of Hollywood because the Gresham was one of the grand hotels of Dublin where the great ones came to rest, study and play in the land of saints and scholars. I learned later that this was of course not true but for now the important thing was to get the damned job. It is approximately six miles to O'Connell Street from

Perrystown and all went well up to the point and time I reached O' Connell Bridge, the main bridge that spans the Liffey River that flows through the heart of Dublin City.

The skies opened up and water poured down. The wind blew fiercely in from the sea and I was almost blown around the statue of the great Daniel O' Connell which stood in the center of the north side of the bridge named in his honor. I gave up the idea of cycling on the road and sought the shelter of the buildings on the west side of O' Connell St. I appreciated the protection from the wind as I continued my journey cycling the sidewalk. All went well until a Garda (policeman) stopped me as I cycled by the General Post Office.

"Where the hell do you think your going this hour of the night on your bicycle?" he coolly asked me, as though the time had some mystical quality about it. "Don't ye know your not allowed to be cycling on the pathway - and without a light?" he said, exhibiting that satisfied look - his night's work was just about to reap rich rewards for the Fathers of the city. After he said, "without a light," I knew I was in trouble. He was now beginning to let me know in that unique Dublin way that I was not going to get away with this horrendous offense. "And where do ye live?" he inquired.

"I live in a cottage in Perrystown," said I.

"And what address is it?" he inquired further.

"There's no address on the door, said I."

"Surely to God on High, ye know the number of your house?" he said, his voice tattered by the roar of thunder.

"I forget, because we never use it," I screamed back at him as the sky's symphonic inferno rumbled across the rain battered city.

"Do ye have a letter or something with your name on it so you can identify who you are?" was his next question.

"No officer, I do not have a letter with a dent in it," I replied. I immediately got the bull's look from him, which indicated to me that he was not impressed with my acting dumb.

"I want ye to listen to me good and carefully," he said.

"Do ye know what a letter is young man?"

"Yes officer, I do know what a letter is but nobody writes to me so I do not have one in my possession," I answered.

"And how come nobody writes to you?" he said with a touch of sarcasm.

"Because I do not know anybody I can write to and if you really must know, the truth is I cannot write very well. Does that explain everything satisfactorily sir?" I said indignantly.

THE SECOND PURPOSE

As good Garda do in self-questioning body language, he placed one hand on his jaw and the other beneath the elbow of the one hanging from the jaw - more or less exhibiting the semi military Napoleon look and he said. "I think your full of shite and I don't like little blaguards making a mockery of me." I was really hurt by his last remark as I truly felt I was a little bigger than small. I stood looking stunned and hurt and this natural response of hurt feelings bore some fruit but not the kind of fruit I wanted because the next question he asked completely threw me off guard. He asked me which team I played football for. I was in a terrible state at this point because I knew if I named a team he did not care for, he was likely to double the fine. I entered into the great look of stundness, hoping the garda would forget about the question and just give me a ticket, but that was not in his plan.

"Ye know, I really don't like repeating myself but if it's not too much trouble, would ye mind telling me who do ye play football for?" he said, a touch of irritation honing his voice.

"Sorry sir but have ye heard of St. Agnes'," I said.

"St. Agnes' ye say. Is that the team out there in Crumlin?"

"Yes sir, it is and I play for the under fifteen team."

"I thought ye had the look of a footballer about ye," he said and went on to ask me what I was doing in the town on a bloody awful night like this and I told him. He looked at me with the more relaxed Napoleon look and said. "Maybe I'll see ye on the field some day and we'll battle it out but ye'll have to put a few years on ye yet and ye'll have to be pretty good when ye come up against Clanna Gael." And with those remarks he bid me good luck.

I was a little mixed up at this point because I truly thought I was going to be fined. I asked the Garda if he was letting me go. He replied. "Yes, young man. The ground we are standing on has been stained with the blood of those who bought our freedom with their lives. It was here Patrick Pearse and the gallant few took on the British Empire. Right here where we stand, Patrick himself read the Proclamation of Independence and I am not going to defile this place of honor by doing a little bit of business." With those words, the big Garda wished me well in my interview at the Gresham Hotel and reminded me once again to get a light on my bike, which I never did.

Taking leave of the Garda, I walked across O' Connell St. towards the glittering lights of the Gresham hotel. It was then I noticed the slurping sounds - my boots were leaking. Momentarily I thought about forgetting the interview, but I had come so far - why not go for it? I put on the look of importance the best I could as I entered the main doors of the Gresham but upon observing the elite of society lounging in the lobby, I wanted to melt into something and it didn't matter what it was.

At the far end of the lobby, behind the reception counter stood a young woman leafing through a ledger. Placing each foot as gently as I could, I gingerly moved towards her but the squelching sound from the deep recesses of my water logged boots swished in bouncing echoes through the grand halls of the hotel – a sound that would put mariners to sleep.

Nevertheless, undaunted, I stayed on course but upon observing the receptionists sparkling blue eyed gaze upon me, I idled to a full stop beneath the crystal chandelier whose glittering sparkles reflected in the wet glaze of my oil boots. I suddenly appeared something like a lost, dripping kaleidoscope – my moment of stardom had arrived but it was a moment I did not want. Lost beneath a chandelier in the lobby of the Gresham, my mind closed down in a hollow of darkness as the rain drops from my clothes dripped around my feet into the rich, plush carpet. By nature I was shy and this effect of my make-up blossomed into outright fear. Should I run? Should I say I'm an undercover nun looking for charity to aid the poor people like me, or should I faint? The latter seemed the easier. But while my mind limped through the foggy elements of confusion, the blue-eyed lady spoke.

"Is there something I can help you with," she asked in a soft, gentle west Irish brogue (accent). Oh, how truly lost I was at that moment for I indeed felt what a wet rag might feel if it had feelings. But I did have feelings, so much so that I fell in love with the lovely lady from the west coast but instinctively knew it was not in my best interest to impart my feelings towards her on the matter, so I lied!

"Excuse me Miss," I said. "I hope ye don't mind but I'm a reporter for the *Perrystown Irishman* and we're looking for jobs to advertise in our paper."

"We have no jobs presently," she replied as I nervously slid the soles of my rubber boots through the now soggy carpet beneath my feet.

"O how terribly disappointing to hear that, Miss. You see! I've cycled all the way from Perrystown, specifically to meet with you. My boss, the editor in chief of the newspaper is a very kind man in that he helps poor people secure employment. He asked me to meet with you in regards to the ad. in the *Daily Mail* about your needing a ball boy," I said with a feeling that I was gaining some measure of togetherness.

"We are not in need of a ball boy but we did have an ad running for a bell boy. Unfortunately, that position has being filled," she said, dismantling any vestige of enthusiasm about my job mission.

"I'm sorry to hear that terrible news but I guess that's life," I said, the look of blossoming gloom saturating my face.

"That is life indeed," the Gresham girl said. "We can't get everything we want and that is the way it should be, otherwise; if things are handed to us on a plate there is no sense of accomplishment," the lovely one said.

"Accomplishment!" I said, exasperation dancing in my voice. "I almost drowned coming down here to try to secure a job for some poor person. I don't think that is being handed something on a platter," I said forcing the conversation back on to the Gresham's girl's plate.

"I'm not saying what you are doing is not without sacrifice and that is just my point! When we accomplish our goals through perseverance and dedication, then we can feel good about the accomplishment because it made us fight for it. That's what makes it worthwhile. The goal is a living thing. It speaks to us but so often we do not recognize its call and that is sad because it's the challenge of the goal that truly keeps us alive. If there is no challenge there is only a sleeping life - usually a worthless one," the girl with the west Irish brogue softly said. I did not know how to respond to the wisdom or stupidity I had just heard, so I kept my mouth shut; an unusual employment of that factor for me as I awaited the girl from the west to continue, and she did.

"I'm certainly impressed with the good work you're doing, but you know, it would be nice to know your name?"

"I'm John Gabriel from Perrystown, a small, little village around Terenure and Crumlin," I said, my voice quivering like an eagles feather in a blustery wind.

"A small, little village, you say? Now, you're sure it's not a big, little village," she said, teasing my cutely flawed English as she gently placed her hand on my shoulder pushing it slightly.

"That is funny isn't it… a small, little village… sounds cute, almost as cute as a big, little village," I answered, my self-assurance in tatters.

"And where are you from, if ye don't mind me asking?" I asked the lovely one.

"I'm from Connemara. Have you heard of Connemara?" She asked inquiringly.

"Yes, I have heard of Connemara and I believe it is the most beautiful place in Ireland. Perhaps, even in the world but not as beautiful as you," I remarked about her loveliness almost as an after thought. Then, my face turned red, as red as boiled beetroot.

"That is a very lovely thing to say," she said looking straight into my eyes and continued. "Quiet frankly, I don't know what to say right now other than you look like you could do with some tea and biscuits. Would you like some?"

"That would be lovely indeed – that is if it is not too much trouble," I said, hoping the biscuit plate to be overflowing with Mikado's.

"Sure not a bother, John… you wont take off while I go to the kitchen, will you?" She laughed as she slipped from her seat and gracefully walked across the foyer and down the hallway towards the kitchen.

As I sat in the plush ambience of the great hall, my mind wandered to rivers and mountains, the music of Shenandoah singing in my brain. How beautiful that song, I thought. And the more I entertained its haunting call, the more it absorbed me into the magic of its reality - the voices of the voyageurs singing to the rhythm of their paddles as they coursed the rivers of the North American wilderness. How I wished to be there - to follow in the wake of the great explorers and to know the freedom of it all. But the sound of the water's lap against the paddles splashed the fire of imaginings as the voice of the receptionist nudged me back to reality. "Hear you are, John Gabriel from Perrystown, a nice cup of tea and some Mikado biscuits… just for you," she said smiling her lovely smile, her light blue eyes sparkling their dance.

"You know? I never did get your name," I said. "Do people from Connemara have names?"

"O yes, John. They have the most handsome Irish names. Mine is Aisling. In the Saxon language it means "Dream or Vision".

"O how magical, Aisling . . .how illuminating," I muffled as I scoffed the biscuits down my throat as politely as any nice mannered pig might do, the odd flake and crumb gathering around my rubber boots as the rain water oozed from their tears.

"And you, John Gabriel! Something tells me you have not told me your full name. What is it?" Aisling asked as though she could see into my very soul.

"You are very perceptive Aisling. I like my middle name, Gabriel, that is why I use it when I introduce myself but McDonald is my family name… any of the McDonald clan out your way in Connemara?" I bantered.

"Not that I know of but their could be if you were interested!" she said smiling her lovely smile, then changed the course of conversation.

"Will you please be careful traveling in such terrible weather John Gabriel McDonald, and before you go, I want you to leave the phone number of the

Perrystown Irishman with me so I can give you a call when jobs become available."

At this suggestion I began to panic because nobody in Perrystown had a phone and there was no such publication as the *Perrystown Irishman*. I had two choices - to lie or not to lie. I lied. "Aisling, I must tell you that the *Perrystown Irishman*, as an newspaper publication is just a few weeks in operation and it will be a few months before a phone is installed but as soon as we get it hooked up, I will give you a call," I said, knowing full well that the lie I was telling was about to slap me very hard in the face but my foolish pride would not allow me to tell the truth.

By now, the water sitting at the bottom of my rubber boots had reached a temperature between high and medium and I thought if I left my feet in them for another fifteen minutes they might begin to simmer. It was time to depart. "I promise you Aisling," I said, a hint of longing in my voice, "I shall stay in touch, I really will and, perhaps one day we can visit Connemara together."

"Perhaps one day, John Gabriel, but I can tell that there is a bit of a traveler in you," and with that comment, Aisling picked up the tea tray, looked straight into my eyes and said. "It will be a long time, John Gabriel McDonald but we will meet again, that is for certain." Then with the charm and elegance of a goddess beautiful, she turned and gracefully moved across the foyer. As I walked out through the doors of the Gresham, I knew I would not see her again, at least not in this lifetime and I wondered if that is what Aisling, the dream lady meant when she said. "It will be a long time John Gabriel McDonald but we will meet again".

As I cycled home in the rains unrelenting misery, I wondered how Aisling could possibly have known the traveler's thorn lay buried deep in my foot. Meeting her, somehow gave impetus to my innate feelings about life and the craving for the open road. I felt our meeting had little to do with the bellboy job; its real significance was for Aisling to encourage me towards my true journey.

THE MAKING OF A SOLDIER

Still, I needed a job and I got one – one that didn't pay.

Off I went to join the F.C.A., a cadet wing of the National Defense Service. Here I learned about basic soldiering and weaponry.

Said Sergeant Flannagan as I stood to attention in the front lines of the ranks - a terrible place to be, because those in the front line were always under the scrutiny of those in command: "Mr. McDonald, I've been observing you," said the massively out of shape sergeant. I figured he was impressed with my soldierly professionalism and I immediately thanked him for his troubles. "Thank you sergeant Flannigan, just doing me bit ya know - just like everybody else sir." The bulge in his eyes and the deep reddening of his very fat jowls told me I should have kept my mouth shut. "Never, ever call a sergeant 'sir', McDonald, and that goes for the whole damned lot of ye, de yis hear me." And we all heard sergeant Flannigan because he had that kind of voice that required a frequent touch of oil.

"Can ye tell me what a soldier looks like McDonald," he roared at me with classic military authority as he stepped back, pushing his chest out and placing his head in the look-down-at you-position.

"Yes sergeant Flannigan, I can," I answered.

"De yis hear that soldiers of Ireland? McDonald knows what a soldier looks like and no doubt he's going to tell us what a real soldier looks like, aren't ye boy? His voice of chronic squeakiness demanded attention from his subjects, who, to a man, wanted to shoot him.

"And what does a real soldier look like McDonald? Please do tell us - we are all ears just for you private," his greatness said with a large touch of sarcasm. I became tongue-tied, my voice frozen in the summer wind. The square was silent, too silent. The large sergeant responded to the stillness. "Today, private McDonald, would be as good a time as any to answer the question, if that of course fits into your personal agenda," he roared into my face, showering me with an ocean of spray from that great cave wherein his teeth dwelled. Silence again hung across the square as I searched my strangled mind for a person who looked the image of a soldier. A spark ignited somewhere in the depths of my cranium; my search was rewarded.

"Moses, Sergeant Flannigan! Moses was a great soldier and looked the real image of a real, live, good soldier," I blurted with great confidence.

"Moses, Moses, Moses! And who in the name of God is Moses, McDonald? The sergeant bellowed.

"He was a desert fox, sergeant - just like Rommel," I answered. The sergeant's imposing frame displayed disbelief but I kept going.

"Yes sergeant - Moses, like the great Rommel, led his people to and from the desert, battling the enemy all the way and both were successful evading their adversaries," I said confidently and gallantly.

"That's the greatest load of shite I ever heard in all my days, McDonald," said the bold sergeant.

"It's not a great load of shite sergeant. Moses and Rommel did indeed get their people out of harms way against all odds and that is fact! It cannot be denied. Really, they were the greatest generals that ever lived, if you care to look at it that way," I said with an air of innocent authority.

"If I care to look at it that way McDonald! What the hell have you been reading to unload such a load of horse shite on top of me this lovely and glorious morning? It sounds to me like you got your information from a bottle of warm lemonade," the good sergeant bellowed, then with chest out, arms wrapped around his lower back and his face giving bulls looks to the cobblestones of the square, the sergeant continued. "Do carry on McDonald, I would just love to hear more about Moses and Rommel from one of authority, such as you," he growled.

"I can't really impart much more information about those two desert foxes sergeant because that is all I know about them. They simply knew how to take care of their people," I replied, hoping the sergeant would drop the topic.

Silence reigned supreme across the square once again. I knew I had the better of the sergeant and this self-congratulation was bolstered by the elbow in the ribs from my good friend Paul, whom I had met on signing up, indicating he was impressed with my lunatic performance. The silence became uncomfortable, broken only by the squawk of a lone seagull winging the high winds of late morning. The sergeant slowly stomped the worn cobblestones, the steel heel clips of his boots marking time. We waited. We waited and suffered. We waited and waited and suffered some more.

"Did Moses and Rommel like sausages, McDonald?" The sergeant eventually said as he spun his great personage on the heels of his brilliantly polished boots, bringing his hugeness to the stand-at-ease position.

"No sergeant," as far as I know, Moses liked lamb cooked over a fire and Rommel liked sauerkraut," I answered.

"And what is sauerkraut McDonald?" The sergeant asked, exhibiting a measure of interest.

"I don't know sergeant - a friend of mine told me the general liked sauerkraut, that's all I really know on the subject," I said with a hint of sincerity.

"And do you like sausages, Private McDonald?" The sergeant asked, as though he were about to cook me some.

"Yes sergeant, I love sausages."

"And do ye like them cooked on a stove or over a fire like Moses had his lamb cooked?" The sergeant said as though he was planning a trip to the Egyptian desert, for his elite fighting machine.

"It doesn't matter sergeant, as long as I get them, I don't mind what way they are cooked," I said.

"McDonald, one day I am going to make a good soldier out o' ye, now get the hell the whole lot of yis into the mess because its sausages yis are having for lunch." And with that directive the big sergeant let a bellow of laughter - that laughter conducive to a very large man with a hidden sense of humor as we made as much distance from him as fast as we could.

As the sausages and spuds were demolished as politely as soldiers can demolish things, our Sergeant addressed his hungry soldiers.

"To-night boy's I am going to make real men out of yis. Yis are all going to assemble in the boozer and there take yer fill of porter until yis are good and drunk and make no mistake about it I want yis all present."

And the whole platoon turned up at the bar and did what good fighting soldiers should do on their time off – sing, drink and be merry. However, the following morning was a different story.

"Men," said Sergeant Flannigan, "I have not seen such a disgusting performance in the entirety of me whooooole life. Yis are making me asssshhhamed of yis, yis bloody rotten bunch of shitehawks. Me poor grandmother, the good Lord rest her soul, would put the whole bloody lot of yis to shame." And he went on. "I bet at midnight in the any cemetery there would be more life than what I am looking at right now. A few pints of Guinness and yis can't show up alive. Jesus Mary and Joseph - it's a good thing yis are not off to war - yis'ed die of fright before yis managed to get into yer uniforms," he roared at us - then silence slapped across the square.

The silence was chilling and the bold sergeant kept it that way, broken only when he told us that there was more color in a bottle of milk sitting in a snow bank than there was in his sad looking fighting machine. Then on a sudden he bellowed. "Men of Ireland (he didn't call us soldiers), today I am going to show yis all something about piecing a rifle together and yis better listen carefully because one day yer lives may depend on your ability to disassemble and reassemble your firearms. Do I make myself clear?" he barked at us.

"Yes sir," we answered with as much as enthusiasm as a group of men waiting to be shot.

"Good… good… good God help me make something out yis. Now the last man up the stairs and into the drill room gets to clean all the rifles," the sergeant's voice squawked into the heavens as we bolted across the square. The scramble was massively disjointed as we pushed and shoved our way through the drill room door, the last three men pushing through together making it impossible to tell who was last.

"Gentlemen, this is a rifle, not a gun," the sergeant lectured as he stood in front of a long wooden table, upon which a forlorn weapon looking oddly out of place awaited dissection. "I am going to do this only once and yis better remember what I am showing yis because I will be asking questions in a few minutes," he said tauntingly. After securing twenty per cent attention from his one hundred percent dead troops, sergeant Flannigan had the rifle disassembled and neatly laid out in pieces.

"I take it yis all know what part of the rifle the round (bullet) travels through and since I feel unusually comfortable in knowing yis know what part of the rifle a bullet passes through, we shall concentrate on the parts that make up the firing mechanism of the weapon. If yis learn nothing else in the army, yis better learn what I am about to show yis, because your lives well may depend one day on this knowledge - are yis with me so far, o great sickly looking fighting men," he said with a generous amount of sarcasm.

"Yes sir," we shouted in unison, giving the impression to each other that the other was generating a measure of life in his emaciated body of paleness. Even the sergeant betrayed a tad of hopeful surprise at our budding resurrection.

"This is a bolt," the sergeant said as he held that thing which resembles a door bolt in his hand above his head. He then placed it back on the table gently (as though it were the only piece of smoked salmon left in the world and he was being very nice to it before he chewed it to death) and selecting the firing pin, he dutifully displayed it from his right hand, which hung at ease above his great mop of blazing red hair. "This is the firing pin," he continued. "This is the twin brother of the bolt I just showed yis - one must be attached to the other in order for the firing mechanism to work. Are yis with me so far o great palefaces," the sergeant bellowed.

"Yes sergeant," we responded - a measure of weak strength creeping into our voices.

"Good, good, good," the sergeant said. "Now I want ye to tell me Mulligan what a firing pin does and what a firing pin looks like and I want ye to do that right now Mulligan, so lets hear ye boy," the sergeant concluded.

Mulligan stood about six foot six and was a pretty smart fellow. He paid attention and generally knew how to give an adequate answer. "The firing pin, sergeant, is a small piece of sharp metal that screws into the top end of the bolt - it is that part of the firing mechanism that strikes the bullet causing it to detonate on impact," Mulligan said with the ease of one who knew exactly what he was talking about.

"Excellent Mulligan and can ye tell us what will happen if the firing pin is not screwed all the way into the head of the bolt," the sergeant asked.

"Yes sergeant. If the firing pin is not secured tightly into the top of the bolt, it will be impossible to lock the bolt into position, therefore rendering the rifle useless. It is absolutely essential that all parts of the rifle fit together precisely but the most important aspect of the rifle's function as a weapon is the firing mechanism - the pin and the bolt must fit to precision," Mulligan modestly concluded.

"Did yis hear what this good soldier just shared with us o great warriors," the sergeant bellowed.

"Yes sergeant," we roared back as though a promise of life was given to each one of us for one more day. We were beginning to get over the hangovers and shakes from all the booze we had consumed the night before with a little confidence creeping into one or two of us.

"Why the hell is he going on about the firing pin so bloody much, Paul?" I asked.

"Dunno, maybe it is that part that can really cause a problem if it is not closely watched," said Paul. Why I paid so much attention to the sergeant and his demands that I know how to assemble a rifle blindfolded and resolved never to forget about the firing pin can only be left to conjecture but it was a good thing I did because in the years to come in the great wilderness of a far away country, an event would unfold that would demand the knowledge the good sergeant so thoroughly hammered into my brain.

MADMEN AND FOXES

As my marksmanship improved to that of less than good, I decided to become a huntsman. I took membership in a Dublin hunting club and soon I was traversing the fields of prey with great and daring hunters.

The late hues of evening painted the landscape as the huntsmen trod the tranquil autumn farm fields. We were about twelve in number. Ahead, on the high banks of a ditch, the dogs displayed the excitement of the kill – they had sniffed out a den. As the terriers burrowed fiercely, the hunters covered all exits to the lair, except one. The raw chilling yelps barely distinguishable between man and beast echoed across the fields into the grayness of the distance and as the shades of twilight intensified across the plains of Meath, a sack twisted and rolled with the terrified cries of a cub – the vixen had made good her escape and from a distance she watched.

In the circle of the hunters, the blood sacrifice was offered. It seemed I was standing in a miniature Roman Coliseum as the call for blood echoed and re-echoed into the beyond. There we were, a group of men armed to the teeth circling a cub while one of the boys called to grant a young terrier its first taste of blood. I turned to Hanus, the head hunter, pleading to let the little thing go. "Don't worry John, it will be over in a minute and in time you will get used to it," he said as though the killing was as natural as waxing poetry.

"But why do you want to kill the cub?" I said raising my voice, but my call was lost to the savage growls of both man and beast

The young terrier was loosened upon its defenseless prey, its first taste of sacrificial blood. I was in shock, in disbelief at the spectacle I was part of. I didn't want to be but I was. I wanted to vomit. My total focus was on the little red fox as it so bravely met the rush of the terrier. Oh how little red fought and I thought for a wishful moment it might get the better of the dog. But the little cub succumbed to the inevitable - then the rest of the dogs were loosed and through my blurred vision I watched as the cub was torn apart.

I was totally disillusioned with all of what life was about and as we made our way across the fields in the first strengths of darkness, my heart cried silently. Little Red was now an indelible part of my makeup and so too was the insanity of moments ago. A great rage was burning inside the very depths of my soul. A reflective mood took hold and I wondered about the Man on the Cross and I wondered too about the art of killing as a soldier.

THE DUBLIN ZOOLOGICAL GARDENS

While the only recompense I received in the F.C.A for my soldierly dedication was in the form of sausages, eggs and firing a rifle, my friend, Paul, imparted good news to me that had nothing to do with soldiering. "I heard through the grapevine that they are looking for a cook at the Dublin Zoo, John… might be worth looking into since you are still in need of a job," Paul said with an air of encouragement. And so it was, I packed in my soldiering and went to work at the Dublin zoological gardens. My responsibilities were to prepare food for those who therein dwelled and the very important purchasing of the most excellent North Sea herrings for our delightful seal-sweethearts from California. However, purchasing the finest fresh sea herrings had its difficulties.

One day I called Mr. Buldoon, the fishmonger, to my office. "Please be seated Mr. Buldoon. I have been asked by my boss to address a certain issue with you. Apparently you have been told before never to bring fish for our California seals that are other than herring and it seems that you are not responding favorably to that request. If I find you in violation of this agreement one more time, you are finished as a supplier to our institution, sir! Do you understand me sir!?" I said with a flair of authority, and continued. "You see, Mr. Buldoon, California seals and all other seals for that matter cannot swallow fish that have sharp and pointy dorsal fins, because such fins may cut the seals epiglottis and perhaps even choke our California darlings to death and we are truly fed up with this kind of fifth rate service," I said, feeling much pleased with my controlled lecture.

I knew humans had an epiglottis somewhere beyond the boundaries of their teeth but I was not sure if seals did. However, I felt it sounded educated and professional. Mr. Buldoon seemed somewhat taken aback by my firm demands but as coolly as a fish slides over ice he scaled his response perfectly. "If I told the youngster at the plant, I told him a thousand times not to put anything in the boxes other than the freshest of herring. Shur if ye don't do it yerself it might as well not be done at all," he replied thoughtfully with a hint of sad desperation toning his voice. Still, his answer left me much to wonder about.

"Mr. Buldoon, you should know also that Marty, my boss, told me to tell ye, that if ye don't do what is asked of you in regards to the agreement of the contract, I will be out of a job and you will not be allowed on these lovely grounds ever again," I fired back at his unusual answer. In response to my warning, Mr. Bulldoon left the office, walked to his truck, reached in behind the seat, pulled out a carton of camel cigarettes and presented me with them. "Seals do not smoke cigarettes Mr. Buldoon and I don't smoke them either. All we want here is what we ask for - fresh herrings and fresh herrings only. Is that too much to ask? I think not," I said with a bit of a rage building in me as I continued. "Good day to you Mr. Buldoon and remember – nothing but the freshest of herrings or your account is closed for good. Is that clear," I concluded.

"It'll be done, Mr. McDonald. Don't worry about a thing. I'll make sure there will only be the freshest of North Sea herrings for your California darlings," and with that comment, he slammed the door of his dilapidated fish truck and drove from our gardens just as Danny, the monkey keeper approached me - an expression of apprehension on his face

"John, I need your help. Horace the monkey escaped from the zoo grounds by swinging himself over the high fence into freedom among the trees in the Phoenix Park and we have to go get him. Would you mind coming along with me to round him up," said Danny. It was not a wise thing for Horace to jump over our fence and skip off into the park because it's against the law for monkeys to swing in Irish trees outside zoo grounds. Out we went in search of Horace and it was not long before the little biped was spotted. I had no idea how I could help entice a monkey from a tree but since I was the zoo cook and I knew Horace loved his daily feed of bananas, I thought it wise to bring along a few bunches to coax him out of the tree.

Negotiations went on for some time with Horace but Horace was not responding favorably to the banana offering. This was made evident as the bananas I threw to him came back and hit me in the face. I had a feeling that he was quite happy in his little republic without bananas.

It was the fall time of the year and as evening time began to gray the light, Mr. Murphy, the superintendent, suggested the worst. "I will have to get the gun and shoot Horace in the behind," said Mr. Murphy.

I was not sure why Mr. Murphy was going to shoot Horace in the behind but Danny was quick to question the tactic. "Any particular reason why Horace is to be shot in the behind Mr. Murphy," Danny asked in his quiet way.

"Oh, that is the best spot to shoot a monkey with a tranquilizing dart," said Mr. Murphy. "It reduces the chance of hitting his bone structure, thereby avoiding unnecessary injury to the little fellow," Mr. Murphy explained to us as though he was a veteran of such undertakings. I was glad for Horace, as I did not want to see the little furry creature executed for escaping from his enclosure. "You see boys," Mr. Murphy continued, "If Horace gets out of our sight it is unlikely we would ever see him again and if perchance he bit someone, there is a strong possibility of that person contracting rabies, therefore we must put the little fellow to sleep and take him back home, however, when I shoot him, it might take a few minutes for the drug to take effect, so I would like you John and Danny to stay behind and bring him back when the inevitable happens," said Mr. Murphy as he aimed the rifle and shot Horace in the behind.

The aim was good and Horace let out a bit of a screech as the tip of the dart penetrated his behind. But Horace held on... and on... and on. It was decided that I climb the tree and bring Horace down. Up the tree I went. Down the tree went Horace and took off like a bat out of hell across the lovely green lands of the Phoenix Park. Off went Danny after him. From my perch I could see Danny was not making much ground on Horace the monkey. Then Horace decided to stop running and climb a tree. Up the trunk he went, grabbed the first outstretched branch and hung on. From that position he did not move, at least for a few moments. He hung from the branch by one long arm and seemed to sway to the light breeze of the evening. The ground beckoned to him and Horace could not resist. He remained motionless on the ground. The drug had taken affect. As Danny and I walked back to the zoo grounds with Horace sleeping soundly in a sack, Danny changed the conversation from monkey business to Gaelic football. "I hear your team, St Agnes' is in the final against Ballyfermot Gaels this Sunday. Are you on the team, John?" he asked with a sense of interest.

"Yes, I am playing goalkeeper and I really don't think too much of our chances but you never know," I replied.

"Well, I'll have my fingers crossed for you and your team even though I come from Ballyfermot" Danny said jokingly as we walked in through the gates of the zoo grounds with our sleeping monkey.

FIELD OF CHAMPIONS

The afternoon had a bit of a haze to it as the teams took to the field and our chance of winning was doubtful. Ballyfermot was a tough team, one coached by the Christian Brothers and the Christian Brothers were excellent coaches. However, my father decided to attend the game, a most unusual occurrence. This visitation by Dad was indeed odd because in all the time I had played Gaelic football, Dad had never come to support us. Nevertheless, that morning he made up for all the games he had missed. I swear to this day that he fired up a team that had neither seen him nor heard of him but whatever chemistry took hold on the field that day, he bawled the Ballyfermot Gales to defeat.

The cup belonged to St. Agnes' - a sore throat to Dad and great mutterings to the Christian Brothers.

O' Father, dear Father, why cans't thou speak? A few weeks passed before

Mother could understand her husband's mutterings. A massive case of laryngitis beset itself upon Dad's vocals - a souvenir from the field of champions but proud the good man was of his newly adopted team.

It seemed my career in Gaelic football was under way. The football scouts who attended the championship game found favor in my playing abilities. I was selected into the roster that would determine the team to represent the Dublin minors that year. I felt privileged and proud - honored to wear the blue and white colors, which represented the Dublin Gaelic football team.

It was a warm cloudy Sunday afternoon as the team jogged on to the field of Croke Park. The game was just a preliminary one but it was the proudest day of my life. I stood with the boys in the blue and white of the Dublin Minor Gaelic football club on the field of greatness, which I had dreamed about since the early days of childhood. I was sixteen years old. When the contest was over, I was informed I was selected to play in the next preliminary game. That meant I was getting closer to being a part of the final selection to represent Dublin in the All Ireland League. But life has its twists, and instead of pursuing my football career, I found myself standing on board a ship sailing out from Dun Laghorie harbor. I was on my way to Winterthur, Switzerland via England.

THE LAND OF WILLIAM TELL

A Swiss construction Company advertised in a Dublin newspaper for tradesmen and general laborers. I fit into the latter category and secured the laborer's humble position of much work and little pay. Still, I was happy. My life as a wanderer was finally under steam and I was on my way to the land of William Tell and a country that produced the best yodelers the world over.

It was in this land of the great Alps that I would meet the indomitable Tom Kilroy a native of Kiltimage, County Mayo - a self educated man and versed in no less than seven languages. It was here too that our small band of Irish workers would meet the man called Johann.

Johann, a Catholic layman, seemed quite concerned about the sinful attractions of the city nightlife and made every effort to ensure our spiritual needs were taken care of. This good soul meant well but we were tired of the guilt-ridden preachings of Mother Church. Still, twice a week the good man showed up at the Company's rooming house to lead us in prayer but in time the group dwindled until the last of us found refuge in the drinking establishments. It was ironic that at the time before Johann's visitations, we were not interested in the bar scene but that is where we found refuge from him.

Eventually, Tom told Johann on behalf of the group, that although we respected his efforts and concerns towards our spiritual needs, it would be more beneficial if he were to spend his valuable time on those more interested in his religious instruction. He seemed hurt but accepted our decision. Before he bid us adieu, he invited Tom and me to visit St. Gallen, a town of historical and religious interest. We agreed. The following Sunday we arrived in St. Gallen and were duly impressed with the town's distinct architectural features. St. Gallen (St Gall) was a monk of old, who had left Ireland sometime in the middle ages, traveled to Switzerland and preached Christianity. It was in this area he settled, preached the word of Christ and remained till the end of his life. We walked the old trails and sat by the river where the Saint fed and cared for the sick and injured wild animals, including bears and wolves. After, we visited the Cathedral named in honor of the Saint and I was impressed with the simplicity of its inner spiritual and artistic expressions. I was thankful Johann had taken us there. Nevertheless, the escape from Johann and his religious preaching gave rise to a solid interest in the very thing Johann tried so desperately to steer our group from – the lure of the mystique of the night life and the amber liquid.

A year had passed since my arrival in Switzerland and although I was very much at ease in this lovely land, I was growing restless. The way of the wanderer began to gnaw at my spirit. The land of Germany beckoned to my curiosity. Tom, too decided to call it quits and soon we were train bound for Germany. As night descended, I watched the inviting countryside change from colorful hues to soft grays and soon I surrendered to the call of sleep but not for long.

In the small hours of the morning, a woman of great largeness rudely awakened me. I had been sleeping in an ordinary compartment in the sitting position, while Tom lay stretched out on the seat opposite, contented in his snores. Much was my disgruntlement with this great intrusion. The large lady, without pause, swung her belongings upon the rack above my head and then in that 'here I come' sweeping motion, swung her formidable person into position on the seat, which I occupied. In an instant my modest figure took on prominent physiological changes. There was not enough room for both of us in the seat and one of us had to go - and go, I nearly did, through the side of the train and out into the quietness of the German night.

THE SECOND PURPOSE

Many inches of flesh were removed instantly from my sides only to be added to my stomach and chest, as the latter were pushed outwards and upwards in front of my nose. So there I was, in the cozy comfort of human squashedness, fighting fiercely to engineer my lungs back to working order. My gestures of appeal went unheeded as I tried to call to Tom who was in deep consultation with the spirits of the little death. I was under the impression he didn't give a damn about his friend who was truly lost in the body of a big woman he did not even know. O how I suffered! Poor me, hardly seen and not heard as the excess carriage of the lady of great muchness swallowed me into her confines.

Tom snored peacefully as the good woman comforted me against my will. She talked and talked so bloody loudly, I was convinced Tom's heart had given up the ghost because he did not as much as break the cadence of his sleeping music. I had no idea who she was talking with but if it was to me, she would have had to make a concentrated search to find me. As the night passed on I called out to the good Lord and promised Him I would never say a bad word again or think bad thoughts, and any money I earned, I would give it to charity. Whatever it would take - but please release me, let me go.

Well, I tell you! The good Lord must have heard my mournful begging, for no sooner were these words uttered, her ladyship decided to go in search of those places for private and personal relief. As she stood up, the pressure was released from the sides of my body and the sudden jolting of my organs catapulting back into their proper places caused me great discomfort. Nevertheless, I did not tarry and made a bolt through the door and into the safety of the corridor.

Here, in the confines of the hall I would see the night through and welcome journey's end when the train rolled into Stuttgart at early morning. I eventually met up with Tom, who immediately expressed his concern about the weight I had put on overnight and suggested I go see a doctor but after a quick explanation, we laughed a tired laugh and went in search of breakfast.

Breakfast was enjoyed to the fullest and whether it was tiredness, homesickness, or the love affair I had with the big lady against my will in the little compartment of the train, I do not know? But I decided to return home to Ireland. Tom on the other hand figured on traveling to France.

After breakfast, I bid adieu to Tom, moved out towards the highway and hitched a ride to Amsterdam. From Amsterdam I caught the ferry across to England, rode the train to Hollyhead and then the ferry to Dublin.

My first priority back in Dublin was to secure a job. The opportunity to make chocolate bars presented itself, and soon I found myself gazing at the yummy creatures rolling along on a conveyor belt.

FLAMBO SHAUNESSY AND THE CHOCOLATE WALTZ

Flambo Shaunessy was a talented fellow. There seemed always to be a song passing through the lips of Flambo and a smile to go with it. He was jolly indeed and popular with the lads - even more so with the ladies. Flambo was also a passionate dancer and when the urge to dance beckoned to his pleasure, he'd simply grab the nearest idle thing to him, which was usually a mop or broom and off he'd go, waltzing along by the conveyor belt, singing his favorite love song: Elvis Presley's, "Are You Lonesome To-night". The girls just loved to see the Flambo do his thing as we boys entertained a little envy. I think perhaps watching Flambo acting as though he were truly as free as the breeze and not in the least self conscious about his uninhibited expressions was the element that caste the slight hint of envy upon us. However, a most unusual happening was in the offing, one that caught Flambo by surprise, as well as the flower of the factory, Sheila Mc Nulty.

One morning, Flambo, being in a rather high-spirited mood, decided to perform the latest jive introduced to the world of dancing. With great flair and a good measure of expertise, Flambo took to the floor with such remarkable agility that any mop would have been complemented to share in his artistic endowments. He exhibited an extraordinary demonstration of physical agility, complete with the most up to date facial contortions, as he twisted legs, arms, back, belly, face, ears, toes and nose into what can be described as an octopus trying to scratch itself in one of those hard to reach places.

Nobody seemed to give a damn about the chocolates rolling on by, piling up at the end of the conveyor belt. The Flambo was at his best and we were all captivated by this man's dancing genius. Unfortunately, the most shocking happened to the poor Flambo. Flambo, dedicated to that peculiar state of mind, in which he therein dwelled, twisted his frame a little too close to the rolling conveyor.

It happened in the twinkling of an eye. The waist-belt that supported Flambo's pants somehow got caught in the conveyor machinery and off came the dancers pants - dropping fully to the floor. Normally such a happening is not such a big deal but in Flambo's case he was not sporting underwear.

Dancing in one's birthday suit with one's pants down around one's legs, no doubt has to be one of the most difficult undertakings in the world and Flambo seemed bent on being a part of that endeavor. Apparently, it had not dawned on Flambo that his pants had removed themselves from his person and that his most private of privates were being displayed. In an instant, Sheila Mc Nulty was up on her seat leaning over the conveyor belt roaring at the top of her voice. "Look at it! Would ye for God's sake take a look at it! Ah Flambo... ye poor thing." But the lovely Sheila in her moment of excitement, leaned a little too far over the conveyor belt and the next thing we know - Sheila was traveling with the chocolates.

In the panic that followed, nobody seemed to know how the conveyor belt switched off. Parties from both sides of the conveyor belt endeavored to assist Sheila but in the confusion of how to handle her "poetry in motion," the poor dear was almost pulled apart - each side trying desperately to pull the lovely one to their side of the belt. Sweet Sheila, was just a couple of feet from the automatic stamping plates and there was no way on God's green earth she was going to make it through the stamping devices without being seriously injured - perhaps even worse. Someone screamed, "lift her up for God's sake!" In an instant all hands had the lovely Sheila airborne. There she was suspended above her chocolates as they rolled on by under her lovely person. Now the character of Sheila was indeed something to behold, because instead of crying or screaming for her mammy, she began to laugh. But it was no laughing matter because nobody knew how to turn the machine off.

By now Flambo had, to some extent, returned to the world of reality and finally seemed to realize he was not in Hollywood but on duty in a chocolate factory. It eventually dawned on him he was out of uniform and in his embarrassed panic to redress himself, the poor Flambo lost his balance. He tried desperately to stay on his feet, as he hopped, skipped and jumped to maintain control but slowly, ever so slowly, Flambo moved in the direction that one does when one is going to execute the arse over heel maneuver. And so it was, the Flambo ended his exhibition with a most unusual bow. This being done, he secured his pant's to his person, reached around one of the support pillars of the building, snapped the lever and shut the power off. Flambo returned to work as though nothing had happened, and Sheila, perhaps in a mild state of shock, sat back on her seat.

The conveyor belt started, the chocolates rolled and the great Flambo grabbed another broom, whistling merrily as he went about his chores

IN THE TRENCHES

Kilroy soon followed my homecoming. His stint in France had proved useful to him. He got a job working as a farm hand. While he had enjoyed the French culture, he had missed his native land. It was good to see him. He looked forward to returning to his home in Mayo. He invited me to spend some time at his home as soon as he was settled. I looked forward to the visit. It was not long before I bid adieu to the lovely Sheila, the dancing Flambo and the chocolate factory and hit the trail to meet the great Kilroy.

I had not been to the west of Ireland before and I was not disappointed. I loved it out here where people were few and the land clean and magical. Out in this sparsely wooded wilderness, roaming its hills and valleys, I dreamt my dreams by the pristine streams where the curlew cast its song to the breeze. In from the sea blew the crisp winds to touch the timelessness of the land's soul - a land unhurried, untainted, a land exuding a defiance to wasteful change, here in lovely Connaught.

"My young Dublin friend," said Tom. "I have a hell of a proposition and I want ye to listen." And so, John listened to what Tom had to say. "The government has been generous of late. They have offered the good sum of one shilling and eight pence per dug or excavated foot of soil to improve the drainage system of the land." And with further emphasis on the foot stuff, Tom went on. "That is, Mr. McDonald, one long foot by one foot wide and two feet deep so we may convert the terrain into productive farm land. And just imagine," he further emphasized. "Since you are an expert on digging trenches, you could spend the rest of your days out here in the West shoveling shite."

I thought about what Tom said for a quick moment, a very quick moment and decided against the offer. I was fond of the land but not so fond of it that I wanted to dig trenches in it for the rest of my life. "You are a generous man Tom," I said. "Your jokes are of a poor quality indeed but I will stay a while and dig in with you." With that said I grabbed a pick and shovel, wandered down the field with Tom and dug in. We dug and dug and dug, day in and day out. I thought if I could engineer my life to such precision as I demonstrated while digging trenches, that I could really make something of myself but what that self might be, I had no idea. I put the question to Tom.

"Mr. Kilroy, what is it that causes discontentment in a man's soul?" I asked.

"That is a loaded question my friend. Is your question about all men or is it just about you?" He said.

I paused for a moment before I answered. "It's me, Tom. Truthfully, I am not sure what the hell I am doing. I feel like I am running away all the time, not able to or not wanting to fit in. It's really bothersome." I said.

"Perhaps you are not meant to fit into a structured life my friend. I have noticed how you spend time in the hills. Yours may be a different path and it is only you that can find that path." And he continued. "I too am a wanderer but I have found purpose with life. I am a writer. You have yet to discover yours," he said.

"And how do I discover my purpose Tom?" I asked him.

"That, my friend, is something you must search for. Some Indian tribes of North America believe that one will find purpose in the silence of the wilderness. Perhaps that place is for you, to discover what you are about." Then he concluded. "I feel you may have many difficulties along your trail but in time you will find meaning to your journey."

Restlessness again stirred within and pretty soon I was bidding my good friend farewell. It was the last time I would see him and I wondered if he would succeed as a playwright. His thoughts and ideas were sound, as were his intellect and his great heart. There should be no reason why this good man should not succeed, no reason at all. Still, I wondered what life was truly all about.

It was across the Irish Sea again, this time to visit my brother, Lawrence, who had left Dublin some years earlier to study psychology at the Tooting Bec Institution in London. He invited me to take up studies with him but since I could hardly read and write I felt it inappropriate to attempt it and for that matter I was not interested in the study of the mechanics of the mind. Working with a pick and shovel seemed more suitable to me. Good wages were to be made working the London underground train tunnels. I wasted no time securing a job there. It was not a nice job. Much of the time I spent picking myself up out of the mud or helping pull someone else out of it. It was cold, damp, muddy and slimy - everything purgatory must be: that place of great grayness and perpetual mist.

After work, there was no place to wash or clean the mud from our persons. Indeed, it was a purgatory because we looked like the living dead as we made our way up the elevator shaft and out into the light at work's end. Working these foreboding places under such unsafe and miserable conditions left no doubt in my mind what human discount was. This underground was not a pleasant place to be. But for one reason or another, men gave it their best and through the misery found a way of easing the insanity of it all by finding something to laugh at, something to lighten the load. For sure, down in this hellhole I was learning that a sense of humor would serve me well. It would see me through difficult times. It was important I develop it, hang on to it, take it wherever I go, use it freely and to hell with the seriousness of it all. The road ahead was not going to be easy. I would, in time, need every assistance from those who walked the road before me to pull me out of the hell I would eventually venture into - a hell, still some years in the future.

I grew tired of washing down the mud with pints of Guinness or a host of other drinks available for such purposes. I was now beginning to develop a tolerance for the stuff that was supposed to make a man of me. Although I was not overly fond of the taste of alcohol, I was attracted to its social setting. To wander home aimlessly after a few too many with the road flowing ahead of me, did not for some peculiar reason impress upon me the oddity of the inebriated state of being. It seemed to me that the effects and after effects of a night's drinking were natural biological occurrences and should not be questioned. It was an accepted activity of life, drinking, getting drunk, having a good time and it was all right to sleep in a doorway along the sidewalk, on a park bench, or in a garbage dumpster for that matter and I thought again about the disappointment that happened in the garden of yesteryear.

GOOD CHRISTIAN SOLDIERS AND THE CONGO

I became restless in the perpetual bustle of London and longed to travel the open road once again. I bid adieu to brother Lawrence at the hospital and my buddies from below the earth and set out for mainland Europe. A train to Dover, a ferry to Ostend, Belgium and once again I was on mainland Europe. In Ostend, I checked into the youth hostel and later that evening at a local tavern, I met Brian of Dublin. And Brian of Dublin said. "Didn't I see you somewhere before?" And soon it was realized that we both had worked at the chocolate factory back in Dublin.

After a few pints of beer brought about comfortable chatter, Brian imparted to me some adventurous information. "John, word has it that there is a bar in Copenhagen where soldiers of fortune meet," he said more quietly than the sleeping whispers of the summer pines.

"Men of fortune? I don't understand. Are they wealthy? Do they have lots of money? Please explain Brian?"

Brian explained, "Soldiers of fortune are good men who take up arms against rotten bastards who cause great misery to innocent people."

"I see. So what you are saying to me is: a whole bunch of these fortune fellows meet at the pub, say prayers and go off to fight for the rights of those oppressed."

"No John, that's not what I am saying," Brian replied. "What I am saying is this! After soldiers of fortune take a break from the good Christian work they do, some of them come to Copenhagen to visit, drink lots of beer, find women, have a good time and head off to the war fields again."

"What's so Christian about that kind of behavior," I said.

"Nothing in particular," said Brian, "other than most of them are Christian."

"So, where is all this leading," I said.

"There's a lot of money to be made in the Congo operating as a mercenary and if we play our cards right, we can meet some of these fellows who have finished their tour of duty and get the low-down on the situation." I thought about my military experience back in Ireland and felt that I had enough training to enter into combat on the side of the good Christians and beat the crap out of the dirty swine that brought misery to the impoverished. I looked forward to meeting real men, real warriors who fought for the cause of justice and I was going to be one of them. I thought that in the Eyes of God, killing bad people would be O. K. and I would not go to hell for getting rid of filthy murdering swine. God would give his blessing towards this work and I would be seen favorably in His light. The following morning we set out for Denmark.

It was a miserable winter's evening as we entered through the doorway of the Copenhagen tavern; our ears treated to familiar songs of home by a couple of wandering Celtic musicians. In short time we met the boys from the Congo. I felt privileged to be among the bravest of the brave. Wine, beer and whiskey were the order of the evening; as songs were sung, men talked real talk and the women were proud to be among the worlds finest. The evening moved on and as conversation opened up to the real nature of what was happening in the Congo, I was beginning to become greatly unsettled from what I was hearing. The good Christian soldier was not as Christian as I was led to believe. A good belly of disgust was developing in me towards those who lived by the gun. To see an individual smile as he took pleasure in describing how he murdered defenseless women, children and men, and then empty cans of gasoline over their bodies, drop a burning match, stand back and savor the fruits of their day's work, was beyond my comprehension. I had much to learn about the real nature of man.

I had heard enough. I told Brian I was not interested in listening to any more bullshit and I was leaving. He too had had enough of big mens' talk and prepared to leave. Just as we were polishing off the last of our beer, the unexpected happened. Two of the mercenaries got into an argument and decided to settle things in the back alley. Everybody figured on a fistfight but when each combatant produced a knife, the mood of the onlookers changed considerably. Dismay was in vogue and perhaps a killing or two. Someone addressed the combatants. "Now boys, now, no need to settle something of no importance by killing each other. You know, the best way to solve anything is to clarify what the dispute is about, over a pint or two."

The voice was having little or no effect. The dangerous men with knives seemed bent on making the deadly steel draw blood. They circled each other. I watched in horror. I could not comprehend the madness of the event. We, (about ten of us), stood in a circle, just as I had done in the Irish countryside in years past with great hunters, watching dogs tear a beautiful fox to pieces. Here again, the scene of such a disgusting event was about to unfold. The voices fell silent. The fighters moved slowly, circling each other, gauging each other's depth of madness. It would be just a matter of moments before one of them lay on the cobblestones in a most unhealthy state.

Nobody seemed to know what to do. We just stood there like frozen zombies, detached from our senses, watching and waiting and scared. Then a miracle! In this dark and miserable wintry laneway, the silence of madness was shattered by the earsplitting cry of an alley cat. One of the fighting morons scared so badly he let his knife drop. The rest of us spilled our jugs of beer over each other. The screech of the cat seemed to snap us back to reality and someone told the combatants it was too cold to be killing each other and contest should be put on hold till summertime. Brian began to laugh, the cat let out a screech one more time; the fellow who dropped the knife was told his fly was open. That comment diffused the seriousness of the confrontation. The madness was over with, at least for now. I wondered about the scene I had witnessed but still did not make the connection between the insanity and the amber colored liquid.

Brian and I had had enough of the tough talk. We took leave and headed to Koge, a small town on the edge of the North Sea. Brian and I secured work at the local lumber mill but the bitter winds whipping in from the North Sea, were not something I was prepared to deal with. I decided to pack up and head out for the kibbutzs in Israel. Brian was not interested in traveling to the sunny south. I would go it alone.

It was bitterly cold standing on the autobahn in the middle of February, my thumb extended to the wind. In time a Volkswagen stopped. I was picked up – really picked up except I did not know it at the time. As the grayness of evening approached, the driver, Jesper, suggested we stop overnight at a hotel because it was too far and dangerous a drive to continue on to Munic non stop. I agreed.

"I think it would be a very good idea if we shared a room and bed for the night," said Jesper. It was one of those times when one is certain of what one heard but needs a repeat to be sure.

"What did you say Jesper?" I asked.

"I think it a good idea to share a room and a bed together so we can save a few marks," he reiterated.

"Jesper, I want you to listen very carefully. I do not sleep with men. In fact, I still have to experience the sleeping thing with a woman, but it will be with a woman I will sleep with when that time comes. I do not need to save a few marks that badly - shall we leave it at that?" I said. And so it was left at that or so I thought.

Jesper did not speak German. It was left to me to make the arrangements. This being done, we packed our gear into the hotel and settled down for the night. The cheapest way for us to go was to rent a room with two single beds. I felt pretty uneasy about my situation but there was not a whole lot I could do about it. I was exhausted. It was not long before I was in a deep sleep.

It was, I believe, about three o' clock in the morning when I awoke to the desperate cries of Jesper. He explained he had been sitting in his bed reading a book while sipping on a glass of water and as he turned a page in his book, he somehow lost his grip on the glass and the fountain of life poured over his bed. He asked if it was all right to share my bed. It is a rare thing when I get badly upset and Jesper managed to do just that. "Jesper," I said, "get used to your water bed because you are having nothing to do with mine"- and Jesper did exactly what he was told.

At morning, we were back on the road arriving in Munich late afternoon. It was farewell to Jesper and off to the Hoff Brau Haus beer hall to indulge while I mulled over my maps and plan my journey to Israel. Late afternoon turned into evening as the tempo of life in the great hall quickened. All was well in my world as the music played and the beer flowed. Around midnight, I think, a tattered looking soul presented him self to the rather large number of patrons, most of whom were American soldiers. The tattered looking soul stood upon the long wooden beer table and addressed the multitudes.

I had some difficulty discerning what this good fellow was up to because the fog had thickened somewhat in my brain and it was not easy for me to define, visually, who was who and what was what. I had, however, an uncomfortable feeling I knew the fellow who stood limp among the steins of beer; he looked familiar. He rambled on about this and that and whatever to a largely inattentive crowd but gained complete attention when the idiot shouted across the hall 'Yankee go home'.

Silence gripped the hall and an American soldier gripped the tattered looking soul by the throat and in one swift movement threw the idiot across the floor. But the idiot was not alone. He had help. And the fool who went to help the idiot was none other than one of the two mercenaries who were scared by an alley cat in Copenhagen. The other was unconscious on the floor. Like a wobbling rhino he lunged at the soldier. The soldier steeped aside sweeping his foot into the lunger's arse driving him head first into the hard wood of the table's leg. Both mercenaries were asleep within seconds of each other. One soldier had taken care of things.

Moments later a bucket of ice brought the Congo fighters back to earth and as they were being hauled away by the police, one of them turned to me and said. "For God's sake, come and get us John, we're counting on you." I was startled. How on earth did he recognize me? I did not know. The police threw them in the German paddy wagon and hauled them off to jail. I sat again to nurture my beer, to dream my dreams and scheme my schemes. I tried to forget about the idiot and the fool but my conscience would not allow me.

THE ROCKY ROAD TO SPAIN

The blast of winter's icy wind slapped at my face, giving me the impression that I was still alive as the sharp, piercing sounds of the police sirens split the early morning silence while I wandered in search of the jailhouse. Common sense told me not to go to the place where the cars with noisy sirens were going because Zack and Jock, the mercenaries were there and I should avoid them at all costs. But stupidity overruled common sense and so it was, I was able to secure the release of the terrible duo.

What was it in my nature that caused me to step into troublesome unpredictability? It was an ingredient in my makeup that would cause me unwanted trouble time and again. Was it a passion operating in a guilt-ridden mind to try to do the right thing? Was it part of a massive sense of insecurity? Was it low self-worth that would cause me to play out a martyr-like lifestyle? It never entered my head to dwell on the more worthy things I had accomplished. That was it! I suffered the inability to take into consideration the good I had done. So what the hell was causing such a negative flow of energy through me? I did not know. Would St Christopher, the patron saint for travelers gone to get them out of jail? Perhaps he would have! He would have seen the good in them and that is what was important; the feeling of doing a compassionate turn in helping my fellow man. So I reasoned I should do as St Christopher would do – that I should go get the trouble making fools out of the jailhouse.

There release secured, Jock insisted on thanking me by sharing his latest wonderful idea. "What idea would that be," I asked him expectantly.

"If we buy a car, we could drive through Switzerland, France and Spain, sell the car in the port city of Cartagena, Spain, and travel by ship across the Mediterranean to Haifa, Israel," he said.

"Some great idea that is Jock," said Zack, "but where do you think we are going to get the money to purchase an automobile, the gas and insurance to get us there?"

"Let's look at it this way," said Jock. "You have an international license, so we don't have a problem as far as driving is concerned and as far as insurance goes we automatically get that when we buy the car."

"Well that's just goddamned wonderful," said Zack, "now that you've sorted us all out for the traveling, who the hell is going to pay for the auto?"

"Well, if we all chip in, I'm sure we could get an old beater to take us to Spain for next to nothing, " said Jock. I was not too sure where all this was leading - the money part that is but I thought it a good idea and said so. However, what I did not realize was, that I was being set up. I had the money and Zack and Jock were intent on getting me to loosen it up so they could sit on their arses at my expense, driving in plush comfort all the way to Spain. And got me they did.

Jock had about fifty German marks to his name and Zack had about the same. I had about five hundred marks, so it was reasonable to assume the financing of the trip was going to come from my pocket. Off without delay to the place where cars were sold and before long a car was purchased and owned by Zack. It was Zack who possessed an international drivers license, therefore it was Zack who was able legally to purchase a nice little red Volkswagen with my money. Zack was doing very well out of the deal. He had not laid out as much a penny on the car and it was he who owned it. I was out four hundred marks, which had taken me a few months to earn and was now stuck with two guys who possessed unpredictable natures. Where this journey was going, I was absolutely uncertain.

The promise of working on an Israeli kibbutz was very attractive to me. I looked forward to visiting the Promised land. The picture Zack had painted of half-naked, beautiful women picking fruits from the vine made the journey even more desirable.

The road to Israel lay open. We were on our way. Out of snowy Munich, Zack drove our little red auto, which we appropriately named Little Red Riding Hood. It was nice traveling in the comfort of Zack's auto. Excellent time was made and by evening's end we had made it to Winterthur in Switzerland. We booked into an old castle, which had been converted into a hostel and made plans for the next day. Morning came far too early but the open road beckoned and truly it seemed the Esso pictures from my school days had come alive. It was exactly how I had envisioned it. To awaken a free man, in a free world, without a bother and owing nothing to anyone. It was indeed a wonderful feeling. The weather was beginning to warm a little as we slowly moved south away from the cold reaches of northern Europe.

On we went, secure in the knowledge that our Little Red Riding Hood would give a faithful and excellent performance. I personally felt like a tourist and I was comfortable with the way Zack was driving. In fact, I was beginning to form a different viewpoint on these two mercenaries and my judgment of them being murdering bastards was beginning to soften. But, as sure as God would deliver a sun each morning, my changing view on my traveling companions was about to receive a woeful slap in the face.

It was late evening when we reached Basel. Somewhere on the outskirts of the city, we pulled in at a hotel, decided to have some beers and take stock of our progress. We were much buoyed by the progress we were making and the reality of it was that we were going to make it to Israel. To be sure, we were on our way to work alongside those beautiful women in the fruit groves and as the beer made its journey to my stomach, then, to my blood stream and eventually to my house of thinking, the magic and enthrallment of the journey took on biblical proportions.

I do not know how long I was in that world of loveliness but I found myself rudely snapped out of it by the unmistakable concern in the waiter's voice as he cried, "Bitte! Bitte! Dumkopp! Aus, aus, schnell, schnell." It was a terrible thing indeed to be snatched away from my delightful dreamland by the unpleasant activity of the waiter strangling Jock and tossing him arse overhead across a table.

"For the love of Christ," I called out to Zack. "Can we not go anywhere without this idiot causing trouble?" I was indeed mightily pissed off and I could see now that no matter where we went with this Jock fellow, there was going to be trouble and lots of it. I immediately moved in between the waiter and Jock, explaining that I was extremely sorry for the behavior of my traveling companion and that I would remove him immediately from the premises. However, this was far more easily said than done. It seemed that once Jock had some beer in his belly he was bent on destruction.

I was just as much alarmed at the placid behavior of Zack in these rather unpleasant circumstances. It seemed he gave his full approval to Jock's violent excursions and I was quick to tell him so. I told him that if it was not too much trouble, would he kindly help me get this goddamned troublemaker out of the hotel before the police came and threw us all in the slammer. I did not want a repeat of what took place in Munich but it sure looked like it was heading that direction. The seriousness in my voice seemed to grab Zack's attention and strangely, with a little encouragement from Zack, Jock surrendered his madness and removed himself from the premises. They disappeared into the night. I apologized profusely to the waiter and told him I would make sure we would not come this way again. With those words, I handed him a twenty-franc note and made my way back to Little Red Riding Hood.

I had waited some time for the deadly duo to show up at the car but it was beyond me as to where they had disappeared. I was still at that naive age where it would not enter my head that they may have headed off to another bar. I waited and waited and then the thought struck me that I should grab my gear and disappear. However, this idea soon dwindled into nothingness because the car was locked and Zack had the keys. I was furious with myself for allowing this type of situation to occur because at this point all I wanted to do was get away from these madmen. As much as I desired to make my exit, I could see it was not going to be easy.

The beer I had consumed in the bar was now taking effect. My head felt heavy, my eyes sleepy. I sat by Little Red looking up at the starlit Swiss sky wondering how I was going to make my escape. The booze took full control of my senses and soon I was fast asleep.

It was around two a.m. when I awoke to the proddings of the two missing mercenaries. Zack was in glorious voice, singing the Universal Soldier Song to the presence of the multitudes of nobodies and clearly, had a voice that made my father's sound as sweet as the nectar of the Gods. They had returned from a watering hole they had no doubt found by mistake after we had left the previous one. It seemed they had behaved themselves and this gave me a little comfort of mind. The night was not too chilly and we decided to camp where we were. I fell back to sleep listening to the God awful strains of Zack torturing some unfortunate song.

The morning's hazy sunshine greeted our fuzzy minds and overloaded bladders. The French border was not far. It was a matter of hours before we reached it and passed through without difficulties. It was wonderful traveling south through the French countryside. By nightfall we had reached Lyon and then turned southeast and crossed the French Alps heading towards Marseille. Tiredness brought the drive to an end. We pulled off the mountain highway to rest the night. Zack was a good driver and even he was impressed with the guts of Little Red. The weather in the French Alps was kind to us. A good breakfast at sunrise, a wash in a mountain stream, and we were on our way to the port city of Marseille. Since we had left wintry Munich, the weather had warmed considerably.

The dock of the port city bustled with life. I had a sense of being here before. At any moment I felt someone might say, "Hello John, its nice to see you again," but perhaps that was just a reflection of my Celtic imagination. Basking in the brilliant Mediterranean sun, Marseille manifested life at its fullest, a rich tapestry of humanity busy weaving its destiny.

All to soon, it was time to move on. Little Red had the most arduous part of the journey before her. The next stop, the city of Perpignan would bring us ever closer to the great mountainous citadels of the Pyrenees. Late evening saw us roll into the city. We decided to rest the night in Perpignan before we attempted to cross the Pyrenees the next day.

The following morning, happiness danced through my veins, as I looked forward to reaching Cartegena and then,… to Israel. All was well and wonderful in my mind but such thoughts of exciting adventure were about to suffer a severe setback. Indeed, it was beyond belief what was actually taking place. My two companions decided to turn back and travel to Denmark. I was dumfounded. The silence within was deafening, broken only by the thoughts to kill. To kill or not to kill, that was the question. Then, a little bird told me to forget about such nastiness, it was not the right thing to do. Besides, the boys were far more experienced in that department and it was more probable that I would end up dead.

IT'S A LONG WAY TO LONDON

There, not so far away as the crow flies, the Pyrenees stood in all their majesty. Across those mountains lay the land of Spain and I wanted to go there but the two crazy bastards I was traveling with had reneged on the plan. More than that, it was my money that bought the car and it was my money that got us this far. Now I was really pissed off and there was not a whole lot I could do about it. I too, was almost broke and it was only by selling the car in Cartegena we could afford passage to Israel.

"Please make a little sense to me," I screamed at them. "Do tell me, if it is not too much trouble, why the hell you want to go back when we are so close to crossing the sea to Israel". Then our world grew still but only for a moment. I continued, "You pair of thick bastards, you have been nothing but trouble since I met you. You conned me, didn't you, you pair of useless shite hawks? If ye had a brain between ye it would be the most lonesome thing in the universe," I roared at them. I was on a roll. The debasing names that I unloaded upon their cowering frames were coming to mind thick and fast. I unloaded volley after volley, smiting the creeps with the vomit of my ire. I became more enraged as both of them held their silence, neither one fueling the fire of my rage. I'm not sure if I began to do an old ancient Celtic war dance but in reflection, there may have been a strong possibility of such a happening. I think I was on the verge of offering myself up to the gods when at last the voice of Zack broke the bout of morning madness.

"We can't cross into Spain because my driver's license has expired," he explained. At the Swiss and French customs we were asked only for the car insurance, not my driver's license. However, at the Spanish border, I will be asked for both driver's license and insurance and that will spell the death of the trip."

"How come we're just finding this information now?" I spat back at him.

"Last night when you and Jock were sleeping I went into the town for a beer. There I met some Australians who had just arrived from Spain and they told me there is no way we can cross the border without a driver's license; they will impound the car if we try it."

"Why can't you renew your license? Surely we can do that, cant we?" I spat at him. No we can't because when we bought the car in Munich, the dealer did not ask for my license and it was a good thing he did not. It was already two years expired. Nothing but chance got us this far.

Oh Lord! Here I am in the lovely warm fresh winds of dear old France listening to the greatest load of pure shite I ever listened to and not a blasted thing I can do about it except take a long hard look at the elusive Pyrnenees and surrender my dreams of picking oranges and parsnips on the kibbutz in the Promised Land.

Sad was my heart when Little Red pointed her nose to the frozen European North and moved ever so faithfully towards the land of the winter snows. The morning passed on into evening, back into morning and little, very little was said as we steadily moved into the cooler temperatures of the north. It was the second evening of our trip when we arrived back in the city of Basel, Switzerland. After the long journey, we decided to go for a beer and mull over our next move. That move was not long in coming.

Unknown to me, perhaps to all three, we had unwittingly stopped at the hotel where Jock had caused the trouble with the waiter some days before. The waiter recognized us immediately and insisted we leave at once which we did except for Jock. Jock decided to make an issue out of it and this time a full brawl got under way. The waiter received a punch across his chops from the fist of Jock, which sent him reeling backwards into the beer parlor. However, this waiter was not about to take an unfair wallop across his chops. With the dignity and composure of one well versed in the higher arts of human behavior, the good waiter removed his spectacles, placing them with the grace of a saint upon a table, dusted his clothes appropriately, fixed his tie, then moved towards Jock.

It was one of the most marvelous experiences my eyes were ever treated to. It must have been close to the speed of lightening before the foot of the waiter stopped abruptly in that very sensitive area of the physical known only to the male gender. Absent were the appropriate facial expressions to fit the dynamics of the equation but they were on their way, a trifle slow at first, then quickly to full maturity. Poor Jock, I thought to myself and then I thought, "Ah, serves the bastard right!" And so the waiter served the bastard right and left and right and left and out through the front door and down the street. He then dumped him for good measure head first into a garbage can and belted him with the lid. Then, as one might well have desert after a good meal, the good waiter picked up the bin and emptied the bloodied limp frame of Jock by the sidewalk.

I wasn't surprised at Zack's decision not to step in and help Jock. Zack, I'm sure, still had the memory fresh in his mind of the thrashing he received back in Munich because of his buddy. I wanted to say something to the waiter but the waiter had everything under control. He didn't need to hear my apologies for the one lying on the street. He had heard them a few nights before and he wasn't in the mood to listen. He walked towards me, not in a threatening manner but in the fashion one might cordially leave a table after a delightful meal. He brushed his clothes as he addressed me. "That fellow lying in the street is a very bad bucket of shit and you should not be mit such bad things as him. I vent easy on him only because he vos mit you. I should not hang around mit such - he for you vill only trouble bring," he said as he strolled back towards the hotel. I nodded my head in agreement but said nothing.

I thought it was the last of the spectacle but the waiter had other ideas. He re-emerged from the hotel with a bucket of sloppy water and gave the Jock lad his final blessing as he poured it over the stricken warrior, then as though it were all in a days work, bid us farewell forever.

Zack and I removed the bloodied but peaceful Jock from the street, placed him in the back of the car and headed north to the German Swiss border. He had been beaten senselessly but he would live. The dear fellow remained quiet for the remainder of the trip to the town of Essen, Germany, where I stepped from the little red car and bid the boys adieu forever. With them went my Little Red and an end to my disappointments and frustrations. "Lord help the people they run into in Denmark" was my last silent remark as the Volkswagen disappeared into the distance of early morning.

Luck was with me in catching rides and by late afternoon I had made it close to the Dutch border. In due course while thumbing, a motorcycle policeman stopped and checked my passport. "May I see your papers please," the winterized policeman said to me politely.

"Yes sir, I have my passport here in my pocket… ah yes… here it is," I responded in the same courteous manner as the policeman.

"Ah, you are an Irishman," he said quiet happily as he leafed through my papers.

"Yes sir, I am from Dublin. I am on my way to visit my brothers in London and I hope to make it to Rotterdam before nightfall," I said as I smiled a relaxed but weary smile.

"Excellent, excellent... then I will help you have your wish. Please hop on the back seat and I will take you to the border... yes," he said as he nodded for me to sit on the rear seat of his motor bike.

Down the highway we motored towards the border of Holland and in due course the policeman pulled up by a transport at a truck stop along the highway. "Hello in there," he shouted up through the window of the driver. Soon a head appeared to query the call.

"Yes, Mr. policeman what can I do for you?" the driver of the truck asked.

"My Irish friend needs to travel to Rotterdam and I see by your plate that you are going there. Can you take him with you?" The German policeman roared up to the Dutch driver.

"Of course, of course, I can take him along," the Dutchman said smiling a broad smile as a puff of smoke from his pipe was lost to the winter air. I could hardly believe my luck. I was on my way.

"Take it easy Irish and have a good time with your life," the policeman said as he helped me with my backpack into the cab. And with those words he laughed a laugh to the broad greatness of the sky and with a wave and a smile disappeared on his motorbike into the creeping mistiness of the icy gray twilight. The Dutch driver fired the engine of his freight truck, welcomed me aboard and headed down the highway towards the border.

Back in London I hooked up with my brother Larry and also brother Gerrard, who had joined Larry to study in the field of psychiatry at the Tooting Bec Institution for Mental health. They invited me to stay at their apartment. I was impressed with the way in which they were both developing purpose and meaning in their lives. Often times we would sit over a pint or two and chat about the business and the mysteries of life and where it all may lead. The answers were always in other questions - without end. Still, we respected each other's views on life and its mysteries and when the debate grew too heavy, Larry had a way of dismantling the impasse as he did on this occasion.

"John, do allow me to treat you to the finest fish and chips in London," Larry shot at me out of the blue. I was surprised at the offering because I was not in the least hungry.

"And where would ye be about obtaining the finest fish and chips in London, dear brother," I replied.

"From my future wife, of course," he said with a bit of a shy smile.

"Your future wife," I said with great surprise.

"Yes, my future wife. Her name is Sunday. She is from Greece and she cooks in the restaurant at the institution. If you play your cards right, John, we can get you settled with a nice Greek lady," he said with a hint of smugness. "As a matter of fact, you will also have the pleasure of meeting Gerrard's future wife. Her name is Sofia and she, too, is Greek." I was impressed with this Irish / Greek foursome get-together but my instincts kicked into high alert. Was I the third member of our family to meet his soul mate at the great restaurant of fish and chips? I must be careful, 'ere my wandering days suddenly surrender to the beauty and charm of a Greek goddess.

In the great bland hall of tasteless institutional food, I was introduced to the ladies from the land of Greece. Sunday and Sofia were indeed ladies of loveliness and to be sure, they did make excellent fish and chips. Still, it would take more than fish and chips to end my wandering ways. My Brother Gerrard, saw to it that I was given this opportunity. Without excusing himself, he walked off to the kitchen and returned with a most splendid goddess of the universe. She was lovelier than the first rose of spring and I immediately fell in lust and love. Katrina, a gorgeous redhead from the "seat of democracy", Athens, possessed beauty and charm that would make the screen stars of Hollywood seethe with envy. What to do, I did not know. I stood at a turning point talking heartily to myself. I thought what a dirty swine my brother is for screwing up my free roaming mind and on the other hand I was elevating him to that hard to get position of sainthood. My mind was still turning at the turning point place, when Sofia, aware of my scattered state of togetherness, took hold of the reins. "Wouldn't it be lovely if we all meet after we finish work and go for a nice cup of coffee," she said, breaking the strain of the disquieting moment.

"He doesn't know what the hell a coffee is Sofia," Gerrard said and continued. "A bloody big glass of beer maybe but not that god awful stuff that looks and tastes like iodine. Its definitely a beer for brother John and Larry - as for me and you lovely ladies - we shall watch as they get drunk and ascend into the shitetalk stuff, arh, arh, arh," he finished with a grand helping of sarcasm.

"Oh what a lovely idea," Katrina said, as she smiled that smile that would cause the instant melting of an iceberg. I was hooked on the charm and loveliness of the Greek goddess and the only thing that I had going for me that would ensure my freedom for the road, was the chance that Katrina possessed not an inkling of interest towards me, otherwise my fate was sealed.

Late evening arrived, as did the ladies and men folk. We stood for awhile on the side walk outside the institution, wondering which pub to visit. Larry suggested we go to the Tooting Bec common - the common name for a park in England - and visit the green grass and flower patches. It was an unusual suggestion but it had appeal. However, we decided against it and went to a pub. The usual searching for easy chatter dominated the scene in our little corner of the pub but as the beers flowed down my gullet - searching for something to chat about became a thing of the past. Words flowed from my mouth as water might flow from a tap. I was in full command. I had an audience and I was going to impress upon them my hidden genius. Even Larry, who was no slouch at the talking bit, respectfully held silence while his brother of many words held all ears hostage.

"I told you his talking would sooner or later ascend to the shite bit and I would strongly suggest that we all tell him to shut up before he drives us mad, listening to that load of precious dung coming from his mouth. You first Sunday - you tell him to shut up; he respects women and he really will listen," Gerrard said as he gently nudged Sunday with his elbow. Sunday simply smiled her lovely smile and told me to pay a little attention to Katrina. I listened to Sunday's request and immediately asked Katrina to marry me. Katrina suggested I ask her about the question of marriage when I was not under the influence of the bottle. I felt comfortable with her answer and jumped instantly into song mode, singing for her, Elvis Presley's song, "Are You Lonesome Tonight." This singing and romanticizing bore immediate fruit. The barman told me to shut up, that I was not allowed to make noise in his establishment and if I continued he would show me the door. I took offense to his nasty deportment and decided to show him a thing or two.

"Dear sweet Katrina, brothers and future sisters, allow me make this night one to remember - one that will hold well in memory - something to look back upon from the years ahead," I said in a hushed, semi-benevolent tone. I must have had some sense of direction about my input because it seemed I had every ones attention at our table.

"I would just love to hear what you have to say, brother John - I'm all ears - please do inform us," Larry interjected.

"I, dear brothers and sisters, am going to sing that ballad of the great hero, Kevin Barry and I am going to do it now," I said.

"Good for you, John, boy. I never heard of anything so bloody courageous in me whole life - shall I call a hearse before you get started or will I do that when they kill you," Gerrard said with a little concern but, only a little. The girls hadn't a clue what was in the offing but that was about to change.

THE SECOND PURPOSE

As great performers do, I took a very deep breath, looked somewhere into the ceiling and began to sing the ballad of Kevin Barry.

> *In Mountjoy jail, one Monday morning*
> *High upon the scaffold tree*
> *Kevin Barry gave his young life, for the cause of liberty*
> *Just a lad of eighteen summers,' yet, that no one can deny,*
> *As he marched to death that morning*
> *Proud he held his head on high.*
> *Shoot me like an Irish soldier; do not hang me like a dog,*
> *For I fought to free old Ireland, on that cold September morn.*

By the time I had reached the second verse, the bar had grown silent and the barman who had threatened to throw me out earlier, stood glaring at me as though he wanted to cut my throat but he remained quiet. Other patrons began to hum as I broke into to the second verse.

> *Just before he faced the hangman in his dreary prison cell*
> *British soldiers tortured Barry, just because he would not tell*
> *The names of his brave comrades, other things they wished to know,*
> *Turn informer or we'll kill you; Kevin proudly answered no.*
> *Shoot me like an Irish soldier; do not hang me like a dog*
> *For I fought to free old Ireland on that cold September morn.*

"Lovely song mate, bloody right's yeh know. We 'ave no bloody business over in that land of yours," said a Londoner who sat at the table next to us. "Bloody shame that this bunch of ours can't seem to mind their own bleed'n business. Everywhere they go, they have to grab anything they can get their bloody greedy hands on, the bleeders… never mind though, one day you'll 'av the whole lot back again. Mark my words… nobody got the right to take anything that does not belong to them," the Londoner concluded. I thought, that must be how the term, "bleeders," originated - the killing of people - the invasion of their lands. But I didn't dwell on the origin of the word. I was on a roll. The bar which was patronized by an international mixture of humanity had turned their attention to the singer but the little man who had told me to shut up earlier, summed up enough gumption to rudely snap up our drinks from the table and tell us to get the hell out of his establishment.

"That's enough of that behavior - no rebel songs allowed in 'ere or any other rubbish for that matter," the little man said, leaving no doubt in my mind that he was the most cheeky bastard on the face of the earth. The Londoner, who had been enjoying the outburst of song, responded favorably to the little man's rude behavior. He stood up from his table and approached the little one, who was now cradling his jaw in his hands, throwing bull's looks directly at me from the end of his long, polished bar. The tall, slim Londoner, made his way loosely over to the little boiling man at the end of the long, polished bar as though he were about to apologize for our behavior. He then stopped by the little man, whispered something in his ear and poured his pint of ale over the little man's semi-balding head. "There now, yeh cheeky, little creep, 'av a bath me 'ol cock 'n spara and try to be a little nicer to people," the Londoner said to the little wet man, leaving me with the impression he was some kind of expert in the art of baptizing with beer, people he did not like. I was impressed with this very fine Englishman's behavior. For this wonderful act of unsolicited Christening by beer, he was given a rousing round of applause by all in the bar, then our company and the Londoner got to hell out of there. We finished our song outside the bar, bid good night to our new-found London friend and escorted the ladies home.

My head spun, my eyes looked like they were hemorrhaging but I felt the social activities the night before were worth the suffering. Still, even though I had been introduced to a very beautiful lady and given every reason in the whole world to stick around London, the call to the open road was too strong for me to resist. It was as though I really had no choice. It seemed my trail was predestined and this assumption would make itself clear to me in the not too distant future. I bid farewell to my brothers, my future sister-in-laws and to Katrina. I wanted to stay but I knew I had to go.

THE SPUD DIGGERS

The road to Jersey Island beckoned, one of the Channel Islands situated a few miles off the coast of northern France. A few days later would see me arrive at the port city of St. Hellier, Jersey Island's Capitol. It was on this crossing I met Dermot, an aspiring adventurer from that lovely, quaint town of Bray, in the county of Wicklow, Ireland. It was on this trip that I would also meet with the crafty and delightful lady, Monica, who had a great love for port, sherry and more port and sherry.

THE SECOND PURPOSE

Dermot and I, being men of manners and respect, particularly towards the ladies, any ladies, were about to learn a very valuable lesson. This lady, Monica, on in her years, quickly took Dermot and me into her confidence. Before one knew it, we were outdoing each other to see Monica's glass was never in need of want. Monica kept us hanging on the hope of a nice place to stay as soon as we reached Jersey. With our minds operating on the promised security of room and at the cost of next to nothing, Monica's cup overflowed with joy.

I couldn't wait for the ferry to dock. This business of supplying Monica with the essence of her wishes was costing both Dermot and I a good amount of what we didn't have to spare - money. It seemed Monica had quite a taste for the stuff in the glass. I was at last beginning to piece ever so slightly together, the measure of which a human being became vulnerable to the insidious lure of the magic glass, endlessly inviting the unwary into the folds of its unlimited ugliness

I began to see at last why some perfectly decent normal human beings became blathering idiots from the effects of alcohol. It particularly bothered me to see a seemingly lovely lady become quite unattractive in character and mannerism, as the magical potency contained in the glass stole from mind and body the fundamentals of common human decency. This annihilation of self-respect, followed by a journey into the listlessness of a drunken sleep, seared in my mind the utter ugliness of life devoid of grace, all measure of grace. And the scene that summer's day in the garden some years past came to my mind as I witnessed the destruction of things beautiful.

Dermot and I bid adieu to the sleeping Monica as we made our way off the ferry and on to the docks of St. Hellier. Then it was uptown in search of the bed and breakfast place Monica had so lovingly spoken of. Eventually, we came upon the place of loveliness and introduced ourselves to the receptionist as friends of Monica. We were told rather bluntly but politely that the name Monica was not familiar in the establishment and only people who had made reservations could be admitted to the place of loveliness. That indeed counted Dermot and me out because whatever reservations meant, we had not made any and it can be said that we were not lovely either

Said Dermot of Bray, to the lady behind the desk, "Miss, please, if ye don't mind my asking, what do ye mean by veneration?" I could see Dermot had caused an unexpected twist to the flow of questions because it seemed the lady was a little confused by the meaning of the word veneration. This was not difficult to notice because the pencil she had being so professionally businesslike with found its way into her mouth to be chewed as though it were a fresh piece of smoked herring. Dermot knew he had started something and did not let up on the veneration bit.

"If we knew we had to venerate, we would not have come here," said Dermot. "This man here is a Catholic and I am a Protestant and I don't mind telling ye we are not about to make veneration's to anybody including you. I find this most insulting and unsettling to my spiritual make-up," he said. I wondered what kind of spiritual make up Dermot possessed. The dear girl eventually got a word in edgeways, explaining that she had said reservation, not the word veneration and she was truly sorry for any hurt feelings she may have caused. I just stood there, being part of the picture but doing my best not to fit into it. Dermot had turned forty shades of red and was at a loss as to what to say next when the receptionist broke the silence by inviting us to the lounge for a drink. She then told us that she would talk to Raquel, the manageress about securing a room for us.

Raquel De Bussy was an eighteen-year old beauty. She had no difficulty in firing my tired but potent imagination. Her sensuousness did not escape Dermot's eyes either. Raquel was the daughter of the owner of the hotel and welcomed us to her fold. "I hear there was a little mix up," she said with a smile. It seemed Raquel was impressed with Dermot's spiritual blustering and asked if he would like to continue on the same subject. Long into the evening I listened to Dermot expound on the subjects of religion, mysticism, spiritualism, Confucianism and the good and rotten state of things in the world. I had no idea what Dermot was on about but Raquel was totally immersed in what the enlightened one had revealed to her. And the more Dermot revealed his knowledge of the unknown, the more Raquel revealed to Dermot.

Before Dermot and Raquel embarked on a more intimate journey with the aid of the stuff in the bottle, the receptionist told us she had secured two rooms. I wondered why two rooms had been secured, because, unless Dermot had a small fortune, they weren't going to be paid for. However, Raquel arrested my fears with the assurance that it was all on the hotel and I shouldn't worry about a thing. Then she took Dermot by the hand and invited him to tour the building, leaving me to the hush of the evening's moods and the unsettling thoughts of what the morrow may bring.

However, for now, all was well. I made my way to the appointed room and as I drifted into the sleep of sleeps, my thoughts centered on Monica. Was she o. k? Did she make it off the ferry? Was she passed out somewhere? I did not know. I also did not know that the pattern set for a disruptive life through the partaking of John Barleycorn had fully established itself in my body's chemistry - the same insidious pattern that gripped the body of Monica

Sunshine broke through the curtains as I stirred to meet the day. At breakfast, plans were laid for our future on Jersey Island. Raquel set about searching the newspapers to see what may be advertised in the way of jobs and accommodation. It was not long before her efforts bore fruit.

In the Parish of St. Lawrence, there dwelled the Vatts family. As it turned out, Mr. Vatts was in need of two potato diggers. It was something I happened to be good at. Dermot as young as he was, a year younger than me, almost had a heart attack at the prospect of working a garden fork. I could see nothing wrong with making a living that way but poor Dermot was mightily opposed to the idea as any educated, lazy philosopher might be. However, accommodation was also available for the chosen potato pickers and we could not afford to turn the job down.

My father had great enthusiasm about the potato: the life, times, genealogy, history, texture, color, eyes, size, thickness of skin, flouriness and above all, the taste. In fact, I often wondered why my father had not worked on developing his very own spud, imbued with those characteristics indigenous to the land behind his house and name it the "Perrystown spud." There is no doubt, however, of my inheriting a portion of his interest and loyalty concerning the spud. At last I could once again watch the fruits of the soil jangle on the tines of the fork. Once again I would smell the richness of the earth in my Garden of Eden.

It was a fond farewell to the lovely Raquel as we set off on the bus from St. Hellier to meet with Mr. Vatts the potato farmer.

"I hear you are looking for two potato diggers sir," I said to the farmer.

"Yes I need two potato diggers - are you gentlemen capable of such work?" He replied in a heavy British accent. I explained to him that my father was an expert in the field of potato digging and that he had taught me the fine art of extracting the potato from the ground without injuring it with the tine of the fork. He seemed receptive to my know-how of the potato kingdom and when I began to rattle off names of the potato family, he was most suitably impressed. He asked me if I had studied the science of the potato at Oxford. I told him I had not, that any understanding I possessed of the potato was imparted to me through the knowledgeable teachings of my Daddy. Dermot was impressed beyond belief with my apparent ease and confidence in which I addressed the potato issue, that is until the dog, Lassie, friendly to say the least, decided to smell Dermot's privates.

This unwanted happening put Dermot in a bit of an embarrassing situation. The dog was doing what was natural and as Dermot went from pale white, which was his natural color, to pink, to light red, to crimson red, to fire engine red, to deep purple. Mr. Vatts noticed his uncomfortable predicament and told Lassie to be a good doggie and look for a mouse to play with. To Dermot's relief, Lassie complied with her master's request and Dermot returned to the familiar North European skin color of his birth.

"Let's get you some grub and we'll go over the plan of the potato digging," Mr. Vatts said. This done, Dermot and I were introduced to his family. Winnie, Charles's wife of the true French bloodline, Ian, the eldest son, Andrea, the eldest and only daughter and Alistair, the youngest boy. There was not enough Winnie could do for Dermot and me in her efforts to make us feel at home. So began a two-year stay at this home of much happiness.

The digging went on and on and on as the spuds came up and up and up. It was a fine year for the farmers of the Islands as the weather conditions were perfect for growing, thereby yielding excellent crops. Poor Dermot did not fare too well for the first few weeks as his body had to adjust to the physical demands of digging, picking and stalk removal from the potatoes. In the meantime, he developed a touch of laryngitis, which, in his own kind way, he insisted on sharing with everyone within the household and all those he came in contact outside of it. He was by no stretch of the imagination, a selfish sort.

He coughed morning noon and night, creating great disturbances within the rank and file of the house. It was easy to dislike Dermot intensely on account of his persistent hacking because during the day he was my work partner and at night he was not more than five feet from me in the sleeping quarters. However, he was nursed back to health before he was strangled, saving us all an easy decision on Dermot's future. Nevertheless, the good fellow from Bray proved as capable a worker as any of us and by the time the last potato was unearthed, the philosopher had graduated from the field with honors.

"John and Dermot, now that the digging is finished, you must go to the employment office and get yourselves a job," said Winnie. We agreed. Off we went to see the one who gave jobs to people. We were fortunate. Jimmy Le Houquet was a successful businessman in the construction industry. He required two good men to help on the work sites and Dermot and I were just the men he needed. I enjoyed working for Jim and in my spare time I played for the St. Lawrence soccer club. Life for me was full. But soon that would

THE SECOND PURPOSE

change

One day, on the field of soccer, a ball came my way. I had to go get it because I was the goalkeeper. Out I went to get the ball with great abandonment and flair. However, there was an element of danger in obtaining the ball. It was on the toe of the opposition's striker and it was his intention to put that ball into the net that I protected from any such violation. I had the uneasy feeling that he was prepared to kill me if necessary to obtain his goal

Behind him galloped my defensemen who were intent on murdering him if they caught him. However, the striker seemed to realize his predicament if my troops closed in and began to distance himself from the marauders. "Oh my God!" I thought, today I am going to die. And so began my advance towards the brilliant center forward of our arch rivals, the indomitable Grouville United, a powerful soccer machine and one not prone to losing.

The forward was a good thirty yards from me and because of the speed he was moving at, I knew he could not shoot the ball. There was no way he could slow his pace, steady himself and fire the ball cleanly. if he tried that move, he would have been trampled to death on the spot by the defense men who were now almost upon him and in a position to legally destroy him. As I watched the forward move closer, I knew the only chance I had of stopping him was to dash out directly towards him and dive at his feet in the hopes of taking the ball from him. Not the safest choice - but the only one.

If one has never experienced such an undertaking, it is as exciting as rushing headlong into a stampeding herd of buffalo with the intention of bringing the leader to its knees, removing its horns, then standing up and telling the rest to go back to where they came from. As I made my move (diving at his feet), the forward had no choice but to shoot the ball and as he did, my hand deflected it moving it from his line of fire. The forward could not stop his foot from carrying through and its full impact sank deep into my thigh. The pain however was lost to the future as my defense, unable to rein in, galloped over me. My destruction was complete.

My leg, now in a cumbersome cast, rendered me incapable of working or playing soccer. "Have no fear John, we shall soon have you up and about but the first thing we must do is get you out of that cast," my coach said.

"I don't understand what you mean Al, do you have some miracle cure?" I asked.

"Not I, my good man but I know someone who does and we are going to see this good person tomorrow," Al said.

"And who is this good person Al?" I further inquired.

"He is a man who practices the art of faith healing and he will cure you," Al said confidently.

Monsieur De Champlain and his wife lived on a farm in a beautiful and tranquil setting in the Jersey countryside.

Monsieur De Champlain and Al carried me to a chair in the kitchen, which I was placed in. The cast was ripped away exposing a fleshy mess of twisted knots as distasteful as the colors they dwelled within. Madame De Champlain had prepared a basin of warm water to bath and clean my leg as her husband began to massage the injured muscles. It would take a few treatments to bring my misery to an end but that is exactly what the De Champlain's accomplished. They had given me my health and freedom back. But even more than that, the De Champlains had infused in me what my good mother always knew and tried to teach me: in humility lies fullness of life and love and the truest sense of freedom. And as Mother had always said, "John, everything will be alright." And truly, everything turned out just as Mum said - alright.

One day while visiting the De Champlains for a treatment, I met the coach of the infamous soccer club Sporting Club Française. I was invited to join the club as their goalkeeper. There was no conflict of interest with my St. Lawrence Club as both teams were relegated to different leagues. I accepted the honor.

In due course, Sporting Club Francaise was invited to the French mainland to partake in a soccer tournament. I asked my boss, Mr. Le Hoquet, if I could have time off to travel to France. "And what is happening in France that requires your presence, Mr. McDonald?" asked Mr. Le Houquet.

"I have been asked by my club, Sporting Club Francaise, to represent them as their goalkeeper in a soccer tournament which begins on Armistice Day," I replied. Jimmy Le Houquet was a man of medium stature who tended to stand in a rather business-like posture but with a totally relaxed expression about him. I had never worked for a person quite like Jimmy Le Houquet. He appeared to be one of those people who was capable of reading a person's mind from a fair distance of forty miles or more. I awaited an answer.

"Have a good time over in that big land and try to come back in one piece," he eventually said, in his distinct Jersey French accent.

It was Sunday morning when the old twin engine Hercules rumbled down the runway of the Jersey airport. On board, the members of Sporting Club Françoise chatted gaily as the old craft fought to gain height. It was my first time on an aircraft. I was stone sober and very much afraid. From the moment the craft began to rise, it flip-flopped through the sky leaving me the impression I was safely in the hands of death. I expected the craft to break in two at any moment and the only reason I did not sit in a corner and cry was because I could not find one. It did not help matters when the hostess screamed for everyone to buckle up as she herself presented characteristic qualities of the terrified.

The captain of the team, Roy Ballston noticed my dilemma. Realizing his goalkeeper was about to die from fright, he instantly produced a bottle of cognac which I immediately glugged as much as I possibly could. From the aircraft's agonizing twisting, rolling, dipping, swerving, swaying, step dancing and hop scotching, it suddenly seemed to level out and glide like a ship might do on tranquil waters. Somewhere in St. Malo, I awakened in a hotel room. The cognac had done its job.

The French were wonderful hosts. They sent some of their soccer ambassadors to our hotel the following morning, which marked the beginning of the Armistice services, to greet the members of our club and treat us to the best of French hospitality. "Monsieur goal keeper," said Pierre, "A toast to you and your gallant team," as he handed me a glass of the finest French wine. I couldn't help but admire the French. They simply had a delightful way of feeding one's ego and my ego had an exceptional appetite. So with glass in hand, I saluted Pierre of France. It was truly a splendid wine and I was quick to say so. Pierre was delighted that I enjoyed the fruit of the vine and quickly refilled my glass and another and another. There was nothing unusual about this kind of diplomatic interaction between football teams except it was nine o'clock in the morning and the team of Sporting Club Françoise was to be at the city's memorial monument by ten o clock. Here we would pay our respects to the brave men and women who bought our freedom with their lives during the Great World Wars.

Pierre had done his job. My teammates found me with my head stuck out the hotel window singing to a barn door across the court yard. "What in the name of blazes has happened to you John?" said Roy, the captain of our team.

"A French saboteur by the name of Pierre offered me a cup of special coffee and it has done something to my head," I replied. This they found hard to believe because they knew I did not drink coffee. In fact, they paid little attention to what I was trying to relay to them as they politely dragged me from the room to the waiting car in the hotel's courtyard.

I was whisked away to the memorial service in honor of the fallen French and Allied troops who stopped Hitler's Nazi war machine from overrunning the world. It was a very dignified and solemn service and even in my hazy state of semi consciousness I fully realized the horrific sacrifice the people of the free world had made to stop the madness, the evil, the depraved lunatics of satanic perversion from directing their vile ideology upon all that was decent. The president of our club laid a wreath in honor of the fallen to the strains of the French National Anthem. When the ceremony concluded our team was taken to the soccer field.

In the warm-up before the game, I became aware of my sleeping reflexes. I was a little worried, because, if I was not reacting to the speed at which the ball was being moved about in a pre-game warm-up, I wondered how the hell I would handle something blasted at me at the speed of seventy miles an hour or more. I tried not to bother my mind with the inevitable but the inevitable was beginning to unfold.

The teams took their places on the field, the whistle blew and I wished everyone the best of luck as though he were not a part of the contest. In moments however, three French strikers were bearing down on me with ill intent. It must be mentioned at this point that my teammates were pursuing one man but the effect of Pierre's fine wine caused me to see three. The confusion mounted within because our team supporters were yelling at me to stay on my goal line while my teammates on the field were roaring at me to advance and challenge the striker. In all honesty, I do not know what I did to this very day but apparently it was spectacular. In my mind the French player who was thundering down the right wing was one person with three bodies. Three people with three balls were moving rapidly in on me and I had no idea which one to tackle.

Go forth! John and stop the intruder, a voice commanded. I listened and advanced. I know this for certain because I tripped over my feet in the first few steps of my advance. The tripping proved fruitful however because the French striker with three bodies and six legs volleyed the ball as I fell to the ground, my face in the path of the incoming missile. The ball stayed out of the net but I was out cold.

Unfortunately the game was at its early stages. There was no backup goalkeeper available, so I was patched up and sent out to do something but that something was not good enough. The French forwards soon found their mark and buried the ball past me. We lost by that one goal which effectively eliminated us from the tournament.

The games came to a close and all teams that participated in the tournament rendezvoused back at our hotel and much was the merriment.

Singing, dancing and drinking were in vogue and would remain so for the following few days, after which time we journeyed back to Jersey. The French were wonderful hosts and I was left with fond memories of my visit to St. Malo. The tournament was over far too soon. It was back to Jersey and to work. I did not have to worry about the return trip by aircraft. I did not remember it.

OH, CANADA

It was a damp chilly morning as my workmate Len and I concentrated on our construction chores. I was busy completing some granite stonework while Len collected the rubbish and set about burning it. It was during the cleanup that Len came across an article in a London newspaper advertising for miners in the town of Thompson, Manitoba, Canada.

"I know you want to travel," said Len, as he handed me the wet, moldy newspaper, which had been lying around for some weeks on the construction site. Len was a good sort, happily married and contented with his lot in life. I often envied people like Len who seemed not to possess thorns in their feet. "I had tossed it into the fire but because it was so damp it would not burn, so I removed it to open it up to make it catch fire more easily, that's when I saw the advertisement for the miners," he said with a smile. At that moment I knew I would soon be in Canada. I traveled to London in November of 1967 to be interviewed by the recruiting officers of the International Nickel Company of Canada. Four months later, I sat on a Boeing as it took to the skies over Heathrow Airport, its course - north by northwest. I was on my way to Winnipeg International Airport, Canada.

Approximately ten hours later, I viewed the city lights of Winnipeg as the aircraft prepared for landing. It seemed the trip was not so long in time as I had supposed but this was largely due to the amount of Canadian rye whiskey I consumed on the trip. This rye whiskey was also responsible for the smoothness of the flight and I thought, "this land produces a drink of grand magic - I shall indeed feel at home here." I was greeted by the customs officer in a rather formal but courteous manner. He handed me a document, which denoted my status as Landed Immigrant, then with a firm, and friendly handshake, welcomed me to the great Land of the North. Then, from the past came the words of the great Kilroy: "maybe it's in the wilderness you shall find purpose Mr. John."

As I wandered the air terminal in a rather inebriated state, an announcement caught my attention because it was all about lost souls like me wandering in the wastelands of their mind. The announcement was a request for those people who were aboard the recent flight from London to go to the reception area if they required assistance. I did not delay in responding to the call and so I came to meet the wonderful Greer family. Andy and Betty Greer were just good caring decent people who helped newly arrived immigrants. And so it was, a group of lost souls were invited to the Hotel St. Norbert, to unwind, have a few drinks and a taste of Canadian nightlife. It was in this hotel I would sleep my first sleep in Canada, sing my first song on the music stage and quickly develop a taste for good old Canadian beer.

The next morning saw me pack and prepare to board a train for the mining town of Thompson in the far north. It was bitterly cold, the temperature thirty degrees below zero. It was my first experience of such horrible weather and I did not like it. Andy and Betty were kind enough to see me off as I embarked truly on a journey into the unknown. Had I known what lay ahead of me I never would have left my dear native Dublin, not for one moment.

As the train pulled out of the station, I waved a fond farewell to Andy and Betty. I was glad to have come to know them. I felt an unusual closeness to these good people whom I had known only for a measure of hours and to see them wave to me as the train made distance between us left me with an uneasy feeling of separated connectedness. I thought, "there is someone taking care of me - I just can't see them." In time I would, however. In time I would be left with no doubt that there is a beautiful power taking care of me. In time I would see it and there is nothing anyone can say or do to remove that belief - no not a belief but the absolute truth. However, that time was long into the future. For now I would cast my eyes over the great wilderness - the place of timeless silence.

It was about three in the afternoon when the train pulled into The Pas, a small town about two hundred miles north of Winnipeg. It was at this moment I was introduced to everything that was to my mind traditionally Canadian - all in a minute or two. A group of children boarded the train. With them they carried snowshoes, skis, puppies, beaver pelts and an assortment of other wares associated only with the land which I was traveling through. After the children came the parents, in-laws and trappers. It was the tail end of the annual event of the trappers' festival. I had arrived just in time for the last of its rugged expressions.

A little blond haired girl said, "What's your name?" As I sat there mystified with all that was taking place around me. I looked at her inquiringly, wondering if it was me she was addressing. "Yes sir! You sir! She said as her sparkling brown eyes filled with curiosity settled intensely on mine. She repeated, "What's your name?" I thought, what a cheeky little urchin as I half-willingly surrendered my identity to her.

"My name is John and if you don't mind young lady, would you please tell me your name?" I replied.

"My name is Kathleen and I would like to know where you got that funny accent you have?" I was not too sure how to answer such a rude question put to me by a child, so I asked her why she thought my accent was funny. "Well," said the little blond girl, "our teacher has an accent like yours and I don't mean to say it's funny but different."

"I see. And where is this teacher of yours from?" I inquired.

"He's from Ireland and he taught us a bunch of Irish songs," the little blond girl said. And without a further word, she and her friends sang "Clancy Lowered The Boom."

It was hard to believe I was on a train somewhere in frozen Canada and not in some part of my own country. But then again, perhaps I was, for these lovely children had, through their singing, released from the corners of my mind delightful memories of my past. And I thought, perhaps the past is not so passed as I may think it is as the melodious strains of the children's voices awakened the sleeping memories of my childhood.

I felt very comfortable among these good people who were absent of the typical European uncertainty of another's presence until a measure of time brought comfortable trust to them. I was accepted into their fold instantly and before long they were sharing an assortment of foods with me, which I had neither seen nor tasted before. By the time the feast had ended, I had tasted bear, beaver, deer, moose and duck, followed with a washing of beer, whiskey, wine, brandy and hooch. I was getting pretty drunk but I was enjoying every moment of the trip. I knew I was in a land that would sear its spirit deep into my heart. In time I would come to love and respect the very heartbeat of this land, just as much as the land in which I was born. Here, on a slow moving train through the northern icy mists of Manitoba, a whole new world unfolded its veils to me. I thought, as sleep took hold of my tired and intoxicated mind, that I was surely traveling the veritable highway of life - life at its finest. Indeed I was. Yes, indeed I was.

The train clattered to a stop in the early hours of a new day in the town of Flin Flon, located on the Saskatchewan, Manitoba border. I had awakened just in time to bid a hearty farewell to the family of trappers who had adopted me that afternoon. Flin Flon was their hometown. The little girl who had snapped me from my daydreaming that afternoon was fast asleep in her father's arms. Through the train's frosted window I watched them fade into the darkness of early morning; young Kathleen dreaming her dreams wrapped in furs in her father's arms. I would not see them again.

Later that morning, the train rolled into Thompson. Like so many others who were coming to Thompson to work in the mines, I tried to look like I wasn't lost. My breath seemed to suspend in front of my nose like a cloud of fuzzy ice. It was cold in this Canada, bloody cold. My body was beginning to creak and moan with the slightest movement. I thought that this had been a very long way to travel to freeze to death. I was not amused. While I stood stiffening, a taxi driver hollered to me wanting to know if I was going to the INCO camp. I said I was. He told me to hop in. "I'm dropping a lady off on the way, so it will cost you pretty close to half," he said. With that good news, I creaked over to the cab, threw my luggage in the trunk and maneuvered my frozen framework the best way I could through the back door of the cab and onto the seat.

The lady that sat in the back of the cab was dignified and beautiful beyond belief. Dressed in the most striking and exquisite garments of Native design, she sat looking through the window, her gaze seemingly lost to the distance. I knew I was seated beside a princess. I wanted to say hello to her but I didn't have the courage. What was it with me that I couldn't open my mouth and say a simple hello! What the hell was it? Yes sir, just what the hell was it? The cab pulled into the driveway of her home. Not a word was spoken as she left the cab and moved towards her house. I was not infatuated, nor did I fall in love or lust. In fact I wasn't up to much of anything because I was still frozen and a light thaw, as far as I knew, was setting in. I'm not sure what was happening to my mind but I was thinking that it was a fine day back then when Sitting Bull had laid a hammering on Custer. Too bad Sitting Bull did not have a whole lot more days like that.

REBELLION

That morning I was issued a Company identity card and shown to my room at the trailer site. I had made it to the land of the "True North Great and Free". I was tired, very tired and now I would sleep. The following morning

THE SECOND PURPOSE

I reported to the security office to be briefed on behavioral expectations, company policies, etc. After, it was off to the changing rooms, then down the shaft to become a miner. I did not like it. I did not like being underground. I could not help thinking I was entombed in the loneliest, coldest, most dreadful place in all of eternity and the more I thought about it, the more I feared. I could feel the walls of the mine closing in on me. This was my first experience with claustrophobia. I was terrified.

Digging deep into my mind, I dwelled on pastoral settings, rippling brooks and moo cows in an effort to shun my fears down in these depths of darkness and I swore if I got out alive, I would not come back. I got out alive and I did come back but I still did not like it and the only thing that could ever make me accept this work place of utter blackness was a connecting of the human spirit with my workmates and, as slim as such a chance was, it took hold.

I was elated when, at the end of each shift, I surfaced from the blackness of the mines to be greeted by the light of the world. To see the sun in the blue, blue sky of Manitoba gave me a feeling of belonging to a world I did not understand but was elated to be a part of. Truly the light at the end of the tunnel was heavenly.

As the days slowly passed, I was beginning to become more comfortable with life in Thompson, but that was to be rudely and abruptly changed. It was day thirteen in Canada as I sat at a table in the Company's cafeteria, eating my supper when a most unusual event took place. Just as I was about to feed my face, a block of butter sailed towards the ceiling and there remained. It was odd indeed to say the least, observing butter hanging from a ceiling with its saucer stuck to its bottom. I was truly preoccupied with this spectacle because it looked so much out of place there. My train of thought was suddenly interrupted as a six foot long seat sailed across the room and out through the window. I had arrived in time for the rebellion.

A gathering of rebels went about the canteen methodically smashing anything that invited their fancy. I had no idea what was going on, except for the fact it was not pleasant and I had lost my appetite. However, I was politely informed by the throwers of things that I should not worry about the destructive measures taking place and to finish my meal in comfort. While I was pondering the assurance given me, cauldrons, coffee brewers, pots, pans and things of likeness were attacked as though they were responsible for starting the last World War. There was much smashing and crashing in the kitchen. Still, I thought it better to seek safer quarters and made my exit as the wrecking crew dedicated their efforts to much disorder. As I prepared to leave, I noticed a lone individual sitting off in a corner. His presence portrayed a definitive bearing and if the wrecking crew had an inkling of what he was about, it is safe to say a hospital or worse awaited him. His presence stuck firm in my mind. I would not forget him. I would see him again many years to the future and in a very different setting of the Canadian landscape.

There were grievances at the INCO camp which needed to be addressed, and it looked like they would have to be. The wrecking spread throughout parts of the town and many instances violence occurred. The beer parlor saw many a nosebleed and the trailers, Company buildings and equipment were subjected to damage. It was hard to believe I was in Canada but I was, and I wondered what the hell was going on.

Meanwhile, the troubles in Ireland were extremely serious and while I was a little more than tired of being asked about the killings and bombings back home. I had a brief respite from such questions as the dispute between the Nickel Company and its employees took on vicious elements. Security guards were subject to nasty beatings and it was feared dynamite would be used as the situation deteriorated. An emergency call went out to the RCMP. That call was put out by the lone figure that sat in the corner of the cafeteria. Overnight, an estimated eighty to ninety Mounties were flown into Thompson and within twenty-four hours, they brought the situation under control.

The happenings in Thompson left me perturbed as the men did have a grievance with INCO. It was a hard grind working the mines and smelters. As soon as you became a hired hand, you were in debt to the company. The employee paid for all work gear required for operations as well as their room and board. It was a hard grind for a family man, particularly if he was from out of town, because he had a double burden of payments to make. The wages were a pittance and the work extremely dangerous. Fatalities were common and the injury rate exceedingly high. For the first time since I had worked in the slop of the London underground, I again felt that uncomfortable feeling of humanity being used to keep the index high on the stock exchange. Thompson was a Company town. INCO, it seemed, owned everything in it, including the workers.

It was ten a.m. Monday morning. I stood with hundreds of miners at the railroad station in the biting freeze of forty below. We awaited the train bound for Winnipeg. It was exactly thirteen days since I had arrived in Thompson, fourteen since my arrival in Canada. Ben, Michael and I had become workmates. They came north to go to work, make a wage and support their families but as it turned out, they were going back with less than they came with. I had twenty-five dollars to my name but with it I was able to purchase train tickets to Winnipeg for the three of us. We were free of INCO but where I was going, I did not know. It was still winter. I now had ten dollars to see me through until I got a job.

Carling O'Keefe, a Major beer brewing company in Canada, had just made a smash hit commercial with the song " Dublin In The Green," and the Irish Rovers had had a number one hit with a couple of their songs, " The Unicorn and the Black Velvet Band." The Celtic influence had come to Canada and the people were humming our tunes. I had a guitar. I had always traveled with a guitar but I did not know how to play one. That was about to change. Beer, whiskey, wine, moonshine and a host of other drinks amazingly appeared from those secret places one holds dear to themselves and very quickly, it seemed all the people on the train were getting very, very drunk. It was absolutely wonderful. I knew the song "Dublin In the Green." I had sung it many times as a boy scout when we went marching over the mountains back home. With this knowledge of singing and being fresh from the old sod, I quickly became a celebrity. The conductors were a good bunch of guys and helped me locate the guitar, which had been stored in the baggage compartment. That done, the partying began in earnest. I knew one chord on the guitar but it seemed it was enough for my musical arrangement of "Dublin In The Green." Life was at its finest as the train rolled over the Canadian landscape– on towards the town of The Pas. There, we would have a thirty-minute stopover.

The world has its surprises and The Pas was no exception. It seemed like a good idea to take advantage of the stopover by visiting the local beer parlor. It was a grubby place we entered. I was with Ben and Michael. We ordered up some beer and sat ourselves down. Some more of the train travelers wandered in behind us. The waitress was busy. One of the guys from the train was insistent on immediate service. The waitress told him to wait a moment until she finished serving another customer. What happened next was quiet unbelievable. The guy who was insisting on immediate service reached over the bar, grabbed the waitress by the breast, placed two fingers on one of her nipples and squeezed it.

Instantly there was a knife at his throat. The white man turned silently pale. The man who held the knife was a Native who had been sitting at the bar and he was making a serious decision. This was easy to discern because by all outward appearances he seemed unconcerned whether or not he killed the violator. I thought I was going to see the makings of a dead person. The waitress was Indian, the idiot, a white man. It was hard to believe he could turn whiter than pale but he did. Without a word being spoken, the one who held the knife brought the weapon down across the fellow's chest, to his arm, where he pressed it home. He was in a bloody mess but he would live. He decided against having the beer and left as quietly as a feather floating on the wind.

By this time of the journey it seemed every man aboard the train was feeling no pain, except the wounded warrior. Perhaps he too would not feel too much of anything until the liquor wore off. The train conductor grabbed a first aid kit and patched him up. He was a lucky man. I had never seen such open violation on the female gender before and an uneasy feeling came to mind. What if the woman was white? Would such an insult have happened? It was a question that would stick in my mind. As I came to know and understand the sociopolitical climate of the vast land of the north, I would come to understand what decimation of the spirit meant. I would also experience the struggle of a people desperately trying to overcome the brutal impositions of colonial insult.

The train pulled out from The Pas. It was about one a. m; on went the party, on and on and on and still it seemed there was no end to the demand to hear "Dublin In The Green." It can be said that the guitar never once in its marathon concert changed from being played in the chord of G. The monotony of its constancy remained but to the inebriated mind it was the most wonderful sound in the universe.

There was many a sick head to be nursed as the train rolled into Winnipeg mid-morning. The party was over, my companions gone. I was tired, sick and weary. I was now a very lonely, isolated individual in the vast cold building of the Canadian National Railroad - my protector from the killing elements - its floor to ponder while reality sank in. My predicament was not good.

DESPERATE TIMES

To put one foot in front of the other and proceed was the call to my sad state of affairs and this I did with tireless resolve. The toe of my shoe became my main focal point, much like a fisherman may keep a sharp eye on his fishing pole, the only difference being the certainty of my shoe not catching a fish. As soon as my head gathered the feeling of wellness I set about taking stock of my situation, planning moves towards the construction of my survival. I had the protection of the great CNR building where coffee, newspapers and washrooms were available. This was a good start. I could enjoy a nice cup of coffee while I scoured the paper in search of a job. My situation was not so bad after all.

In 1968, a cup of coffee cost a nickel and, a beer, a dime. I had ten dollars. That meant I could buy two hundred cups of coffee or one hundred beers. I opted on the coffee course - it was one of my wiser moves. Each morning saw me towel wash in the washrooms of the CNR building, grab a coffee and search the newspapers for a job. Obtaining a job was proving difficult. There was high unemployment in Canada and it was winter. Things indeed looked bleak. From morning till late evening I wandered in search of work throughout the city of Winnipeg but at the end of the day the results were the same - no job for John. My days in Ireland traveling and wandering had prepared me both physically and mentally to deal with isolation. Such experiences were now brought forward and put to service.

The days dragged into weeks and I became unwell from the hunger. The station master, although never asking about my circumstances appeared to understand my plight. He was a kind person. He inconspicuously made available for me the use of a phone, coffee and newspapers. The stationmaster did not know it but he was instrumental in seeing me through the extremes of difficulties. Still, on I plodded in search of the elusive job. However, finding work was not happening. What was happening was a growing knowledge of buildings in which I could take refuge from the vicious, biting winds of winter. Still, the biting freeze extracted its price. Smothered in clothes more suitable for friendlier climates, my hands, nose and ears succumbed to the pains of frostbite. Oh how I wished for the sunny days of Jersey Island.

Eighteen days into my wintry tour of Winnipeg I chanced a phone call to the company, Consolidated Merchants. I had no idea who or what they did. The lady who answered the phone spoke with a soft Scottish accent inquiring politely as to how she could help me. I simply told her my name and asked if there were any vacancies. She told me there possibly were and suggested I call by to see her. I was there within half an hour. Shannon Lea was a delightful person and immediately put me at ease by telling me I could start on Monday morning at eight o'clock. I wanted to hug her so badly but I did not want to get fired before I started. I dropped the idea.

I thanked her profusely as I left her office and promised myself that I was going to sing for two weeks naught but Scottish songs. I was safe. I was not going to starve. I was going to live. I was not going to freeze to death in Canada. Elation built within. Yet, I needed a place to stay and I had no money. I went to the railroad station and asked Mike, the Stationmaster for his daily newspaper, stating I had found a job. He was so happy at hearing the news, he ordered coffee and chocolate bars at the convenience outlet and helped me search the paper for a room to rent.

Jennifer Sweetman was a lovely looking lady. "Madame," said I, "I arrived in Canada a few weeks ago. I secured a job this afternoon at Consolidated Merchants and I start work Monday morning. However, until I get paid, I am without a place to stay. Would it be possible to stay at your place until I collect my wages, wherefore I shall pay you immediately?" Jennifer smiled a smile of smiles, swung the door wide open and ushered me in. At last I had a place to stay. I must have looked in some awful damned state because, without a word, Jennifer took me to the kitchen, sat me at the table, fed me fish, sausages, carrot cake and a bottle of wine. I told her of my journey, the riots in Thompson and about the very big house I had lived in for the past two weeks which was the CNR station. She listened politely and then suggested that we both go to the station to pick up my worldly goods.

At the train station, I introduced Jennifer to Mike as we picked up my belongings. I thanked him for his help and friendship. He was happy to see I had made out okay. Indeed I had made out okay, perhaps even a little too well. Upon returning to the house, I showered and retired to my bedroom. I slept the sleep of sleeps and when I awoke late into the evening, the house was empty. I made some coffee, sat in the kitchen and slowly awakened to the reality of what I had been through. A desperate feeling of loneliness and longing overcame me to the point of supreme depression. In my life, I had never experienced such a heavy sadness. It seemed my very soul was wandering in some bottomless pit, void of light, life and hope; no one to share with, no familiarities, no voice, just a vast expanse of nothingness. I had heard of depression. If this was what it was, it was next door to hell.

As late evening rolled into early morning, I found refuge in my guitar. I did not have to wonder why "Dublin In The Green" came to mind as I began to strum and sing a favorite song of my childhood. My voice went from gentle humming to modest crooning to great hollerings. The great release of emotional suppression was in full swing. When I had finished my Irish aria I felt a piercing silence steal through the house. It was almost eerie. Then from outside my bedroom door, tumultuous cheers split the silence. I was not alone. Jennifer and company had returned from an evening of socializing.

The party went on through the wee hours of the morning into the not so wee hours of the morning, then into the afternoon. Then it was back to the bar from which Jennifer and company had begun the evening before. "Dublin In The Green" was in great demand and because it was in great demand, so was I. I had unwittingly fallen into a nest of serious drinkers and although I did not realize it at the time, my apprenticeship to becoming a full-blown alcoholic had begun.

The dance band played their music into the late spell of the night. Jennifer looked at me lovingly and said, "John, I would like you to meet my good friend Michelle." And so I met Michelle. Again Jennifer addressed me. "Go take Michelle for a dance, you make a grand couple," she said smilingly. The last part of the comment worried me immediately. I was not a dancer and normally I would do everything possible to stay off a dance floor and now I was on the spot, because Michelle took me by the hand and led me like a little drunken lamb to the dance floor where upon she immediately snuggled into my body. I thought, what a lovely forward girl.

Everything was going according to the way it should go under such circumstances. Life was so much more exciting than working under the great landmass of northern Canada. Then, while being preoccupied with my private lustful thoughts, the singer of the band announced the engagement of one called Michelle to one called John. Now I was drunk, really drunk but there are those things that are said in life that makes one afraid no matter what state of mind one may be in and for me, this was one of those occasions.

The band member seemed to take some personal satisfaction in the announcement because he wandered from blessings to the lucky couple to how impressed he was at the sexy loveliness of Michelle. While he expounded on the beauty of the woman who was going to be my wife, Michelle took every opportunity to show how much she was in love with me right there on the floor. As it turned out, the band member had been engaged to Michelle. They had had a disagreement and Jennifer took the opportunity to create the element of jealousy by pairing Michelle with me. However, Michelle did take a shine to me. Suddenly I felt the winds of structure knock on my rambling nature. I became concerned, but for now, I was having a wonderful time and tomorrow was so far away.

The party over, the loving at rest, it was time to go to work. I had begun work at Consolidated Merchants. My wages were a mere sixty dollars a week. It was not a lot but it was a step in the right direction. I joined the YMCA, spending my mid-week evenings in the gym rather than in the beer parlors - a positive move. I also attempted to undertake a night school course but it proved elusive. However, I did complete a Career Interest Test and its results were fascinating. I was told I was suited for a career in the music and the forest industry. I had reason to be fascinated by such results because I knew a whole lot of nothing about those professions.

The weekend parties at the house began to wear me down. The fascination with the drinking and more liberal form of expression through alcohol use began to trail off. It had been fun for a while but its continuation did not interest me. I was searching for something more fulfilling in my life and I was not finding it in the bottle nor at the parties. In fact, I was becoming rather disconcerted with the way of the bottle and it hurt me deeply to see my friend Jennifer under its influence. I could handle seeing men passed out from the bottle's effects but to see a woman passed out or drunk ripped at the pit of my stomach. Michelle escaped this type of lure and I was happy to see she was safe from it. We spent a lot of time together and I became very comfortable being with her. For the first time in my life, I began to see women in a very different light from what I assumed or was conditioned to thinking.

Things began to deteriorate in the house due to drinking and I decided to leave. Where to, I wondered? I made a phone call to Andy and Betty, the couple who had been so kind to me on my arrival in Canada. They were happy to hear from me and offered me a room in their home in Fort Garry. I was on the way. Jennifer knew she was in trouble with the booze and did not offer any useless excuses. She also understood the reasons why I was leaving. I would miss her. She was a decent person and it made me sad to see her a slave of John Barleycorn but that was life. Wandering on the wrong road extracted a price - sometimes the price was life itself.

TONY MCREDMOND

"There is an Irish singer by the name of Tony Mc Redmond entertaining at the Airport Inn tonight, would you like to go see him," Betty asked expectantly.

"Sounds like a great idea Betty, I answered enthusiastically. Thus began my introduction into the entertainment world. Tony introduced me to Dave Gallavan and Jack Beaty, both Dubliners, also to George of England, via India and to a very beautiful lady by the name of Judy whom I became attracted to. Soon I would leave the good home of the Greer's and move in with the boys from Dublin.

A few weeks after my arrival at my new residence a party was held in honor of my moving in. At exactly midnight while Jack had everybody's attention singing his rendition of the song, Forty Shades of Green, a knock was heard on the door. It was opened and in walked two unfamiliar faces. They were party crashers. Jack asked them to leave but they insisted upon remaining, thus causing the singer to take charge. I became a little concerned, because Jack weighed, soaking wet, no more than one hundred and twenty pounds. On the other hand, the newcomers looked in pretty good shape, bristling with all that muscle stuff. "Gentlemen," said Jack in tones of urgency, "please leave these premises before I call my good friend at the Winnipeg police department." That ultimatum had the reverse effect of what was expected. At this point, George of England via India quickly stepped in.

Sporting a glass of gin, in his most polished Oxford accent he eloquently addressed the intruders. "Gentlemen, I feel there is an issue which needs to be addressed. We are a gathering of simple people who are delightfully interested in modest pleasures of life, a little wine, a little dancing, a little singing and while one is present in our company nothing more is expected nor asked for." I think we were to a person mesmerized at the command with which George addressed the gathering. And George went on. "So gentlemen, I say this to you. It is only in the interest of camaraderie, fun times and common respect for each other we are gathered here." George really had our attention until he began to get a little biblical and self-righteous about his address. He really blew it when he let a most massive belch express itself, causing the gin in his glass to take flight and find refuge in his pinstriped, Harris tweed, three piece suit.

He blew it! He lost the initiative. This was made perfectly clear when one of the unwelcome told him in no uncertain terms to go far a field and fornicate. I had no idea what he meant by such a statement, so I turned to Judy and asked her if the fellow had complimented George on his speech. I got this strange, almost sympathetic look from Judy as she shook her head, saying to me, "No John, that is not what he meant, my dear. I think things are going to get rather unpleasant and it is best we leave." But leaving was unthinkable in a situation like that. In the quietness of our minds, the decision to stay was made.

As Jack always seemed to do when he felt he had something of importance to say, he placed his two thumbs behind the lapels of his jacket and moved his fingers through the air as one may use one's hands in the execution of a musical masterpiece played on the flute, except in Jack's case, there was no flute. But such fingering skills were impressive and they caught the attention of all present, even the two rednecks. "Now boys," Jack began, "No need to take it any further than it is. We're all here to have a little fun." And turning to obtain our approval which he received admirably by the nodding of our heads, carried on with his presentation. He ended with the statement that everyone was welcome to have a nice time except the two ugly looking bastards who were not invited and if they didn't leave walking they would leave airborne. His speech finished, he looked at Judy, throwing her "the nod and the wink," and said. "Isn't that fact, Judy?" Judy, who was resting her hand on my shoulder with a glass of wine in it, let it slip from the shock of what she had just heard, emptying its contents down the back of my neck. I too wondered if Jack was expecting Judy to throw the two guys out the door.

Jack went on. "So now you gutless shite hawks, get to hell out the door before ye go out the window." With that said, poor George, who was much smaller in stature than Jack, received a terrible punch in the ribs from one of the troublemakers. To my amazement, George protested in his most polished Oxford accent, saying, "That's not cricket my good fellow," and with the speed and accuracy that would make any martial arts champion rage with envy, planted his foot in that delicate area of the attackers person, rendering the fellow's sexual reproductive organs non-reproductive. There was a great hush within our ranks, respected even by the wounded interloper's friend as the unfortunate sank slowly to his knees, displaying a look of saintly reverence upon his face as his eyes turned upwards to the heavens. His last word of the evening to whomever he had set eyes upon in the heavens was a long drawn out, *awwwwwwww*. For a moment he knelt, immovable, and then grasping himself in that most personal and private place, fell over on his side with a thud

"You'll be leaving now, won't you," said Jack to the one who was still in good health. Without a word being spoken, he helped his buddy to his feet. It was the last we saw of them. Poor George of England via India received a broken rib from the unexpected punch thrown at him but he was a proud man and little though he was in stature, a powerful life force coursed his veins. Poor George of England via India was far from being poor.

How easy it was to forget the sleeping Monica and troubled Jennifer. How convenient it was to push such ominous signs aside. Such fearful things surely could not happen to me. After all, I was in the prime of my life. It was not the time to question the uncommon actions resulting from the consumption of alcohol. Alcohol had opened doors for me. It removed my inhibitions and shyness. It made me feel like I was somebody. I could discuss any subject with great confidence and alacrity while under its influence. Its consumption seemed ever to solicit aid from the wings of my soul, injecting me with the knowledge that this heavenly nectar was indeed prescribed by the gods for the goodness of man. This indeed was a good thing.

Perhaps the man in the garden was right. "Give it time and it will make a real man out of ye," he said, exhibiting a characteristic authority, an authority associated and released only by the magic of the bottle's content. Alcohol was the panacea of life and I thought, if only the brewers supplied the great masses with their product, life would at last be meaningful and undisturbed. However, what was not noticeable about the drinking patterns developing in my life was the absence of reflective thinking while sober. Analyzing my drinking behavior when sober never crossed my mind. It seemed two separate worlds existed – neither one overlapping into the other. They were in effect two separate entities, one real and the other an illusion. It was the world of illusion that had the stronger appeal for me but unfortunately, I did not realize that the world I felt more comfortable associated with was the one of deception.

Nevertheless, I was still a young man and while such negative thoughts about my drinking alcohol was far to the periphery of my mind, I was more interested in developing a successful career in something and, whatever that something should be – I enlisted the help of my friend Dave Galavan to determine my course of action. Dave was no slouch in the matter of business smarts and quickly directed me towards a career in Life Insurance. "Mr. McDonald, winter is approaching and I think I can help get you started in an exciting and rewarding career," Dave said. I wondered what the hell winter had to do with an exciting and rewarding career. "I have been chatting with a good fellow this afternoon and he needs people like you," Dave continued. "It's a lucrative business, fair and rewarding. I think you will do very well at it. Go see Archie in the offices of Sun Life Assurance. Tell him I sent you." I did not like that statement, "Tell him I sent you." That was a statement my father used most frequently and I never knew what the hell I was getting myself into. But it always left me with a little curiosity as to what it might be all about. Since it was about insurance it might not be so bad, because Tony Mc Redmond, my balladeer friend had tried his hand at selling insurance. Not only did Tony like selling insurance but he opened his very own insurance company.

It was no accident Tony was successful. He was one of the most unassuming friends I ever had. His personality exuded fairness, honesty and a quiet dignity – that pleasantness about the human spirit one feels comfortable being around. In some respects I envied him.

"I think you will be happy with our company and I shall assist you in every possible way," said Archie. With those words my job in Selkirk came to an end and so began, "the death of my selling." I liked Archie. He was a good and fair man and did assist me in every way. He saw to it that I got a loan from his bank to purchase a: car, suave looking brief case, Russian style head cover to keep the nasty winter from freezing my brains, long buffalo coat which was in vogue in the Winnipeg winters, gloves that resembled puffed out tabby cats, mukluks (padded boots) to help my feet from turning into blocks of ice and business cards to add the ultimate touch of professionalism. Indeed, had Archie given me a rifle, I would have been ready to patrol the Arctic front, helping keep Canada safe from unwelcome intruders and making every polar bear who came my way green with envy at the assortment of furs I sported to shield me from the bitter Canadian winters.

The thick of winter is not a good time to start anything in Winnipeg unless it's a car going south to Mexico. I gave my sales career a shot. I couldn't handle it. I could not relate to a world that needed to insure anything, everything, even life. When I began to tell prospective clients that they really did not need what I was trying to sell them, I knew the death of an insurance salesman was imminent. It was soon over for me. My career as a salesman had ended almost as quickly as it had begun.

One afternoon while visiting with Judy at her home near Stony Creek, I was taken to marvel at the great breadth of the Canadian landscape. It was here as I gazed at the ever-changing moods filtering through the horizon, I decided that I would travel this great land and come to experience its spirit – its unending magnificence. But how, I didn't have a clue. Still, my resolve was to put one foot in front of the other and proceed.

As Judy and I stood looking out towards the horizon, she turned to me and said, "You are going away, John, aren't you? You are going away and I have a feeling I will never see you again." The emotions of the moment were very real. She was sad and hurt. I did not know what to say. I just shook my head in the affirmative, then, held her. I did not realize that she has detected an air of restlessness in me but Judy was right - I was on my way. It seemed there was nothing in the world that could calm my restless nature. It was the last time I would visit the landscape of Stony Creek. It would be the last time I would walk the farm fields with Judy.

THE GREAT WARFIELD

Four mornings later, the outskirts of Toronto came into view. It was midsummer. The sun was on the horizon and the irritations of the mechanized world were slowly but steadily creeping upon a slumbering land. Fatigue gnawed at my mind. I pulled over in a shaded area to catch some shut-eye. It was later in the afternoon when I awoke from a long, deep sleep. I was hot, sweaty and uncomfortable. The heavy humidity, which seemed to build in the atmosphere the farther I drove east was not to my liking. Chancing upon a stream, I welcomed the revitalizing energies of its cool waters, bathed and moved on feeling invigorated.

It was towards late evening when I spotted a hitchhiker in the distance. I had become comfortable offering a lift to travelers. Apart from the odd rude smelly individual, the majority of people were rather pleasant.

Warfield Hogan stood about six feet six into the sky and appeared to be in great physical shape. Says Warfield, as he sat in the front seat with the top of his head solidly imbedded in the car's ceiling, "Thanks for the ride buddy, I sure appreciate it." I told him he was welcome and asked him how far he was going. He said he was on his way to British Columbia but as it was getting a little late he figured he would return home and try hitching a lift in the morning. We spoke a little about the country to the west and before long we were talking ourselves into turning the opposite way and heading towards the Rockies.

I had very little money left but between the two of us, we figured we could make it to the Rockies by picking up hitchhikers and asking them to share in the fuel cost. It worked like a charm. On we motored across the Canadian landscape in the faithful little auto, sometimes one hitchhiker with us, sometimes eight or nine. We were never without company and never without a great bellyful of laughter, story and wit. I was beginning to learn a little about the makeup of my fellow man. We all, it seemed, were in search of something; what it was we did not know.

On we rolled over the low lands, the flat lands, the hills, dales, prairies, valleys and mountains. I was tasting freedom at its finest. All who traveled with us had a goodly supply of bread and peanut butter. That was about it! Not too much of anything else in the line of food; the only variation in peanut butter being the brand names. I had never in my life heard of peanut butter before I came to Canada but by the time we got halfway across the prairie, I was so sick of it, I would have given my right leg for a potato - any kind of potato - cooked, uncooked, bad, good or just plain rotten. Still, peanut butter was affordable and nourishing and would remain the staple of our diet until better times surfaced over the horizon.

Somewhere in Alberta we picked up Melon; a woman as wealthy as Warfield and me but endowed with all the trimmings of physical loveliness. She was pleasant and fun to be with. We had a long way to travel and were low on cash, food, gasoline, and very much in need of a dip in a stream. Said the great Warfield Hogan, "Pull in at the next service station and I'll trade my watch for a tank of gas." This was a tough one for the great Warfield because of the sentimentality attached to the watch but our situation was desperate.

It was some sight to behold watching the huge bulk of Warfield saunter across the tarmac of the service station that hot summer's day. He even looked back toward our little faithful Acadian auto with that look of martyrism about him, as much as to say to the car, "I am doing this for you little one, now it's up to you to get us to the Rockies after this painful sacrifice."

It was almost peaceful, lying slouched back in my seat waiting for the important transaction to eventuate; the distant sound of a train's whistle breaking the sleepiness of the hazy summer evening as the prairie winds buffeted the hapless tumbleweed.

Through the window of the sedan, I observed a man rather small in stature, approach and address Warfield. I could hear only slight mumbles at first but that all changed presumably when Warfield asked the question. "I'm sick and tired of your type stopping here, day in, day out, with your bloody useless wares, expecting me to bail you out of your sad state of affairs," he ranted and raved at Warfield. Melon obviously feeling a little concerned for the predicament Warfield suffered, suggested she go and try to smooth the situation over.

It was something to behold watching the body of Melon sway to the rhythms of her sexy loveliness, as she sang her physical attributes across the open pavement to where the one sided debate was in full swing. The trader had just finished bad-mouthing some travelers who had stopped by on their way to the Yukon some hours before, in an attempt to barter a kitten for a can of oil. It was clear the businessman was going to die soon if he did not stop his ranting and raving, not from a swat from the great Warfield but from his own highly charged blood pressure system. The trader's high-pitched soprano voice garnished with the trimmings of a crows cawing seemed to tone down an octave or two as the goddess beautiful entered the scene. The sway of Melon's hips was enough to shame a complete female swing band into retirement. She had a body that would make Venus De Milo green with envy and breasts that would stop a train in its tracks. The trader's ranting and raving, dwindled away to the whispers of a mouse suffering from a bad case of laryngitis, as the beautiful one approached the scene of great disconsolateness.

Upon the wind, the voice of the trader was heard. "Yes miss, eh . . .what may I do for you?" The goddess informed the man that she was the wife of the great Warfield, that they were trying to get back to their little one in B. C. and the fellow in the car, who was me, was trying to get them back home. She went on to explain that we had been traveling for three days and while attending church service the previous evening, her handbag, which had within it her last few dollars, was stolen. By the time she was through her masterful presentation, she had managed to have the tank filled with gasoline, an extra five gallon can to fit in the trunk, bottles of Pepsi Cola, cookies, candies, hot dogs, marshmallows and a twenty dollar bill. The trader was as close as one can get to outright sobbing from the story Melon had shared with him. A profound sense of altruism seemed to fill his soul.

It was obvious the trader was suffering from a mighty visitation of lust but the outcome was a release of charitable bounty upon our sad state of affairs. Jeb was a good man indeed and offered apologies for his rude outburst to Warfield. Melon was good, real good - so damned good that I felt proud she was on our side.

THE BLUE CANADIAN ROCKIES

The Rockies lay to the west four hundred miles as the crow flies. On we went into the setting sun buoyed with the charitable donation from the trader. Later we pulled off the highway to rest the night and grab a bite to eat. It was a wonderful experience dining out on the prairies beneath the moon, our little fire glowing as we barbecued hot dogs and marshmallows. In the distance, the call of the coyote echoed through the deep purples of the flatlands. As one world prepared to rest, another awakened to the nocturnal call.

Early morning saw us move on as the rising sun gave birth to a brand new day. If all went well, we would reach the Rockies by late evening. Our little darling car faithfully motored on and on and at last, the snowy peaks of the majestic Rockies rose ever so slowly from the earth beyond the farthest reaches of the horizon. I had never expected to come to this land, Canada. I had known little about it except that there was a fellow who always "got his man," and he was the famous O' Rourke of the North West Mounted Police.

None of us had been to the Rockies before, and now, there they were in all their majesty, mystique and resplendence calling us to their cradles. As I stood there by the Alberta highway casting my eyes across the magnificence of the towering wilderness before me, I knew in my heart that the spirit of this great Canadian landscape had gripped my inner core. What lay ahead? I did not know. What I did know however was, that my journey had become unstoppable and irreversible. There was a place to the west to which we would travel. We would travel there because it was so.

Our plan was to swing north of Calgary towards Edmonton and then due west towards Jasper, then on to Prince Rupert via Prince George. Old Candy's engine was purring like a kitten and the only thing that concerned us was the wear and tear to her tires. With the extra can of gasoline still in the trunk and the tank a quarter full, we figured we would make it as far as Edmonton. From there - God only knew. We had reached Calgary by late afternoon and late evening saw us approach the outskirts of Edmonton. Food was getting low and hunger was belly aching. For the moment we were out of ideas as to how best to improve our marginal circumstances but faith intervened and the unexpected happened once again.

Up ahead, a lone figure standing by vehicle waved us down as we approached. I pulled over to check things out. The man who had waved us down was American. He was having difficulty changing a flat tire. He told us the nuts were rusted on the wheel studs and try as he may, they would not budge. Warfield tackled the problem. I knew Warfield was a big man and quite muscular but when he put his energy into turning the tire iron he made the great Godzilla look almost a little weak in comparison.

There was a creak and a groan and then a slight movement of the tire iron as it was twisted to work. Then came the ahs and uhs of the sideline supporters pinching in for a look at the action. It was a little hard to get a look at the proceedings because Warfield was so huge his shoulders literally spanned the length of the car. It was easy to see that our lives had lacked the curiosities of mechanics as we crowded around the great hulk of Warfield -

showing our interest in the application of physics towards a nut, stud and a wheel wrench. Then, suddenly, a major shift of the wheel wrench and the satisfied smile on Warfield's face indicated that he had broken loose the first one.

Broken it be damned! The steel of the tire wrench had been twisted into uselessness, three quarters of the tire iron in Warfield's hands and the other still attached to the stubborn nutt. Such was the strength of Warfield. That was the end of the tire iron's career. The nut remained on the stud. Warfield's face went from the look of satisfaction to one in traction. However, all was not lost. There was a tire iron in the trunk of Candy - perhaps we would fare better with it. We were lucky! It fit the studs of the convertible Chevy. Back to work went the great Warfield, this time the nuts giving way - creating much joy beneath the first crimson hues of the Alberta evening sky.

Brannagh Casey hailed from Kansas City, Missouri. He was on his way to visit his daughter in Edmonton. He was overjoyed with the help we afforded him, not just because his car was back on the road but now he could proceed on his way to see his newly born granddaughter. His daughter had given birth a couple of days ago to her first child and Brannagh was indeed on cloud nine. There are people who can read the soul of others and Brannagh was one of those people. Nothing was ever mentioned in the course of conversation about our rather wanting circumstances but Brannagh knew his helpers were feeling a pinch of hard times. From his wallet he handed the great Warfield a fifty-dollar note, then bid us a fond farewell

The sky was in full flame as we pulled into a truck-stop restaurant. Here we'd freshen up, then, discuss the trip over coffee and French-fries. A strange feeling overcame me as I sat with Warfield and Melon. It suddenly dawned on me that we three had grown pretty close. We made a good team and were very comfortable around each other. Then on a sudden, Warfield reached for a napkin to wipe his eyes. I asked if he had got some dust in his eyes but he did not answer. Warfield was not an over talkative fellow but he had grown a little quieter than usual. Melon also picked up on the unusual quietness of the big fella.

I really did not know a great deal about Warfield's background other than he had appeared on the outskirts of Toronto some days ago and was instrumental in my turning Candy around to head towards the Rockies. Tears welled in the Torontonian's eyes. I was surprised by the emerging emotional state before me. I was not sure why I should be surprised. Perhaps it was because I had not seen a fully-grown man cry before. Maybe I felt they had no right to.

"You have a wife and child back in Toronto, don't you Mr. Hogan?" asked Melon, as she wiped the tears from his eyes. The big fella nodded. The verbal interaction died right there as they held each other. There was loveliness in the silence as they snuggled into each other's comfort. I wondered too, if Melon was hurting inwardly. The big semis split the silence of the outside world as they swept along the highway into the ever growing darkness as evening surrendered to the first stars of twilight.

It was time to move on. Somewhere to the west lay the town of Prince Rupert. I had no idea why I was going to Prince Rupert, other than it was out by the Pacific Ocean. Melon did not like the name Rupert and the prefix of a prince to it made it even more unpalatable for her. I can't say I was overly fond of it. I figured a town needed a name but why not an Indian name? Native names were magical, full of nature's expression. So why not its original name? What was its original name? It was sad to see such ordinary names replace those of beauty and meaning to satisfy the arrogance and ego of the white man but that's the way it seems to be no matter where the Europeans go. Maybe one day they will come to recognize and understand the harmfulness of their superficial superiority but I will not be holding my breath. Melon explained to me that by replacing Indian names with European names was all part of the government's plan of assimilation for the Native - to absorb the Native into Colonial society. The banning of Indian customs, including the speaking of their language and the practicing of their sacred rituals was deliberately designed to destroy the spirit, the mind, and the soul of the Indian. I was dumfounded at what she revealed to me. In fact, I refused to believe it, but judging what had happened in my own land by the ones who came to civilize our nation dispelled any doubts about the revelation. I had much to learn about Colonial oppression and indeed such oppression was alive and well in the great fair land of Canada.

On we motored through the blackness of night into the early part of morning. Somewhere at the foot of the Rockies I pulled over our little faithful Candy as sleep came a calling to our weary minds.

It was late morning when I awoke, my nose given to the smell of bacon and eggs. It was a strange feeling here at the foot of the Rocky Mountains, being a part of a group I had known only for a few days. I felt a sense of belonging. The stream by which we had inadvertently stopped in the darkness gave a sense of ease to our world. I thought perhaps Tom Kilroy was right as my eyes gazed upon the vastness and awesomeness of the great wilderness. Yes indeed. It well may be here I would find purpose to my existence.

Breakfast finished, an invigorating bathe in the pristine stream, then it was on through the spectacular scenery of Jasper national park, across the Yellowhead highway towards Prince George, occasionally stopping to take in the world of perfect beauty.

In the afternoon we stopped to pick up two hitchhikers, one black and one white. They were traveling to Whitehorse, the capitol of the Yukon via Prince George. Although they were polite, there appeared uneasiness about them. The black man's name was Jim and his buddy, Michael. They got right to the point about where they were going and the reason why. They were disillusioned with the American involvement in Vietnam and had decided Canada was a more peaceful country to live in. The decision they made had hurt them deeply but they had seen too many of their high school buddies come back in caskets. They were asking the same question most of the world was asking. Why the slaughter of so many innocent women, children and men? Why a full scale directive of military genocide upon a nation in the throes of poverty? These two men were hurting.

We were about two hundred miles from Prince George when Candy went flat on us. This was the first inconvenience our little Candy had caused us since she came into my care. It was a good thing Candy blew a tire. As Warfield tackled the tire problem, we discovered the engine's oil level was dangerously low and there was little water in the radiator. I was not a mechanic and had no idea how to take care of a car. As far as I was concerned, once gasoline went into the tank that was all that was needed. I could not understand why a car should need water, oil, grease, air in tires, water for the wipers and so on. I was to learn the hard way about proper car maintenance. However, with the help of our two new traveling companions, Candy received water in her radiator and cooking oil in her engine - not professional but good enough for my standards of auto care.

It was late evening when Candy rolled into Prince George. From there, Jim and Michael continued north towards the Yukon. We were headed due west. I felt for those two guys. They had had to make a very difficult decision turning them-selves toward self-imposed exile in order not to take up arms against their fellow man in that far off country of Vietnam. I also thought it decent of the Canadian government to allow people like Michael and Jim to enter Canada and apply for citizenship so they could avoid fighting in a war that seemed only to diminish the wholesomeness of their great nation. I felt fortunate to be free from the wars and the killings, to be here in the majesty, the exquisite splendor and freedom in this incredible jewel of the North American continent.

The freshness of the late morning breeze gave hints of autumn's approach as we watched the exiles move further into the distance, then, they were gone, lost to the depths beyond the first rise on the road to the north.

Five hundred miles lay between the Prince Rupert and us. I turned the car towards the west and stepped on the gas but scarcely moved a hundred yards - we were out of gas. Within moments however, a good-hearted fellow stopped and offered help. I was impressed with his seemingly concern about our plight. In his company sat two delightful-looking ladies and they too were quite adamant about helping us.

THE KIDNAPPERS

The good fellow offered to drive me to a gas station to obtain the necessary goods. I bid adieu to Melon and Warfield with the assumption I would be back in a few minutes. Had I known what was in store for me, I would have walked the rest of the way to Prince Rupert.

Bronson was a lad who liked his beer and so did his girlfriends. Introductions were made all around and I was thankful that when my nationality was made known, they were polite enough not to ask me to sing "Dublin In the Green."

"We'll get you to a gas station up ahead - it's a few miles but we'll have you back in no time. In the meantime, help yourself to a beer," Bronson said assuredly. I thought it awfully nice of the fellow to share his bottles of beer. I did not refuse. We all had one, then two, then three and on and on. Before long we engaged in windfalls of useless conversation. It had not entered my head however, to ask how far away the gas station was and after a while I did not really care. Penny was a pretty looking girl and kept telling me how much she loved my accent as she nuzzled into any part of my body that was available.

Sometime later it had dawned on me that we had left the highway. This change of direction was obvious by the swirling clouds of dust that enveloped the car as we sped along to somewhere. It seemed that my life and destiny were in someone else's hands and there was not a whole lot I could do about it. I did not, however, question my destiny because I was drunk and I really did not give a damn where the hell I was going.

Bronson, who was not much of a talker, other than repeating the idiotic statement: "God damn, aint' I some wonderful driver," accompanied with a foul-mouthed belch, indicated to me that he was probably one of the most boring human being the great God had created. As I pondered the psychological make-up of this extraordinary numbnut, my eyes closed down to the world about me. Haziness beset my mind as the voices of the ladies faded into obscurity. I knew I was going to rest with the spirits and I thought, if we don't make it - I won't even know.

But Bronson did make it and to be sure, awakened me to inform me of his arrival at Canada's last outpost. "Irish," Bronson bellowed at the top of his voice, "told ya we'd make it," finishing his address with the usual, "God damn" and a great blubbery burp. My head was reeling from the effects of the booze, my stomach churned and I knew I had to find a place to empty its contents. While this messy turmoil of negotiating was going on in my head, Bronson was welcoming himself and everyone he did not know and who was not with him to this one and only wonderful place on our planet. I did not think he was losing it - I knew instinctively he lost it a long time ago. We stood on a patch of cleared earth approximately one quarter mile square. In the center of the cleared area stood a partially constructed building. At the far end of the lot, shoulder to shoulder, stood a number of house trailers neatly in rows against the backdrop of the forest. I had no idea where I was, nor did I care - I just wanted to throw up.

"I've got to go over to the bushes for a while Bronson," I said. "I don't feel too good - be right back."

"Okay Irish," he replied. Oh how my head swooned and the earth moved beneath my feet as though I were walking on a waterbed. It was a long way to the trees and I was not sure I was going to make it. The sailors "deck-walk" in a stormy sea, was all in vogue as I moved across the open ground to the seclusion of the forest. "Keep going dear son of Ireland, keep going,... almost there... hang on now... just a few more yards," I kept repeating as though I was completing the last few footsteps of some heroic mission. Each yard seemed like a mile and the urgency to throw up was immediate. Suddenly the waterbed seemed to open up and swallow me as down I went, face forward into the grasses at the edge of the forest. Here, I bid adieu to the contents of my stomach, my dignity and my self-respect. I then slipped into a drunken sleep.

The sun was to the southwest when I awakened. I had no idea how long I had slept. My body was badly dehydrated and my mouth felt like it had housed a heard of goats for the past two years. I was not in the best physical or psychological shape. I had no idea what I was doing lying beneath a tree and worse! I did not know what part of the country the tree belonged to! Things were not looking good. As my mind cleared ever so slightly, I heard the ripple of a stream to a short distance and made my way to it.

How wonderful water is to a dying system, at least one in my dilapidated condition! I slurped and slurped and slurped. I had never, in all my life, tasted water so sweet and so refreshing. Slowly, the realization of my predicament hinted at my senses. The vision of a chubby man belching while driving a car and two women sitting on my lap in the back of the vehicle began to take on some clarity. Then, suddenly, the whole picture was made crystal clear to me. I had literally been taken for a ride.

I ducked my head into the stream and sipped from its refreshing energies, then walked from the forest. Though my head was still suffering a smidgen of haziness, I was quickly regaining the full use of my senses. Across the open ground, I moved to where I thought Bronson and the girls should be but as I got closer, it was obvious they had left. Not unduly concerned at their absence, my eyes focused on a small red object sitting out on the open ground. I wandered towards it and as I did, I realized it was my gasoline can. Was I abandoned? Surely not! But as time passed, I began to accept that I had been left behind in the jaws of the wilderness.

I had no idea how I was going to get back to Prince George. I had no idea where I was. I knew for sure I was lost somewhere in the Canadian wilderness, alone with an empty gas can. At times, I thought Bronson may have gone off to visit someone in the trailers and he would no doubt come back to pick me up but as the day grew older, I realized it was wishful thinking. It was time to move on.

For some hours I had been walking the road back to the highway when a vehicle came racing towards me. I felt a little hope as I figured it would be easy to hitch a ride out here in the wilderness. As the vehicle came closer, it began to slow and I recognized it as Bronson's. Lord, happiness was my lot indeed - I had been rescued. I could now see Bronson's face quite clearly and as the vehicle slowed some more, I could see the girls waving to me. I felt elated. However, elation was short-lived as the car picked up speed and disappeared into a cloud of dust as the girls waved from the rear window and then they were gone forever.

It is not nice to be left behind in a territory one is not familiar with, standing on a dirt road with an empty two-gallon gas container. Disbelief slapped me in the heart. I was left to the elements of the wilderness, talking to myself, and at times, complaining to the odd shrub about my sad state of affairs. But the shrubs did what all shrubs do - ignored me. Such was my state of mind. To add insult to injury, a noisy cawing crow flew low overhead and did something I had never seen a bird do before. It completely rolled over in flight, upside down as it were, righted itself and carried on cawing. It was quite something to behold, this bird of disgusting vocals flying upside down through the sky. It was a nice show of aeronautical expertise but it did little to remove my feelings of dejection. That all changed, however, when the show-off bird returned and from a goodly distance above my head, bombed me with the waste contents of its stomach. It was an excellent shot and its accuracy annoyed me thoroughly.

There were not many times throughout my young life that I had sat by the side of a trail, confused and lost. But when such times occurred, a voice prompted softly through my mind. It told me to just keep going. I would hear this voice numerous times but truly, as comforting as it was, I did not relish hearing it because it meant I was usually in deep trouble. As I wiped the birdshite from my dusty scalp, I asked the voice if it was necessary for the divine to send the most obnoxious creature in creation to visit me and to have it distribute its belly contents across the side of my head. To such a question, the appropriate amount of silence was always given. Annoyed, but odd as it may seem, I began to smile at the comical state of my situation. The smile turned into laughter.

As the crow cawed its way into the distance, a cloud of dust rose from the road a few hundred yards from the same direction I had walked, a small red truck moving just ahead of it. Here was my transport back to the highway. Dead or alive I was traveling with its driver. As the little red truck bolted towards me, I stood in the middle of the trail, giving the driver no choice but to stop or run me over. Staying in this country with a little red gas can was not an option for me. As any madman would do, I stood my ground and just before the car left the trail and headed into the density of the undergrowth, imprinted on my mind, was the stark look of terror on the driver's face. It was an interesting scene watching the little red truck hop, skip and jump its way through the underbrush of the forest. A great assortment of instruments littered the newly made trail as they bounced from the back of the truck as it danced gaily to a standstill.

BILL DOOKER, THE LUMBERJACK

Within moments, a lone figure emerged from the underbrush and slowly walked towards me. I felt my time had come and I offered prayers immediately to anybody who might listen. As I prepared for my last moments on earth, I felt that it was not right for the great God to have me travel so far from my Emerald Isle to die by the hands of an unknown Canadian.

"God damn - almost clipped you pretty good, young fella. What the hell are ya doing out in the middle of this Godforsaken place?" said the man in a husky voice. I had no idea how to answer the giant that approached me. "Here, God damn, have a beer, looks like ya could do with one. Sure scared the living hell right out of me, God damn," he said. I was so bloody scared that he was just being nice before he executed me that I let the bottle drop. But before there was a drop spilled, the big Canadian had grasped it before it hit the ground. The burly man had a great sense of humor and while I struggled to regain some measure of my former self, I found myself sitting on a log, drinking beer, laughing and listening to a man that had a great passion for life.

Bill Dooker was a lumberjack who had just finished a months work in a logging operation somewhere deep in the Canadian forest and had been flown out of camp an hour or so before my almost fatal encounter with him. As we moved along the trail towards the highway, we chatted merrily and drank heartily from a twelve pack of beer that had survived the bumpy ride through the underbrush. I had not eaten for some time and the beer was beginning to make me feel ill but rather than be a sensible person, I figured I should play the role of the "real man," The "real-man" whom I had heard about so many years before. "Yes sir! Have a sniff," the gardener had said as he shoved a bottle of whiskey towards my nose, "it will make a real man out of you."

Bill Dooker spoke about his adventures in the logging business and just like that shithead Bronson, who had abandoned me, Bill Dooker began and finished every sentence with the words "God damn." Bill loved the life of a lumberjack. This was indeed made obvious by the fact that he spoke only about trees, logs and more trees and logs. As the beer went down and the conversation loosened a little more, the great lumberjack suggested I try my hand at logging, assuring me that I looked the type made to measure for the bush life but I wasn't so sure. Nevertheless, was not Bill Dooker suggesting what the results of my career test indicated in Winnipeg a couple of years ago - logging and music? Was I not in the great wilderness Tom Kilroy had spoken about? Indeed I was here and undeniably the predictions seemed to be unfolding.

The effects of the beer presented a more creative twist to the one sided conversation as Bill now had me operating as his right hand man. In fact, in his mind he had me felling trees, breaking trails, driving logging trucks, building roads and operating as a chokerman. I had no idea what he was talking about. I knew little about trees other than swinging from them and all I really wanted to do was get back to Warfield and Melon. By the time we had reached the highway, I knew what a cedar, fir, hemlock, spruce, pine, and maple tree looked like. Bill Dooker was determined to make a logger out of me.

At last, the highway appeared. Bill intended going north towards the town of Chetwynd and I was on my way back to Prince George with an empty gasoline container. I thanked Bill for the ride and in a woozy state of mind made my way to the paved road, which would take me back to Prince George. As the dust settled and I looked down the trail in the direction from which we had come, I noticed a sign crudely attached to a pole on the side of the trail. It indicated the location of Mac Kenzie - the place I had spent the last few hours. Ten years later, the cleared area, which I had stumbled across to find the refuge of the forest to empty the contents of my stomach, would become a thriving town.

As I walked south along the highway hitching a ride, Bill decided for whatever reason to deliver me to my friends waiting back in Prince George. I did not object, not even to the next drink he uncapped for me. We were on our way to the great Warfield and the lovely Melon and hopefully they were waiting where I had bid them adieu before I was kidnapped.

The sun had some hours left in the sky as Bill pulled over to the side of the road where Melon and Warfield faithfully awaited my return. Bill was a good man indeed for he took it upon himself to explain to my friends what had happened to me. As he presented a wonderful case in my favor, I moved from Bill's car to mine with great difficulty, for I was indeed highly drunk and heavy of limb. However, I managed to make the trip and contented myself in the back of the car holding the empty gasoline container as I wandered off into unconsciousness. A few hours later, I awoke to the music of the radio and the idle of the car's engine.

While I was passed out, Bill had driven Warfield to a gas station where he secured the gas and some groceries, then returned. Before the logger departed he told Warfield not to forget to mention to me that I was suited for the bush life. He was a good fellow, this Bill Dooker. I wondered if I would see him again.

It was time to move on. The first stars of the evening appeared as Warfield took the wheel and headed west towards Prince Rupert Tiredness brought the drive to an end around midnight in Vanderhoof, a town a few hours drive from Prince George. There wasn't much happening around the small town except for the winds intermittent blusters and the beckoning of a dim light over the sign of the local bar. We responded to the light's calling. It was the first bar I had visited since I left Winnipeg. A few sleepy tired eyes came to life immediately when the "goddess," Melon, entered through the doorway of the hotel. Melon was indeed a woman any man would be proud to be with. It was so easy to obtain help and receive information from the men folk when with her. For her part, she seemed genuinely unaware of her physical blessings and only once did she use her sexy endowments in the business of manipulation. That was back on the prairies at Jeb's service station.

Since I left Winnipeg, it was the first time I began to unwind and feel comfortable. The beer tasted good. It led to one more, then another and then it was time to find someone to talk to other than Melon and Warfield. So it was, I met Jim, a middle-aged man and owner of a small sawmill in Fort St. Jame's, a small town located approximately forty miles north of Vanderhoof. Jim needed a few good people to work at his mill and offered the three of us jobs with room and board. It was a decent offer but it was explained that we had to travel to Prince Rupert to tend to pressing business and upon returning we would stop by and take up the offer and the matter was left at that. Later, at a party that simply blossomed from the bar, my guitar was brought into play as we sang and talked about important things until sleep came calling.

This night would confirm my solid entry into the world of illusion. I liked what booze did to me. It waived all inhibitions and opened many doors. I was also beginning to realize the potential of my guitar, not just as a musical instrument but as a tool for creating social interest and harmony. This was a good thing indeed.

Later in the morning I awoke among scattered, sleeping bodies, some of whom looked familiar, some who looked vaguely familiar and others I could not recall to mind. The sun was high in the sky, its heat making the cramped sleeping quarters stuffy and wanting of fresh air. I did not feel good. My mouth tasted as though it had been chewing cobwebs garnished with sour milk and the head upon my shoulder I did not want. I found the washroom and gazing upon my countenance in the mirror, suffered great fright. A shower and a cup of fresh coffee were most helpful in restoring me to some degree of physical comfort. Looking through the window, I noticed my faithful car parked in the driveway and I wondered how it had gotten there. Did I drive it here? I could not recall. I felt extremely uncomfortable at the thought of not being able to remember the events from the night before, particularly not recollecting who drove the car. I had no idea whose house I was in. It was time to move on. I awakened my friends and while the rest of the house slept, a note of thanks was left to the good host and then it was on to Prince Rupert.

The country we traveled through was absolutely spectacular. This was the Buckly Valley country, awe inspiring and majestic as it was imposing. This was the land of the Seven Sisters mountain range, their high mountain peaks reaching into the azure sky, their foothills sweeping down to the streams of the lush, fertile valleys.

Late evening saw us roll into the town of Prince Rupert, park the car and rest for the night. As we discussed our plan for sleeping quarters, a Mountie knocked on the window of our little four-wheeled house. We were asked semi-politely to step out of the vehicle and identify ourselves. So it was we were checked out to make sure we were honorable and law abiding people of the land. To be sure, we were kinda decent folk but suspicion arose in the ranks of the great police force when it was discovered we had two dollars between us and not a shack to call home in the whole of Canada. It became a little more uncomfortable for us when Candy was searched for things illegal. None were found. We got the usual odd look any human being might give three people after discovering we were all homeless with only two dollars to our name. "And where do you plan on staying the night?" the officer asked. I had not a clue as what to say to him but the big Warfield did.

"We are staying in that little car sir. I am going to snuggle up beside this beautiful woman and God only knows the outcome of that delightful contact but whatever the outcome it can only be most desirous. My good friend, Irish, will be sleeping in the front of the car as he has for two weeks. We are not troublemakers and as a matter of fact I happen to be an ex-policeman from Toronto. I left the force because I did not like the bullshit I had to put up with. I was a good police officer and I know that you also are sir and you are merely carrying out your duty. But as I said we are not troublesome and we are all kinda starting our lives over under difficult circumstances and that is the sole drift of it," Warfield concluded with the look of immovability about him.

Well, Lord, Lord, Lord. For a fellow that had hardly opened his mouth in conversation, he managed to leave three people a little dumfounded with his excellent oration. Melon could hardly contain herself. I'm not too sure if it was the promise of Warfield sleeping in the back of the car with her that made her blossom into a bundle of shimmering womaness or the sheer eloquence with which he had delivered his proclamation, but she gave Warfield a rousing round of applause, which really left us all a little stumped. The officer handed my drivers license to me, smiled and wished us good luck. The rains were falling as the great Warfield and Melon snuggled in the back of the car and I distributed myself as comfortably as possible as I prepared to go to sleep with the spirits.

I awoke as usual with my left leg resting on top of the steering wheel and my head buried between the end of the seat and the inside of the car's door. My physical make-up looked a little wanting after a night's sleep in the bent out of shape position but usually, after a few hours, I began to resemble something of a homo-sapien as my body unraveled into the upright position. Warfield seemed not to fare much better than me and Melon had a remarkable knack for looking like she had crawled out of that place where cabbage patch dolls sleep in groups. Nevertheless, we accepted each other, lock, stock and barrel, the cheap judgments of human frailties closed out to genuine companionship. A strong bond had developed between us and although it would remain so, this day would see our company suffer its first fracture.

They looked a little out of place, sporting aprons as they washed dishes in the hotel's kitchen. I, on the other hand, sat in a cubicle drinking coffee and murdering a plateful of bacon and eggs. Melon had arranged with the management to wash the dishes for a few hours with the great Warfield in exchange for breakfast and lunch. She had made a hit with the hotel management and the writing was on the wall. The lovely Melon's time was coming to a close in our company. Jobs were scarce in Prince Rupert. Indeed, throughout Canada, there was a serious recession and it was to last well into the next decade. Warfield and I knew we must move on to find employment. Within days of our arrival in Prince Rupert, we were saying a fond farewell to our lovely Melon. As we were set to depart, she presented us with forty dollars, which she had secured as an advance from her employer.

Departing from this fine lady made me sad but the Great Warfield was beyond consoling. He had grown very fond of Melon and the separation from his family and now a departure from a girl he cared for, left him silent and as distant as the dark side of the moon. We had planned to make it back to Vanderhoof and perhaps take on the job Jim had offered us at the mill in Fort St. James. It was a long drive back and old Candy was beginning to sound a little rough. On we motored however, steadily heading east, past Terrace, on towards Hazelton… and then a flat tire. Within minutes Warfield had replaced it with the spare. We had driven approximately two hundred yards when our Candy blew another tire. It seemed we had come to the end of our road.

An uneasy feeling coursed through my veins as I fully realized that I was truly good and stuck somewhere on the Canadian landscape fully embroiled in a personal economic mess. I had no doubt the same thoughts were flourishing in the mind of the great Warfield. We both sat on the hood of the car lost in our lonely confusion as what to do next. We had no answer. Then the thought suddenly occurred to me that I should convey to Warfield the reassuring aphorism my mother always imparted to me when things were not going too well in my life. "You know Warfield, my mother always said, when things got a little rough in life, everything would turn out O K." Warfield gave me that look of disconnectedness indicating he was not swallowing the comfort of the unknown help that was on its way out of the unseen. The warm afternoon sun seemed to add to the listlessness of time as my legs swung to and fro above the flat front wheel of the car. On the other side of the hood, Warfield was doing exactly the same thing.

THE MAKING OF A LUMBERJACK

Barney Booley stopped to offer his services. We explained our situation, then, found ourselves packed into his well-used station wagon heading towards the hills. He reassured us that our car would be safe where it was and he would organize some people to pick it up the following day. The chill of the late summer evening was beginning to present itself as we left the highway at the village of Hazelton moving north towards the ancient Indian village of Kitwanga. Barney Booley was a logger and resided in a cabin by the mighty Skeena river. This country was prime fishing and logging country. As we moved up the Kispiox valley, I knew instinctively that I was in a special place favored by the great God and I was left to wonder what was in store for me as the old station wagon wound its way along the ancient dirt road towards the home of Barney Booley.

Morning light broke as we awoke to the inviting smell of bacon, eggs and coffee. Barney was heading off to work and left us with the run of the place while he was gone. When he returned in the evening, he informed us that he had organized a job for us with the Bojak logging company. We were to start the following morning. He also organized some people to go retrieve Candy. The following morning he dropped Warfield and me off at the logging camp of the Bojak Company and bid us farewell. I often returned to that old cabin to chat with Barney and loved listening to the stories of his life as a logger and his fondness for the wilderness.

Life as a bushman was bloody brutal and I must say I found nothing remotely romantic (a term for some unknown reason attributed to bush life) about it except when the workday ended. Five a. m. to afternoon exhaustion saw and heard me utter the great unmentionables. I thought this life had to be the most brutal known to man and I could not for the life of me figure out why Bill Dooker felt I had the stuff for lumberjacking. Every kind of dirty thing that flew on two wings bit and chewed me with a vengeance. I was a little worried as I thought I might bleed to death at the loss of so much flesh. However, the cooler days were approaching and that meant winter was on its way. It also meant the dirty little bugs would have their wings frozen and stiffened and that would be the end of them for another season

The Great Warfield was not faring much better. He was finding it as difficult as I was dealing with this new art of survival. He craved relief from it. It was our job to haul across the terrain long wire cables to wrap around the butt end of the trees the fallers had cut down. When this was done, the loop of the cable was placed on a large hook attached to a main cable line on the Caterpillar and hauled to the loading area for transportation to the mills. I doubt if there is an apprenticeship anywhere in the world as difficult as that of a chockerman. I considered myself in pretty good shape but making it out of the bush at the end of the day was as much as I could physically do. As the weeks went by, I began to condition both mentally and physically to the demands of the bush life. Warfield however, was finding it difficult dealing with the isolation from city life - but more so from his children. The strain was showing upon his enormous frame and eventually he could take it no more.

It was a late October afternoon when I bid good-bye to my good friend Warfield as the logging truck pulled out from camp towards Hazelton. There he would catch the Greyhound coach back to Toronto. He had made enough dollars from his job to see him comfortably home. I missed the big fellow. It was the last time I saw him.

The fall weather brought new and fresh vibrancy to the mountain wilderness. It was here at the Bojak camp I met Angus, a superb fisherman, Seventh Day Adventist and teacher at the camp school. Angus went to great lengths to teach me the art of fly fishing and the patience and skill in fishing the fabled steelhead, a sea going rainbow trout indigenous to the waters of the Pacific coast. Weekends saw us fish the waters of the mighty Skeena and the tranquil depths of the mystical Lake Kitwankool. By these inland waters of the Pacific, Angus and I engaged in long conversations about the great Creator and the way to cook fish properly. Life was rich indeed.

Slowly but surely I conditioned to the demands and rigors of the bush life and decided to extend my fishing time to evenings after work. Lake Kitwankool was too far from camp to travel to in the evening, as the early arrival of darkness left little time to get some fishing done. However, there were a number of rivers meandering the terrain not far from camp. Upon informing Angus of my intentions to fish the rivers, he adamantly warned me not to stray from the beaten trail because this was grizzly bear country and to get lost in the bush could prove fatal. I promised him that I would be careful and that I would stay close to the trails.

The autumn leaves, like lazy butterflies, wafted through the cool evening air as squirrels busily gathered the nuts to tide them through the coming winter. In the sky, great flocks of Canada geese coursed their way to the warm lands of Mexico and Texas as the first traces of new borne snow settled across the jagged peaks of the high Rockies.

It was shortly after supper when I headed out from camp down the trails towards the streams. How far the steams were, I was not sure but the walk to reach them was taking longer than expected and I grew uneasy as the shades of evening settled across the land. Then, somewhere in the distance I heard a river's rush. In my excitement to fish the water's, I abandoned all promises made to stay on the beaten trail. It was a serious mistake. I started into the underbrush moving towards the sound of the river. Deeper, deeper, I moved into the forest, until it became quite difficult to negotiate. Further into its depths I ventured, and still could not locate the river. As time slipped by, daylight quickly faded and pretty soon the light of day was lost to the twilight. I decided to turn back.

This decision, although the proper one, failed to succeed. As twilight moved into darkness, I tried desperately to find the trail. My movements became more hurried as elements of panic chipped away at my composure. The dread of having to spend the night in the "wilderness hotel" moved the elements of panic towards outright terror. Full measures of desperation took control. Dignity and self-control vanished from my countenance as I tried to flee the forest's domain. The lashing of the unseen briars across my face gave proof to my loss of togetherness. Then, suddenly, I was by the river. The calming effects of the waters eased my fears as my mind surrendered to calmness. The river blended into the deep purples of the closing night as darkness settled across the land.

It was not a comfortable feeling being stuck in the bush lost this time of the year, because autumn was upon the land and the bears fed heartily on the spawning fish in the rivers to fatten them for their winter's hibernation. This was nature at its finest - the heart of the worlds greatest salmon grounds and home to the massive grizzly, and in this most bounteous and wild part of God's country, I wondered where I was going to spend the night - hopefully it was not going to be in a bears belly.

Climbing a tree in fisherman's boots is no easy task, particularly if the boots are hip-waders. Nevertheless, I had to make a bed but more importantly, to get to hell out of the way of the bears. I decided to remove my awkward rubber long-Johns. This move proved helpful in the art of tree climbing. I climbed as high as it was possible, then set about making a nest for myself. While I was busy doing my domestic chores, I remained comfortably warm but when it was time to retire, the chilly night began to deliver its unkindness unto me. Shivering and shaking in a big cedar tree beneath the gleaming moon is not a nice experience, particularly when grizzly bears are feeding their faces with salmon a few feet below my tree bed.

My feet were the first parts of me to go numb and the numbness moved slowly but surely upwards. After a couple of hours of physical chattering, my body seemed to normalize. Indeed I began to feel a little sleepy. I decided to undo my pants belt and attach it and myself to a branch. This proved a wise move as I did indeed doze off. As fate had it, I fell right out of my perch. It is not a pleasant situation to be dangling from a tree somewhere in Canada while bears picnicked to their hearts content at the foot of my house. To make matters worse, I delivered a mighty fine sneeze showering everything below me with moisturized blessings. Now, let it be known that sneezing and dangling from a tree is not an easy thing to do but I did it and it caught the attention of my furry neighbors

I knew at last what it was like to be suspended in time. I understood the meaning of "stillness of death". I knew silence was not golden as some people claimed. I knew what it was like to be hung from high. I knew I was not in a position to bargain. It was clear I was going to die. It was just a question of how fast mummy bear could climb a tree and swat me into eternity.

Strangely, mummy bear seemed quite content filling her stomach with choice sockeye salmon and paid no attention to the drizzle I sprayed over her. However, her cute little, big offspring was not so inattentive. I thought, you cheeky little bastard, you're going to get me killed just because of your bloody nosiness. The silence became deafening as I dangled from my perch in the early morning wilderness. Little snoopy put his nose to the breeze and pointed it towards my suspended being. I was very cold but hot sweat began to ooze from ever pore in my body and now, I fully understood what the infection by malaria entailed. Would my potential informer keep his mouth shut? I did not know. His stare upon my swinging form seemed to last an eternity as his nose sniffed me out. I became fully aware at this point that I had even frozen the movement of thought as I awaited the outcome of the cub's curiosity. Then, to add more fear to my helplessness, another cub decided to nose in. There they were, two little big potential troublemakers holding my destiny in their paws.

Then it happened! They found my fishing boots and accosted them with great unkindness. In a few seconds my new hip-waders were subjected to a brutal transformation but I was still alive and swinging.

While the bears fished to their heart's content and I was left dangling between heaven and earth, the sound of the first logging truck broke the morning stillness. I knew it was now around five a. m. The cubs lay beneath the tree resting among the tatters of my footwear as Mother seemed to show a little uneasiness hearing the sound of the truck engines as they powered across the hills. Then, as quietly as they had come, the contented family of much fur slipped off to places deeper within the forest. I do not know how long I had dangled from the branch but it was sure nice to be able to uncoil myself and give praise to the good Lord for keeping me safe through the night. I climbed higher in the tree to see if I could locate the direction where the trucks were moving. It was not long before I spotted the headlights of one of the trucks bouncing through the darkness of morning. I now had a bearing. Each minute seemed so very long as I awaited the first rays of dawn. As darkness slowly gave way to the graying twilight, I descended from the tree.

It was not difficult to place my feet in the leftovers of my hip-waders. The upper parts were torn to shreds leaving barely enough material to form any kind of solid attachment around my feet. However, I was thankful to be alive. I had learned a very valuable lesson. Within hours I was back at camp. Angus had informed the camp authorities that I had gone fishing and had not returned. Logging operations were suspended and a full-scale search and rescue had been initiated. I was a welcome sight back at camp but the unspoken word cautioned me not to wander from familiar territory again, at least while I was employed by the logging company. The camp's cook made a fine breakfast for me and then told me to go to bed and stay there until the following morning. I listened to her and did exactly what I was told to do.

THE GREAT CAT SKINNER

After a day's rest back to work I went with my partner, the great cat skinner, Ivan Donnelley. That did not mean he skinned cats as it were but that he handled a D8- Caterpillar bulldozer very efficiently. We made a good team. He really knew how to handle the machine, thus saving me a great deal of energy and frustration in hooking up the logs. We took pride in how we handled the operation because every hookup demanded a new approach. However, overconfidence in one's ability towards skillful logging can prove detrimental to one's health.

It was late Friday afternoon. The work was winding down. We had one more haul left to skid to the landing. The cabled logs were hooked to the main line of the caterpillar. Everything seemed safe and secure. As usual, Ivan puffed on a hand made cigarette as he turned the nose of the machine towards the landing. My thoughts drifted to fishing Lake Kitwankool over the weekend. It was not to be. Through the periphery of my eye, I glanced it but too late. A log that was being hauled by the caterpillar got its butt-end dragged up against a tree stump causing it to flip through the air and smash into the small of my back. The flight through the sky was without effort on my part but the landing quite severe. I lay sprawled across a tree stump, my body twisted to the four directions. I did not know if I was dead or alive and truthfully I was not in the least concerned about which dimension I existed in. My mind was fully at peace.

However, Ivan, apparently recovering from the initial shock of observing me fly through the sky, took to eating the tobacco he had been smoking. He was concerned. The sudden affliction of chronic laryngitis upon his voicebox gives proof to the statement. The engine of the caterpillar was cut, inviting the silence of the evening to add a twist of uncertainty to the outcome of my health. As my mind returned to a smidgen of reality, the fear of my back being broken caused me great consternation. It was not a good feeling to look for feeling where there may be none.

"Can you move at all there me boy, Ivan said, his tone full of nervousness.

"I don't know but I guess I had better find out," I answered. Ever so slowly, fraught with uncertainty and fear at the out come of my physical condition, I anxiously sought movement in my limbs. All body parts responded to the commands. I was going to be okay. Had the tree hit me in the upper or the lower part of the body, the results would have been quite different. Upon seeing a semblance of motion course my being, Ivan, immediately suggested that after work we drink two gallons of Lonesome Charlie, a stash of his finest wine that he had stored in secrecy for such occasions, leaving me with the impression that what had just happened to me was of a regular occurrence in the life of the bush man. I was not far from wrong with that assumption.

The wine, I must admit, was the most disgusting tripe I had ever tasted. I thought if this stuff was the only alcohol available for social drinking, then this world would be a very sober place indeed. However, after a glass or two, Lonesome Charlie seemed to develop a taste superior to the great and distinguished wines of France and so followed great wads of intellectual disputation of which none was left to memory.

My head felt like the sound barrier had been broken in it when I awoke the following morning causing me to swear to the great God that if he would relieve me from my agony, I would never drink a drop of liquor again. Later in the day as I began to feel a little better, I changed the promise to: never again would I partake of that Lonesome Charlie stuff. I really should have stuck to the initial promise.

As mid autumn approached and its full spectrum of color carpeted the land, well below the peaks of the Costal Mountains, the snows' moved steadily downwards. Soon the land would be covered in a blanket of cold white. By the coffee fire, the logging crew huddled against its welcome heat. Sipping from his cup of brew as though it was the Holy Grail, Evan Good, a Native and veteran bushman scanned his eyes across the high terrain. Though close to sixty years old, his youthful appearance belied the veteran's age. In moments, his gaze was transfixed on the yonder. Then slowly he lowered the cup from his mouth and placed it by the fire. In that silent curious manner peculiar to him, he beckoned me to follow.

I did not see the silver-tipped grizzly but Evan did. He reached for a 30.06 rifle, which lay in the rack above the seat of his pickup truck. "He's just gone into the trees up there on the hill - stay close behind me and remain silent," he said. I knew by his soft commanding tone that I had better pay attention.

Steadily and deliberately he paced up the steep hill to where he had spotted the bear. I followed silently. The veteran hunter was in superb physical condition and soon began to outpace me. My legs began to tire, my breathing noticeably heavier as a hot sweat oozed down my cheeks. I was just about to fall to the ground when Evan rested his stride.

He gave me that peculiar look a man gives when he is pissed off. My puffing and panting was not being received favorably by the hunter, but he was polite enough not to comment about it. Then he sat down. Oh, thank God he sat down because my lifeless legs had turned to jelly, unable to support me. While I thanked God for his mercy, I looked back towards the logging operation. The D8 Cats were barely visible and I wondered how the heck Evan could spot a bear from such a distance. Then slowly Evan moved forward and as he did, he indicated to me that the bear was close by.

My heart was in my mouth as we moved ever so cautiously towards the great creature. I wondered why I had put my life in the hands of a man I hardly knew. If Evan missed or wounded the bear, I knew we were both dead - very, very dead.

Just ahead, the land sloped downward then rose in a slight banking arch. From beyond the bank came the sound of a swift running creek. It was by the creek Evan figured the bear might be. I could hear my heart pound as we inched closer to the bank's crest. We had approached from downwind, eliminating the chance for the bear to pick up our scent. Evan lay in against the ridge of the bank, his rifle at the ready, then, peering through the dew-laden ferns, he searched out his prey.

"No sign of him, wonder where the hell he went to," he whispered. I remained silent for I knew I really had nothing of value to say. Then I noticed Evan's eyes grow a little wider and then a whole lot wider as he looked in the direction from which we had come. Then, in an instant, he was to his feet, the rifle placed to his shoulder.

Somehow the bear had picked up our scent and moved around to come up behind us. I turned in the direction Evan was pointing his rifle and found myself looking at the most magnificent creature I had ever seen. He was no more than twenty yards away as he moved slowly towards us, the sheen of his rich fur rippling over its powerful form. A slight swat from such a creature meant instant death to a human. As the gap between us closed, the thought occurred to me of Evan forgetting to load his rifle - a frightening prospect. While my mind was busy dealing with the ifs and ands of such possibilities, the great creature rose on his hind legs, his enormous frame blocking the mid-morning sun. A great sorrow overpowered me as I waited for the sound of the rifle fire. It did not come.

I remained transfixed on the great silver-tipped grizzly as he towered above our miserable frames. My mind was racing in the silence of wonderment as Ivan lowered his rifle. "He might kill us," he said. I did not respond. I couldn't. I was absolutely in awe of the animal that stood before us. "But I don't think he will," said Evan. Then, as though something had been communicated between Evan and the great bear, the magnificent one came down to all fours and moved away unhurriedly, deeper into his domain - his domain since time immemorial.

"Do you know why I did not shoot, Mr. John?" said Evan.

"No, I don't," I answered. "Because the big fella had a great spirit," he said. And with that statement we moved on down the hill and back to work.

THE JERK THAT TRIED TO MURDER ME

Restlessness began to stir once again in my soul and it was time to say good-bye to my friends of the Kispiox Valley. On the advice of my good friend Angus of the church of The Seventh Day Adventists, I headed south to the town of William's Lake where his longtime friend, Glenn, managed a sawmill. Through Glenn, I secured a job at the mill but a yearning for the open country beckoned and soon I found work as a chokerman for the Wild Creek logging Company. I was teamed up with one very ugly human being - Fandangle Shytzenhead. Fandangle was an excellent cat skinner. He could turn the great bulk of a machine cleanly on a dime so to speak. Any truck or machine operator would be envious of his cat handling skills. Fandangle told Paul, the owner of the Company that he was extremely pleased with the way I ran over the hill and around the valleys with the cables slung across my shoulder in search of the prized logs the fallers had cut down. Fandangle could not sing my praises enough, Paul informed me. This was, of course, due to the fact that I carried smaller, lighter cables than I had used up north. The weight and difficulty of handling the bulky chokers (cables) for Bojak logging proved great training for me and truly, I was spoiled by the lighter chokers the Wild Creek Company used. The cats were also fitted with lighter winch lines making the workload at least one third easier than the northern engagement.

Winter settled in across the land and although some loggers favored icy conditions to log in, I was not one of them. Twenty degrees below zero was a normal winter temperature to operate in, sometimes dropping to fifty or sixty below. In this kind of weather things really got miserable and when the body began to creak with the slightest movement, it was time to sit on the engine of the cat and thaw out. My partner knew his job and we worked well as a team, until one Monday morning.

The trucks carried us out at five a. m. towards the logging grounds, everyone but the driver trying to catch a few more winks before the work started. It is not a pleasant feeling to be awakened from a slumber in the middle of the Canadian forest, in the middle of winter, when the temperature is anywhere from twenty to sixty below zero and told to get out of a nice warm truck and get to work. It really is a cruel experience! After the caterpillar engines were fired up, we headed on up into the bush to begin where we left off the Friday before. Shytzenhead was at the controls of the cat as usual but there was something a little odd about his behavior this particular morning. He was non-talkative and the grouchiness of his normal ugly mood seemed to have grown ten fold. There was indeed something uncomfortably ill-flavored about the presence that guided the D 6 cat over the snow capped frozen trails.

The engine of the cat was beginning to warm a little by the time we arrived at our work site. The biting winds of the early morning quickly awakened my sleepy senses as I wrapped the chokers around the butt end of the logs in preparation for hauling. It seemed everything was going according to the regular work plan but that would soon change.

I did not see it coming. The butt end of the tree I was cabling flew up in front of my face, then another and another. I was startled and confused. I had no idea as to what was happening. Branches too, as big as small trees were falling from the sky mixed with showers of frozen snow. I was in a gully. It was still dark and I could not discern what was causing the scattering of the logs nor the deluge from the sky. I moved back from the logs I was attempting to choke and tried desperately to scramble up the bank of the gully but it was too slippery to negotiate. I almost froze with fear and I did not need the help of the weather to accomplish such an outcome. I felt that at any moment my logging career would come to a close. It was during those desperate moments that I noticed the caterpillar moving from side to side, digging its blade into the logs and ramming them in my direction. It was hard to believe but the jerk at the controls of the machine was trying to kill me.

I screamed at the bastard but my screams went unnoticed. He continued to

THE SECOND PURPOSE

plow into the logs which lay scattered over the ground and ram the standing trees. Shytzenhead had gone stark raving mad. I had to get out of the gully. I made my move but my timing was off. I slipped on the ice and fell across the trundling logs. As I lay trapped among the logs, I could see the blade of the cat lie beneath the headlights of the machine, pushing up the snow into its blade as it prepared to smash into the logs I was trapped in. I really thought it was all over as I began to roll and twist in frightened desperation as the logs bounced around me. Then it stopped. I was not asking why and from the scattered logs, I quickly clambered up the bank to relative safety.

A large standing fir tree, of which Fandangle failed to clear the cat's blade, momentarily halted the movement of the cat. It took only a few seconds for Shytzenhead to swing the blade clear but it was enough time for me to clear the danger area.

Shytzenhead did not see the large boomerang shaped piece of stick coming as it bounced off his ugly, scruffy face. He was out cold from the wallop. Had he been paying attention to my position, he would have noticed that I had missed his head with the first two sticks I threw at him but the third was delightfully on target. He fell back into his seat and this was a good thing, for had he fallen out on to the tracks he would have been a dead man - a very crushed, disgusting dead man. The caterpillar, of course, did not know its slimy operator was sleeping heartily at its controls and carried on doing what caterpillars do when their engines are blasting away and throttles are opened wide. It simply carried on doing its work. Before I left the hill, I watched the cat plow into a huge tall tree, its branches fully laden with frozen snow. It's a lot of weight and punch when one is hit by frozen snow falling from a goodly distance of 150 to 200 feet out of the sky and such was the case with Fandangle Shytzenhead.

The crushing force of the cat's power ramming into the tree shook every snowflake from its perch, including brittle branches snapping from the force of the impact. Oh, what a lovely sight! The snow, the ice, the twigs, the branches and, to top it off, the top of the tree snapped, sailing down to add a little green to the snowy coverings of Shytzenhead and his cat. The engine stalled and a good thing it did, because without a doubt its operator would have been asphyxiated. An entombment by frozen snow and a running engine spells certain death.

The gray light of morning covered the land as I made my way down the hill to the landing. The scene below, as the buckers sawed the logs into measured lengths, was indeed a welcome sight. I was upset but I was alive. I hoped the bastard that I had left behind was on his way to the eternal judiciary. I was on my way back to town. I had had enough of bush life for a while.

Later, it was reported, Fandangle Shytzenhead was not in the best of shape when they pulled him from the snow-engulfed cab of the caterpillar later that morning. He was fired instantly and sent packing from the camp. Eventually it became known that Fandangle had met one of his buddies in town the weekend before the Monday morning incident. His buddy needed a job and Fandangle decided to replace me with his buddy. It almost worked. Had I lost my life that morning, it is highly probable, that my death would not have been a suspected homicide.

TO HYPNOTIZE A HEN

In the rustic confines of the Likely hotel, a small, laid back village some thirty miles south east of Williams Lake, four men came together as often happens in drinking establishments. Bill Grisedale was from Elliot Lake, Ontario, Jonah Wilson from New Zealand, Bob Jarvey, a fellow logger and me. As the beer went down and life was philosophized to tatters, the focus of debate eventually fell upon the hypnotizing of hens. I had no idea a hen could be hypnotized; neither did anyone else in the bar but Bob the logger was adamant that it could be done and suggested we travel back to his ranch where he had a flock of such feathered hypnotic subjects.

Sometime around five o' clock in the morning, a car carrying four drunken men pulled into the driveway of Bob's ranch. Project hypnosis was under way.

I had spent much time in my childhood back in Dublin observing the life and times of chickens, turkeys, hens and the odd goose and duck, but nothing, not even my besotted state of mind, prepared me for what was about to take place in this house of hens. The chicken coop had two entrances. The indomitable Jonah Wilson of New Zealand took up position at one entrance while the unyielding Bill Griesdale sealed the second entrance. A chair was placed in the center of the coop and a box of beer placed at the foot of the chair. I had no idea why the beer was placed at the foot of the chair but it did cross my mind that maybe Bob got his subjects drunk before hypnotizing them or the smell of the beer automatically paralyzed them.

Bob sat in Dr Trancelot's chair, then, gave the nod for action as he calmly lit his pipe. I was instructed to creep up on the feathered creatures, nab one and immediately present it to the master for its instruction. However, rather than creep up on a hen, I decided to add a little dancing flair to the whole presentation. It's not easy ballet dancing in logging boots in a chicken coop but I was doing my best and I felt it was a nice touch of ritualistic expression - a prelude to the main event. I knew my efforts were being appreciated because some of the hens clucked in admiration as I pirouetted to and fro. As my dance de la excellence intensified, Bob puffed contentedly on his pipe and seemed to accept that this unusual act of ballet dancing was a nice touch... leading up to the final billing.

At last it was time to make the selection. However, before I pounced, I attempted the very difficult cartwheel execution. This was not a good idea. I could not do cartwheels. The chicken coop came alive instantly as I crashed headlong into the racks, causing hens, chickens, ducks and geese to panic and fly off in every direction. Bob had fallen backwards in his chair and was busily engaged trying to remove his tobacco pipe that had stuck in his gullet. In the meantime, Bill and Jonah went on the attack in an effort to take a prisoner. There was so much dust and feathers floating around as the mad hen house grew madder by the moment. The call was heard to open all doors, before we suffocated from the pollutants and as they were opened, the beautiful wilderness of the Carriboo country came alive, as fleeing poultry headed over the hill and far away.

Hypnotizing a hen proved more difficult than expected and much was our chagrin at the outcome but soon our disenchantment was replaced by the growing excitement of the coming of the William's Lake Stampede, an annual event that saw the laid back town of 10,000 souls transformed into a bustling, fully liberalized community of over 100,000 people and the stampede of 1972 was of the same robust caliber of all that had gone before it – an event where the daring of man was pitted against the provoked rage of the noble animal. Such was the anticipation of those events where man was not always the victor. Nevertheless, any given occasion can produce the most unexpected and the William's Lake Stampede was no exception.

THE GLASS DANCERS

It was a late summer's evening when Bill Grisedale informed me of a party taking place at the nurses' residence. The usual necessities for the occasion were secured: wine, beer, whiskey and a guitar. Later, a young lady whose face smiled from beneath a myriad of hair curlers answered the door bell of the residence that evening. I had just met my future wife.

The usual social activities of such an event ensued and me being a man of shyness, eventually drummed up the courage to invite Erin, the lady who had answered the door to a dance later that night at the Stampede's most elegant dance hall.

Squaw hall was one of the unique social attractions of the Stampede and Squaw hall was not a place to be taking anyone, particularly your future wife. The structure of Squaw hall was simple in its layout. It was in essence, a large square platform, enclosed by four sections of plywood walls, elegantly simple and humble in its 'stampede' design and, was constructed just outside the rodeo grounds proper. This was the place to be when you were tired of life - the wild west at its best - a large outdoor hall without a roof and no special place for the band to perform other than a space of their own choosing. One exit and one entrance, which consisted of the same opening.

Upon entering, a fee was paid and the back of one's hand stamped with some bright colored substance that usually took the best part of a month to fade from the skin. All were welcome to bring their own assortment of liquor to drink freely and merrily. This was liberty at its finest. Squaw Hall was a popular place during the Stampede and at times the action within the confines of its walls would no doubt have made that of the rodeo grounds pale in comparison.

Garbage bins were not a consideration for such a place. When bottles of beer were consumed, the empty bottles were conveniently discarded on the floor-giving rise to a buildup of crushed glass beneath the feet of the dancers. As the night wore on and the tempo picked up, it was not uncommon for the band to be warding off bodies from falling into their midst. It seemed, at regular intervals, individuals lost touch with their balance and found themselves playing a set of drums with their nose, or perhaps lying over the neck of a musician's guitar. Others just got to fighting - the physical expenditure at hockey games came a sad second to our beloved place of dancing. This was Squaw Hall at its finest and surviving an evening of its rambunctious activity without acquiring an injury was considered fortunate if not miraculous.

Hanging around the outside walls of this dancing bastion was not much safer than being on the inside. After the contents of the bottles had been consumed, if they were not dropped to be crushed by the dancing feet of the merrymakers, they were usually tossed over the wall into the crowds hanging around outside. It was this action that saw many a split head arrive at the emergency ward. Squaw Hall was a place like no other and this was the place I took my future wife on our first date. It is not known why the structure was named Squaw Hall but such a title can only be seen as a socio-political affront to the Native people's dignity. The unripe social by-products of the Colonial gestalt were flourishing in ignorance. A prime example of that statement is clearly seen in the hall's characterization – an insult to the real meaning of the name's delightful essence.

PAINS OF THE FIRST NATION

While relative peace existed between Natives and whites, the effects of Colonial policies concerning the First Nations people were obvious. I could see and feel the quiet resignation of the Native people, painfully but patiently biding their time until the roots of their ancient culture took firm hold and flourished once again. Throughout the great continent, the Indian, since the first arrival of the Europeans, had been subjected to the great white lie. They still are.

It was in 1988, that the last of the Native residential boarding schools was closed, ending a government forced attendance policy for the native children. These schools, a manifestation of the white mans paternal control of "their Indians" proved disastrous to the well-being of the Native. Families were brokenhearted as the authorities forcibly removed the children from their homes to be placed under the care of government and Christian agencies.

These schools and what they represented shall be recorded in the ugly annals of Canadian history. It was within the walls of such places that the real push to break the will of the Native was instigated. The children were forbidden to speak their language, sing their songs, practice their spiritual ways or dress in their traditional attire. They were forced to believe the white man's way of life was the proper way and this indoctrination was driven into their minds by the savagery of the stick, the fist and the hand - harsh memories of my past. Children locked in isolation were not uncommon and sexual abuse ran unchecked among the so-called guardians of the little prisoners.

Said my Native friend George, in his soft direct tone to me over a beer one evening. "Mr. John, how would you feel if you owned a lovely mansion and strangers came, took it from you and allotted you and your family the outhouse to live in."

"I wouldn't feel very good, George," I answered. I tried to impart to him that the upheavals in my own country over the past centuries were similar in many ways to the destruction he had witnessed in his land; that our beliefs, culture and unique identity took the brunt of British savagery down through the ages but George held me in check.

"Mr. John, I understand what you are saying but you are of the same color as those people of the Crown and it is easy for you to penetrate their political and economic systems. We on the other hand are scattered across this great big land of ours and we are few. So you see, our situation is not politically or economically as convenient as yours."

"It shall come about," said George, "that our culture and spiritual ways shall come back stronger than ever before, that your people shall find themselves trapped in the makings of their own material mess and, in time, they shall reach out to the ways of the Indian to find hope and peace in their hearts. The Earth cannot be plundered endlessly without her growing sick. Your people are doing a very thorough job of bringing about her complete destruction. They have poisoned all the lands, rivers, oceans and air with pollutants; a result of their ignorance about the true spiritual nature of things and the price we shall all pay for their arrogance and stupidity shall be incalculable. What I say is the truth Mr. John. Greed breathes and nurtures the greatest of sicknesses and evils. Within a few seconds as the Universe goes in time, they have made ill every living thing on the planet. Our earth cry's Mr. John and her tears are ignored; her voice lost to the winds of greed. My friend, in time such transgressions will demand their price – a very great price indeed." And with those words, George lowered his head, looked longingly but uninterested in the glass of beer he was swirling in his large, powerful hands – hands beginning to show the signs of the harshness of the cowboy's life. I did not answer George - allowing the conversation steer in a direction that I was more comfortable with but I knew in my heart that every word George had spoken was saturated with truth.

Even after meeting my future wife, Erin, there was still a strong urge in me to travel and the opportunity arose one day quiet unexpectedly from one who was not prone to travel. "Mr. McDonald, how would you like to travel to Elliot Lake with Jonah and me," said Bill Grisedale. I had no idea where Elliot Lake was but to me it sounded like a great idea.

"So tell me Bill," said I. "Where is Elliot Lake and what would we do there?"

"It is three thousand miles as the crow flies in the Province of Ontario and guaranteed, if we go there, we can work in the mines," said Bill. It did not take long to convince me that it was a good idea and soon, without giving much thought to my relationship with Erin, the three of us were headed east in my faithful old Candy. On we motored across the wide prairies into Northern Ontario and eventually a week later arrived in the town of Elliot Lake.

I had no idea that the type of mining done near the town of Elliot Lake was uranium. I had previously heard through the grapevine that uranium was one of the main elements used in the making of nuclear warheads and this of course made me a little uneasy. Since neither one of our party was knowledgeable on the subject of nuclear science, it was decided to avoid contact with uranium mining and move on to Sudbury to work the nickel mines.

Leaving Elliot Lake the following morning, we headed farther west to Sudbury. As we motored through the outer parts of the city towards its center, I was saddened by the decrepit state of the earth's landscape. It was a lifeless, forlorn, emaciated tapestry of death. Pollutants spewed out into the atmosphere from the chimneys of the smelters poisoning all plant life for a thirty-kilometer radius. One may well have believed one had arrived on the dark side of the moon. Such disrespect for the environment was incomprehensible to me. There was something disgustingly wrong with the way the mining company and the authorities viewed our environment and our relationship to it causing the words of George to my mind's recall. "They have poisoned the lands seas and air Mr. John, all for the sake of greed and stupidity.

Nevertheless, disappointment slapped us in the face when we were informed INCO was not hiring, forcing us to search elsewhere for employment. We decided to head out and try the mines of Thompson, Manitoba. A few days we arrived. We were hired immediately. Jonah and Bill opted to work below in the mines and I decided to work at the smelting plant. Life was rather uneventful until I met Usabio from Portugal. Usabio seemed not to take life too seriously and at the drop of a hat, sang to the moon, stars, the trees, or anyone who cared to listen. I figured the world needed about three billion characters like Usabio. If this were the case there would be a perfect balance between the seriousites and the normal people like Usabio who seemed very much in tune with the happy side of his heart.

Usabio's father lived in Portugal and the nice thing about Usabio's father living in Portugal was the fact that he owned a vineyard and made the best of the best of wine - a hell of a lot better than old Lonesome Charlie, to be sure. Usabio's father's wine had a real kick to it. This I discovered when we decided to have "one" for the road as we headed out to work at the smelter one winter's evening. It brought back memories of a childhood day when I was helping my father's friend work the soil in our garden back in Dublin. From so long ago, the memories of the stuff that made a "real man" out of me was right here in the glass Usabio handed to me. It was exactly the same powerful sweet sickening smell that made the drinker more intoxicated by the second and only by drinking it could its revolting smell be rendered tolerable.

When one partook of Usabio's wine, one went on a mind-boggling tour of all that is unknown. When Usabio sang to his heart's content in his native Portuguese, I felt it only complementary to his rich and noble culture that I should sing in harmony to his fine presentation of the classical arias, even though I knew not a word of Portuguese. The great masters of music would have been right proud of us. Whatever was in that bottle Usabio uncapped, I was determined to introduce my body to it. It was marvelous stuff indeed. I could sing in Portuguese when I drank it. In fact, there was not a language I could not speak when I was under its influence. This was the nectar of the gods and indeed, I felt like a god when its magical substance coursed my veins.

Working at the smelter that evening was a rare and wonderful occasion. It seemed everyone loved and understood me. They understood me for who and what I was. They were also astounded to hear Usabio and me singing a duet in some language other than the common English. Men in white coats and white hard hats with clipboards in their hands were making notes about the great Usabio and me, humbling ourselves by singing in a place where ore was melted down and nickel bars were made - a gigantic blacksmith shop. And here, Usabio and I made our first international appearance as an operatic duo.

"La Scala," was being performed by two humble working men in the smelters of Thompson as furnaces roared their fiery breath and smoke billowed from their bowels through their nostrils and out into the universe. This was opera at its finest. People in the workplace shook their heads in amazement at the performance they were witnessing. Dante's inferno belched its hellfire as Usabio of Portugal and John of Ireland were asked politely but firmly to take the night off.

My head felt like it was being massaged with a cheese grater as the morning bid me its painful greetings. I wanted to die. I showered, went for breakfast and tried to fit into life the best I could. I thought perhaps it was time to leave Thompson and head on back to William's Lake. My lady friend was there and I missed her. As I was mulling things over in my mind, Usabio came by and joined me at the table. I told him I was thinking of going back to William's Lake as I missed my girlfriend and I was really tired of the mining business. He understood how I felt and suggested that we go talk about this serious question of life over a drink of his very special homemade vintage wine - his family's secret recipe. Usabio had a way with words and since it was his family's secret blueprint for instant happiness, I thought it a wonderful idea.

It was almost instant relief - the farewell of my head's discomfort. I suddenly realized how beneficial a good drink of fermented morning tonic was to my sense of well-being. Thank God for people like Usabio, I thought. If it were not for this good man, I probably would never have discovered this drink of many blessings. I knew now that I could drink all I wanted, night and day, sing opera in any language I wished to and when my head was wracked with pain from overindulgence, Usabio's tonic would mend it.

It was not long into the morning when Usabio and I began to finish singing the aria that the men in white coats had so rudely interrupted the night before. I could tell we were doing the piece of music justice as the sounds of our voices wafted out across the Thompson landscape, out where the polar bears roam. Pretty soon, there were people banging their fists on the door of Usabio's room. I thought for a moment that the people had come from all over to pay homage to two of the century's greatest musical performers but when we heard the words, "For Christ's sake, shut up or we'll kick the shit out of you," we instinctively knew some people were envious of our musical talents.

The men who hammered on the door were kind. They could have broken through the door and relieved themselves of their aural agony by killing us. However, they warned us that if they had to come back again because of our noise, it would not be healthy for either one of us. Somewhere from within the foggy canyons of my mind a voice told me to tread carefully, that these hardworking, responsible men were serious. I suggested to Usabio we should tone it down and perhaps wander over to the bar and grace the place with our presence. It was agreed that we go to the place of drinking and, upon arrival, we immediately set about making the lives of the people within, full with musical richness.

I believe we had just begun to sing the second line of Mario Lanza's "Beloved" when the drinks were removed from our hands and the snows on the outer side of the back door shown to us. I personally felt that our talents would be more appreciated at the opera houses of Venice, Saltzburg, or Luxemburg. I had had it with Thompson. I was going back to the West, to the land of trees and rodeos, to the land where hopefully my lady friend would welcome my return.

I confided in Usabio about my intent as we removed our disheveled beings from the place of "thrown through doors" and made our way back to the residence. Usabio was an understanding fellow and proved to be a good friend. He offered to help start my car, which had been stationary in the company's parking lot since we had arrived. Fortified with some more of Usabio's special home brew, we set out to find Candy. Eventually, she was located beneath a goodly amount of snow. Digging began immediately to uncover her. After her extraction, the key was placed in the ignition and just before I turned the key, the words of Bill Griesdale echoed through my mind, "Don't forget to winterize Candy, John, because if anti-freeze is not added to the engine during winter, it will crack when you try to start it." I wondered what he meant.

It does not pay to ignore good advice. However, since I knew little about the mechanics of machinery, Bill's advice fell to the wind. Old Candy seemed every bit herself as she churned, whirred, belched, coughed and hacked - giving a large hint of promise in the prospect of firing her engine. Every crank came closer to ignition and our hopes soared when the engine fired for a fraction of a second. It was suggested by Usabio at this time to try pouring a little gasoline in the carburetor, which I did. There was a terrible explosion as I cranked the engine one more time. Fire and smoke belched forth from under the hood.

I had poured far too much gasoline into the carb. It ignited when I cranked the engine and soon the snow was melting all around. The inky smoke that streaked across the sky spelled the end of Candy. Then, as though the gods of thunder directed her, she imparted one horrific thunderous crack. The engine block had shattered. She came to rest once again, as silently as she had done since we first arrived in Thompson.

It was all over for the faithful old girl. She would never roll down the highways again. Her death was celebrated with the sharing of fond memories and more of Usabio's drink of happiness.

I decided to catch a plane back to William's Lake. A stately farewell party was given to celebrate my departure and a sad state I was in when I was delivered to the air terminal. It was a fond farewell to the best of friends, two of whom I would see back in William's Lake but it was the last I would see of my Portuguese friend, Usabio.

The flight would take me to Winnipeg, then on to Vancouver and eventually William's Lake. It was nice to be back in the Cariboo / Chilcotin country again. That very evening upon my arrival from Thompson, Erin and I took a drive into the country. However, fate was weaving her tapestry as the unforeseen played its game of chess with destiny. This time however, it was not with my destiny alone.

The land was in darkness as we drove back to William's Lake. I observed a road construction sign indicating a detour which I followed.

It was peaceful as I lay on my back looking into a starlit sky. I had no idea what had happened. To my right side, I noticed a large object but was not sure what it was. Soon I heard voices and observed the flashing of lights above me. I felt at peace and was not in the least concerned with the activities taking place about me. I found myself being placed on a stretcher and then carried to an ambulance. Somewhere along the route to the hospital, I realized I had been in an accident and soon, my thoughts turned to the well-being of Erin. The terrible seriousness of the situation began to cause me considerable anguish but when I heard the voice of Erin, telling me she was all right, I calmed down and again drifted off into unconsciousness.

The detour had directed the car to a sixteen-foot hole in the middle of the north/southbound highway. The Department of Highways had located a supply of gravel beneath the surface of the road, which they required to complete a construction project. Besides the cost saving factor, less time would be involved if the gravel was extracted from beneath the road rather than have it trucked in from the gravel pit. That hole cost Erin a fractured vertebrae and me a broken ankle and a cracked rib. Digging up the highway almost cost the lives of two people.

I had four months of crutch time to do before the cast on my leg was removed. During this period of time, I decided to return to school. It was something I needed to do as I had left school in Ireland at the age of thirteen, leaving me quite conscious of my limited education. I enrolled at the William's Lake High-school but truly, I felt like a fish out of water. I just hadn't got it in me to go through with it. However, it was during those few days, that my feeble attempt at improving my education made me very aware of my inner need for further learning. But, my inability to respond to the inner calling was compounded by an extraordinary will to deny myself the need of education's immeasurable value. Thus, I turned my back on the one institution that could give me the means to help make life a comfortable journey, rather than a trip of continuous trial and error.

Since school was put on hold, I turned my attention to the ease of sitting in the Maple Leaf hotel during the morning, afternoon, evening, night and the wee hours of the following morning, drinking beer with the ease of a professional drunk. Since I had lost my freedom of mobility, I figured the only way to meet people was to sit in the bar and wait for them to come in. My plan was sound. Pretty soon, I got to know many, many people. I got to know them so well that I invited them all, each time the bar closed to my residence. We were a happy bunch of drinking lads and as good-natured as we were diverse in our cultures. We were Irish, Native, German, Swiss, Italian, Polish, New Zelanders, Australian, Japanese, English, and one who insisted he was a direct descendant of Christopher Columbus, whom our Indian friend viewed with much suspicion.

My Native friend, George, said to me one day, "You know Mr. John, all that fellow Columbus did, was bring to our shores every disease known to mankind, including syphilis, gonorrhea and the pox and, furthermore; he never discovered the lands of the Americas. We were here tens of thousands of years before any European set foot upon our shores. It was we who discovered your people limping around, exhausted and lost, so what the hell is this bullshit of we being discovered? If I hopped on a boat and went to the shores of Spain or France; does that mean I discovered those countries and that I should take out my blunderbuss and beat the lard out of them until they convert to my way of thinking? That's what it really amounts to Mr. John. A group of Europeans came to my shores with possession and greed in their hearts and when they did, this land was pure, free and clean. Now take a look to what they have done. They have dirtied our Holy and lovely world and it seems very few care about our planet's demise." I had little knowledge of what George had explained to me but it seemed to make a whole lot of sense. While I mulled this information over in my mind, George changed the topic.

"Come with me Mr. John to the Chilcotin river and I will show you how to catch the prized salmon," George said. It was not easy making my way along the steep riverbanks on crutches but that is what I had to do in order to observe the fisherman in action. I wondered why George tied one end of a rope around his waist and the other end to a tree as he prepared to fish the waters of the Chilcotin river. I thought, this is a mighty unusual way to catch fish but the method was foolproof and one that had been used down the centuries by the indigenous people. Slowly moving down the slope of the river's bank, George, secured by the rope around his waist, leaned out over the river to place the net end of a ten to twenty foot long pole in the waters. Here, in the heart of the Chilcotin country, I was witnessing George apply the skills of Native fishing handed down since time immemorial.

The roar of the river's turbulent waters', ceaseless in its unyielding force, thundered its raging song from the depths of its canyon up across the high plateau of the Chilcotin land, dissipating on the humming winds of midsummer rapture. The long pole that George had placed out across the raging waters' faded into the rainbow mist of snowy spray and there was dipped into the water and held as the fisherman's eyes searched the rushing flow for the silvery salmon of the deep. It was nice and cool resting in the shadow of the canyon cliffs, the raging spray cooling the hot summer air. If paradise was lost, then this place by the river, to be sure, was part of it found.

The fisherman's net dipped time and again to lift from the waters' the noble fish that had journeyed inland from the Pacific ocean back to its place of birth, each year since the time the land was young.

It was a wonderful feast that evening as the internationals gathered to share in the catch of the great fisherman. It was only one of so many such evenings but this one had a twist to it as no other social event had had in my life, either before or since.

As the flames of the barbecue readied the salmon for the stomachs of the hungry ones, George, who was sitting beside me on an old pine log, asked me, if I would like to know how it feels to be an Indian. I wondered what he was getting at. "Mr. John, you must go to a quiet place in the forest one day and there dwell upon creation. Go there, Mr. John and when you have blocked the noise of the world from your mind, give yourself an Indian name and see yourself as Indian. See your-self contented with the world before the greedy raped it. Feel the energy of nature at work in the earth where life once was as pure as the mountain streams. Yes, Mr. John, feel the essence of the Great Spirit course your soul as it was with the land when it was untouched by the horrors of mankind.

I went to that place, a place by a gentle stream and whispering pines. There, I sat by the water's and rested in a late evening of early autumn. I gave myself an Indian name, a name promised to secrecy. I sat and gazed across the land and soon was lost to the distance of the past.

I saw the land as it was when it knew not noise, the air clean, without poison. I understood oneness with the Spirit of All. I knew peace within my heart. I knew life as a journey, respecting all things that had sprung from and walked the land. I knew not greed or poverty. I was alive. I was as alive as the great rivers and the gentle streams, the tall trees and high mountains.

As I dwelled upon the power of life and the gifts of the great Creator, I began to long for those days of the past, when war, corruption and thievery were not in the land. To be sure, my sadness was great and my tears full with sorrow. A terrible bitterness flooded my mind as I witnessed the great plunder, the disrespect and savagery towards the natural things within the land, the poisons in the air and in the waters, the sickness of the oceans, the decimation of the animals and the rape of the forests. The land was sick and the people blind. As my mind churned with such affliction throughout the land, the words of George echoed in my mind: we shall come back much stronger, Mr. John and when we do, it is the way of the Indian the white man shall seek, so he may survive the great wrongs he has done to our land and the catastrophes he has brought upon himself.

THE MAKINGS OF AN ENTERTAINER

My experiences in the Cariboo / Chilcotin were of significance to me. Living in the rolling hills of the country had inserted a certain wanting for something far, far, greater than man had to offer, yet I was unsure of what it was but its unseen influence was tapping at the outer reaches of my mind and would not leave me to fall into the comforts of all that are illusionary. Would the answer be found places far off? Erin and I decided to move south to the city of Vancouver to try life in the big city and experience its metropolitan offerings. We rented an apartment in the west end. Life in Vancouver proved challenging to us both but things came together and pretty soon we had established ourselves. Shortly after our arrival, I meet Peter Stony, an accomplished musician and songwriter. We teamed up. Vancouver, in 1974, was not exactly the music capitol of the world and since entertainment was not allowed in drinking establishments, Peter and I turned our attention to other places.

"Play 'Burlington Bess' for my wife," said the big man with the pudgy, sweaty face. "She just loves that song, don't ya dear," he said, looking into the side of her face as he unglued a string of mozzarella cheese from his busy mouth. His wife smiled in acknowledgment and told him to stop eating his pizza like a pig. "Okay, ma dear, you always know what's best for big Daddy, Goddamn, great pizza though. Well boys, what about Burlington Bess, do you know it or not?" he hollered across the room.

Peter addressed the man who ate like a pig. "Sir, I have heard of the song but it is not a part of our repertoire, besides, my partner does not like it."

The big man responded, "Too damn bad you don't want to do it. D'ya mind if I come up and do it for my wife," he said, as he tried to polish off his pizza by jamming it farther towards the back-end off his big mouth. I wondered what he meant by doing it for his wife.

"Come right up sir, we'd only be too happy to accommodate you," said Peter. The big man with the sweaty, pudgy face knocked the table over on his wife as he got up from his chair.

It was not a pleasant scene. The waiters rushed to lend assistance before the wife of the big man tried to murder him. Still, he was undaunted and bent on singing his "Burlington Bess."

The big man, who ate like a pig, cradled the microphone in that way exhibited by the great performers. Rolling it gently in his brawny hands and flipping it from one hand to the other, gave hints of artistic stage qualities not expected from such a massive personage who ate like a pig. "The key of Eeeee flat, boys, that's my favorite key," he said as though he had written the song.

"We don't work in the key of Eeeee flat, we work only in the key of Ceeeee and the key of Geeeee, " said Peter with a hint of sarcasm.

"Goddamn, you fellas are pretty limited, let's try the key of Ceeeee, then," the big man said.

"Would ye like it played on piano, guitar or banjo?" Peter asked.

"God damn, banjo sounds good to me, let's get at her!" said the man with the big cheeks.

The patrons, by this time, had taken an interest in the developing event and an element of curious quietness visited the room. Peter strummed the introductory chord, indicating to the man who ate like a pig, to begin. Now the man who ate like a pig, proved just that, when the first sound that emanated from his mouth was a monstrous, obnoxious burp. "Geeeeeee, sorry 'bout that boys, must be the pizza that caused the burpppppppsing... ah there, I did it again. God damn, anyway, never had a problem doing Burrrppplington Bess before," he said with an air of sincerity as he tried to place his great behind upon a bar stool which was rushed to the scene by a waiter to accommodate the greatness of the man who ate like a pig and was now indicating that he also sang like a pig.

Still, the patrons seemed to be enjoying the unusual showmanship and soon, they too, were a part of the act - unwillingly. Peter strummed the banjo once again, indicating that he was ready to accompany the big man. "I hear ya, me boy... all right... here we go." With those words, he let out a most deafening roar through the microphone, accompanied with the appropriate spray that goes with such uncouth action. The building shook slightly but it had nothing to do with the geological fault, Vancouver, sits upon. It was at that moment, some of the patrons were drawn into the action. Jimmy, the manager, who was in the act of placing a tray full of drinks upon the table of partygoers must have got wind of the great explosion because he immediately took fright and delivered all the drinks upon his very large tray, all at once, all over the table, which he had just delivered four spanking large pizzas to a few minutes earlier. The burping man had to go.

Jimmy, apologized to his patrons, threw his tray on the floor and approached the stage. It was a remarkable scene. He was dressed in the old style red and white vest and straw-hat that suited the attire of a Shakey pizza person but did not exhibit toughness of character in one who wore such dress. But that was not the case with Jimmy. "Get your big behind off my stage and get it out the damned door and never let me see your face again in my establishment," he roared at the big man who was now being pulled from the stage by his very petite wife. "Don't bother about the bill, mam, just get him to hell out of here and do not for, God's sake, ever bring him back, O. K," Jimmy blustered at the little woman. The poor dear was a million or two different shades of red as she coaxed her loved one from the Shakey scene. Jimmy, cleaned up the mess he had just made over his patrons and offered them free fare for the evening and for good measure, threw in a round of drinks for all present - and on the show went - without Burlington Bess.

Thus was the beginning of Peter and John's career in the entertainment industry. From Shakey's Pizza Parlor, we moved to the Horse and Carriage Inn on Alberni St. With this newfound success came extra partying and drinking. The full slide into alcoholism had begun for me.

I had not noticed it but Peter did. He warned me numerous times about how sloppy I was getting during the shows. I tried to curb my drinking but to me, it seemed that drinking and entertainment went hand in hand and that was the way the good Lord meant it to be. However, to appease Peter, I did try to do the show as sober as possible but when the show was over, I made up for lost time. And the recall of the devastation in years past in the cottage garden came to mind but for some reason I could not make the connection to its meaning – its ominous warning – perhaps I did not want to – at least not just yet in my still young life.

Good times were to be had around Vancouver and it seemed we had the world in our hands. Singing, drinking and practicing became my life. This for me was the ultimate. A man could ask for no more. However, my drinking was taking its toll, not only on my health but it was proving disastrous in my relationship with Erin. She was as patient as an angel with my mad antics and why and how she put up with me for so long I do not know. I guess there was some good in me. I went on dry spells from time to time but I would only make up for lost drinking time when I got at it again. However, as far as Peter was concerned, my drinking was out of hand and although he did not wish to, he broke up the partnership. It was a wise move on his part. I was saddened by his decision but it had to be.

Interestingly enough, I did quite well as a single entertainer and had no trouble getting work. The changes to the liquor laws regarding entertainment in the hotel industry opened a whole new world of opportunities for entertainers. Eventually, Peter teamed up with Jimmy Flynn, a brilliant entertainer from Nova Scotia and soon, both were headed back to the land of Flynn where they flourished as a duo. I was happy for them. Yes, indeed, I was glad they made it.

In 1976, my brother Larry arrived with his wife Sunday and their one year old son Larraki, from Europe. They took up residence in the Port Moody area. My brother specialized in the field of psychiatry. Discussing my drinking problem with him conveniently slipped my mind; nevertheless, it was wonderful that he was here in Canada. Larry was also fond of singing and when he came to visit the venue where I was entertaining, he occasionally joined me on the stage, where we sung as a duet or he treated the audience to his own special rendition of Johnny Cash's "My Name Is Sue" and other songs that were received handsomely by the audience. He was a natural entertainer and brought laughter and joy to those who had the good fortune of hearing him sing but his stay in Canada lasted only two years and he and his family traveled back to Europe. I would sadly miss him. Eventually, when I returned to Europe, I would see him for the last time - my brother, whom I had grown very close to.

From Scotland, arrived David, a talented singer and musician. This man would have far reaching effects on my life, so too would the manageress, Irene O, of the "Last Spike" lounge at the Barnett Motor Inn, in Port Moody, a wonderful place to entertain. To this little lounge, the best patrons in the world came - many of them talented. It was as close to family as one could be, without the bickering. I loved that place and the people therein and I loved Irene who really went to pains to see that I was not hassled during my shows. She was my angle. Painful times were not too far to the future for me and it would be with this good lady and her husband Carl, that I would go to in time of need and that place was in the mountains far away in the tranquility of the high country - a place called Tullameen and its sister town Coalmont

The man from Scotland sat quietly at a table in the "Last Spike" lounge. After I had finished my set, he invited me to join him at his table. David Fullerton was studying at the university of B.C. and as a hobby liked to play guitar and sing. The stage was offered to him, whereupon he sang and entertained the patrons with that rich, soft quality of the singing voice of the Scottish highlands. The patrons loved him. This man had a wonderful career in the music industry ahead of him. Dave and I became good friends. Time moved on and soon Dave was securing gigs at various venues throughout the province. Things were really going his way. Then, one day, word came that he was dead. Just like that. He was dead.

During my friendship with Dave, I had not noticed that he was dealing with some issues that needed to be resolved. They were deeply personal, causing him great anxiety. It was under such psychological stress that he ventured to the interior town of Merrit, to entertain at the Valnicola Hotel. It was reported that he booked into the hotel, had supper, then drove out into the cattle country. It was his last drive. In the hills above the beautiful Nicola valley, my good friend David brought his life to an end. I will never know why he ended his life but I sadly missed him.

In time I would visit the beautiful Nicola valley, meet the Mc Cormacs and the Egans, the hosts and owners of the Valnicola Hotel where David had booked into before his death. I would entertain at this fine hotel and come to know the pleasures of the country's domain – its rolling hills, rich fertile valleys and the serenity and joy of canoeing its rivers and lakes. Out here I could reflect on my journey; wherever it may take me. Oft times I would come to realize that the journey was in the essence of the moment and, in one of those moments, I would meet someone I would come to love dearly – my friend and confidant Sharron G. If there was in all creation a person imbued with those things I was searching for – the ease and serenity in life, it was Sharron. The sweet lady certainly had that specialty from the heavens and, in memory, that spiritual delight of that beautiful human being would slowly chip away at my tarnished make-up reducing the wildness within to something manageable for my soul to handle.

TOM BYRNE, THE BEAR AND THE FISH

As Time slipped by I joined the Irish Club of Vancouver and met the man the whole world needs to know - Tom Byrne. Tom was a master of the stage; actor, director, singer, choreographer, adviser, fisherman, and had a wonderful command of the blarney. We shared much in common, such as drinking, singing and fishing - all of which we immersed ourselves in fully. In the late summer of seventy-six, while on a fishing trip, we approached a Native roadblock at the Pemberton Reservation north of Vancouver. The blockade had been erected in protest of the government's policy on Native land issues. We approached it late in the evening. It was our intention to camp by the Lillouette river overnight but to get to our destination, we had to pass through the reservation.

We brought our old, eggshell blue, Chevy van to a halt and waited as five warriors approached us. They stopped a few feet in front of the van, then, stood looking at us. I was becoming a little unnerved and immediately grabbed a bottle of whiskey and drank fully from it. Tom told me not to be a greedy pig as he grabbed the bottle from my hand. Fortified with liquid bravery, I suggested to Tom that he was very good at negotiations and that he should go forth and hope for the best.

After a few objections to my plan, he grudgingly got out of the van and approached the warriors. His voice, a little unsure, addressed the warriors. "Gentlemen, I notice you have the road cut off, would ye mind telling me why this is so?"

"We are tired of the multinationals and government plundering our land and we are going to take it back from the greedy irresponsible bastards," said one of the warriors. "The white man does not know how to tell the truth, he is only interested in money, lying and cheating and we are fed up with his bullshit," concluded the warrior. I was much impressed by the warrior's speech because I fully agreed with what he had said and the only thing I was upset about was that I was not an Indian myself

Here, in this beautiful valley of Pemberton, where eagles soar below the snow-capped peaks, the power of this ancient land and its people gripped me to the very core. Once again, the words of George, visited my foggy mind. "The bastards have to take everything." It seemed we Europeans had a major problem making a deal and sticking to it. Breaking treaties, seemed the right thing to do for the white man and if a treaty was never signed, then all the more reason to swipe the land and to hell with the indigenous people. I felt a terrible shame within coupled with the fact that I was an adventurer within a land that I loved beyond a shadow of a doubt but like others, I felt I was not entitled to the greatness of this magnificent country because the right to dwell here was not given to me by its rightful inhabitants. Right or wrong, that is how I felt then, as I still do now.

However, while my mind was running amok with the shoulds and should nots of human behavior, Tom had begun one of his treatises on the dirty business of the British in our little Emerald Isle. "Gentlemen,' he began. "Do you know we have a great deal in common? The British have done exactly the same thing in our land they are doing in yours. They seem to be everywhere (as though they were some sort of undesirable pest and spraying them with the contents of a large can of insect repellent would get rid of them) and my friend, John, will vouch for that, won't you John?" he roared back to me almost causing me to swallow the whiskey bottle wholesale as I sipped its comforting contents to ease my tension. I did not respond – my mind lost to the haze of the Pow Wow that was in full swing in front of our egg shell blue dilapidated old Chevy – of which characteristics I was quickly duplicating.

"You know gentlemen," Tom continued. "We do indeed have the same troubles in our land that you have here and one day we will be free from it all as you shall be, now ye don't mind if a couple of Irishmen go through to do a little bit of fishing do ye," he concluded.

"Yes we do mind my friend," came the answer. "We will stop you and the God damn army if they try to come through here and that's the end of the matter, now please turn your van around and leave." There was no room to maneuver for Tom. It was time to go and indeed I fully understood the defiance and anger of the people at the blockade and in my heart I wished every success to them but knowing the deceptive skills of the politicians in this great land – any land, I could not see the desired results of the Native people arriving on the winds of fairness any time in the near distance.

The following morning, hung-over, we headed in new directions for a fishing spot.

It was late evening, when Tom pulled the old Chevy van off the trail and into an inviting wooded area overlooking the majestic Lilluoet river. Here, we set camp and prepared for late night angling. Twilight gave way to darkness as Tom and I made our way down a steep slope to the water's edge. It was a bit of heaven - this lovely valley - a fisherman's paradise. Soon, our lures were spinning through the deep, dark flow as we waited in anticipation of a strike. It was not long before Tom's line felt action, forcing me to handle the net. Again and again Tom's line stretched to the limit denying me the chance to cast my line. I was growing mighty envious of the fisherman's luck. One beautiful spring salmon after another grabbed the bait he tossed to them. My envy was constructing a murder plot – Tom's. Then, in my moments of despair, he had hit into an enormous fish, which spent more time in the air than in the water. It had to be a steelhead I thought - the fabled fish of the western rivers. The angling skills of Tom were tested to the fullest as the fish moved into the rushing waters to use its power to try to snap the line. It was up to Tom to see that it didn't but that was not going to be easy for the fisherman. The steelhead had ideas other than going into a frying pan and its struggle soon made Tom disappear downstream on an adventure into the unknown. Tom's departure allowed me to work my line.

My cast was excellent, the lure hitting the water exactly where I had wanted it. I allowed some seconds to pass as the lure sank towards the riverbed. Then it happened. A strike! I pulled back on the rod driving the hook home. I had my fish. As I reeled in the line, I realized my strike was nothing more than a snag. I had hooked into a rock. I was not impressed as I applied maximum tension to snap the line. Then I decided instead of snapping the line, I should wade across the river, shorten the line length and try to work the lure free. It was a good plan and boldly I went forth into the deep.

Beneath the light of the silvery moon I ventured ever so slowly, ever more deeply into the home of fishes. I felt the current build in strength against the calf of my leg but chose not to heed the ominous force. After all, I was in hip waders, which allowed me to move into waters almost waist high. I ventured farther but as I did, the rush of the river against my legs built to such a force that I found it difficult to keep my balance. The gravel bed of the river began to give way to my groping feet. I was in trouble - serious trouble.

I tried desperately to turn back towards the bank but the fast wash of the river made it impossible. There was no sight of Tom returning and even if he did, there was not much he could do to help. I had to make a decision, one that could well be my last. Bracing my right foot against a boulder, I decided to perform a pirouette. This performance would indeed prove sensational, for truly, something of this nature could not have possibly been attempted by anyone before under such circumstances. However, I felt saddened about the absence of an audience to witness this most unusual undertaking. The moon sent its spotlight beaming across the watery stage as the stars twinkled merrily in the upper balcony. The tall trees that graced the river's banks were curtains of the wilderness and the sound of the river's thunderous flow - the applause. The stage was set. I was now ready.

I released the tension of the line so it would not cause extra drag, leaving me less encumbered to execute my pirouette. Forcing my right foot down into the side of the boulder, at the same time raising my left leg from the water, I turned with the speed and grace of a slug only to be literally swept from my feet. My hip waders took on water as a ship would at the bottom of the ocean, as down I went to visit the home of the fishes. I immediately suffered a good measure of shock as the river drew me to its center.

I'm going to meet, St. Peter, I thought, as I was dragged over stones and boulders of the riverbed into immortality which I was not in the least prepared for. I had no time to panic because I was getting walloped left, right and center from anything that stuck up from the river bottom. After, what seemed to be like an eternity, I was jammed in between two boulders, then dislodged and thrown out again and into some more of their kind which were just as nasty as the first. There I remained jammed, freezing and drowning. Suddenly, my body shifted again. This time, my head was pushed upwards and into the light of the moon. I thought this was not what I had in mind for the show. But I was breathing.

It took a few seconds, then, I realized, I was standing on gravel and the strength of the river's run had diminished greatly. The river had pulled me out into its strong current but its flow came back in towards the bank taking me with it. I was going to be all right. Through the whole trip, I never thought of releasing my grip on the rod and I thought, how strange! I hauled myself back onto the bank, cold, miserable and shaken and when I reeled my line in, in came the lure.

While I pulled myself together, the best I could, I heard the voice of Tom, calling from the distance. He was hollering to me to get the net ready. The fish was still on this line and heading back upriver towards me. He had been gone the best part of an hour and still he had the fish hooked. Tom was a good fisherman. I prepared the net as he reeled his catch ever closer to shore. The noble creature had lost the battle. Congratulations were all in order, as indeed, the fish was one of the fabled steelheads of the western rivers. Tom was a happy man and very proud of his accomplishment. However, the euphoria was short-lived.

As we cleaned and prepared the fish to place with Tom's previous catch, it was noticed they were missing. This was mysterious as there was no indication of thievery by prowling animals and it left us to wonder if we had caught any fish at all earlier in the evening.

THE SECOND PURPOSE

It was back to fishing the water's and once again, Tom was latched into another fish and by golly, I managed to hook one myself. Both fish were landed as we struck into two more. I brought mine in, unhooked it, prepared to place it with the rest of the catch and that is when it happened. I turned to place the fish with the other catch, which was almost immediately behind us and had the great displeasure of looking a big black bear in the face.

Looking a bear in the face around midnight, particularly when not expected, is a terrifying experience – at least for me and I could not help but freeze where I stood. The bear on its part turned his midnight stare from my face to the flopping fish on the ground, placed its big paw upon it, then grabbed it between his teeth and began to slowly back away. As I felt my life to be a little safer than it was five seconds before, I chanced to say a few half hearted brave words – "You dirty thieving swine, how dare you take my fish?" The words falling to the wind and hoping the bear did not understand what I called it.

Then out of the blue of the night, Tom responds to the words lost to the wind. "What are you calling me a dirty thief for? Are you going nuts, John?" He said as he swung the rod across his shoulder in preparation to cast his line.

"Not you, Tom. Its this rotten swine here, whose stealing our fish," I replied, watching the bear intensely as he seemed uncertain about leaving with my fish.

"You'll have to shout a little louder, John, I can't hear you over the roar of the water," Tom said, with the air of a confident angler as though the 'big one' was about to bite his lure and the lost on the wind conversation was of no consequence whatever. I decided to shake his confidence a little and shouted loud in his ear that a big black bear was about to bite him in the arse and indeed that bit of news Tom received, seemed to banish instantly the intrepidness of the angler. I could tell by the way Tom became immovable, that he had received the message. .

The great Tom grew still and silent as a dead wind, frozen in time as though he was praying to the goddess of the river. Expecting to be walloped by a bear is not a nice feeling and I could see Tom was busily involved with such thoughts. I took the stealing of our fish with great indignation but the bear it seemed had come to a decision on his momentary indecision. He dropped my nice spring salmon from his jaws and replaced it one more to its choosing. Tom who was now looking more like a midnight watchman gazing across the river, at last broke his spell, to turn around just in time to glimpse the bear as he disappeared into the night with the prized steelhead firmly held in his jaws. It was one of those moments when silence was in order for the voice, and indeed so it was.

Time moved on to the beat of the drum and the sound of music. Tom often times visited the various venues where I entertained and as a guest artist, presented the audience with works of the poet and storyteller Robert Service (1858-1952). Tom was a brilliant performer and excelled in his stage presentations. Not a word was lost to the ear when Tom worked through the poems of the bard - The Shooting of Dan Mc Grew, The Law of the Yukon or The Cremation of Sam Mc Gee. He was truly a master, an authority on the works of Robert Service. Eventually, this talent led him to the doorsteps of Robert Service's cabin in Dawson city, Northern B C. (where Robert Service lived and worked for a time) to recite the works of the great bard during the tourist seasons. Tom was good, very good indeed.

HANGING ON BY A THREAD

It was during the late seventies that I had the good fortune of being introduced to the owners, Bob and Wayne, of the Wheelhouse neighborhood pub in Surrey, British Columbia. We hit it off pretty well. These men, two ex-sailors, who had sailed many a seagoing vessel on the Pacific for a number of years, built themselves a neighborhood pub on Scott Road in Surrey B. C. It was a resounding success. The decor of the pub resembled that of a wheelhouse on a ship, displaying authentic marine implements and artifacts. The atmosphere was that of being on a floating vessel. It was a great place to work. I truly felt at home entertaining at the Wheelhouse. These good men funded the making of my first album, "The Sea Runs Red" a selection of compositions written in protest to the slaughter of the whales. However, the success of the album depended on the success of the singer and the singer's commitment to the bottle prevented the album's success.

It was during these years that my fiancée and I got married and, while there seemed to be balance and harmony to some degree in our marriage, the call to the bottle was truly asserting its insidious force upon me. Try as I might to break the habit, it seemed only to intensify. During this unsettling period of my life, I met the one and only Jack Gibson, sailor supreme. Jack was first mate on the tugboat "The Rosario Straits" which had plied the waters of the west coast. Jack seemed to possess some extraordinary talents. He was a great country and western singer, fisherman and storyteller.

THE SECOND PURPOSE

The Wheelhouse Pub was an attraction to Jack as it was to many mariners and because sea shanties were an integral part of my repertoire and the pub's decor resembled the closest thing to being on a ship, it was not surprising that sea going men found familiarity in its appeal. Jack was one of those good sailors and Jack was a kind man. When Jack got a few drinks beneath his belt, he had the habit of promising me a nice catch of salmon the next time he arrived back on shore from his sailor's chores on the ocean, which were generally a two week spell. He always spoke fondly about his "Rosario" as though it was a faithful old bowser that was always ready to answer his master's call. This expression of sentimentality was most noticeable when Jack consumed one or two "shorts" and spoke fondly of his "Rosie" and how he took care of her every need. Still, when Jack said he was going to get the choicest of salmon - that is what the sailor did.

The Rosie plied the water's of the Pacific coast for more than fifty years and the great Jack Gibson spent more than twenty of those years working aboard her. When out on the deep, he had a foolproof way of catching the prized salmon, a technique, of which he never divulged for obvious reasons and I never asked - I just enjoyed the catch. Jack was also a man that never took life too seriously. He simply enjoyed it, not getting too involved with the philosophies of it, just living it to its fullest rather than talking about it. I liked his character.

My days of entertaining at the Wheelhouse Pub were the beginning of my decline in the music industry. I knew I was hanging on to my life and sanity by a thread and try as I might I could not shake the need or craving for alcohol. I was on a Major downward slide, moving farther and farther away from all I loved and cared for and it seemed there was nothing I could do about it.

I was torn apart inside and out. Music was something I loved and entertaining equally so. I figured, if I gave entertaining a break and tried my hand at some other work, things might change for the better. But what was I to try? All I really knew was the business of logging and perhaps a little about gardening but that was it. Which way to go, I did not know? I was confused but I was willing to give anything a try. I wanted to live. I wanted to survive. I wanted to make a good husband but really, I had no idea how to do any of them. It seemed I was just groping at straws. But groping at straws was a hell of a lot better than not being able to grope at straws or anything else that might steer me in a direction towards finding greener pastures. But, I didn't know which way to go to find the rich green pastures and even if I did find them, it was certain I would not be able to recognize them. I was just running into dead-ends.

Once my life was full with hopes and dreams, unfettered and free. Each heartbeat led towards more curiosity and wonder - a discovery in what the miracle of life was all about - not to be questioned in that heavy, deep, subjective, objective natter but living towards worth in its essence of what it is supposed to be - undaunted by ifs ands and shoulds. Suddenly, all the roar of life was gone. I tried to reach out for help from those who had walked the same path - to listen, but I did not have the fortitude to stick with the map of healing or follow up on the promises I made to myself and to the people who tried to help me.

My mind had closed all channels to the helping powers. I was in essence, spiritually dead, bankrupt in every way. I would try to overcome this deficit by tackling something that was just a replacement but would only allay the nature of my problem for a short while, another band-aid that would not work. But I was trying. Yes, I was really trying but I was losing and I knew it. Yet, I would try again and again and again. To be sure, it was only by the grace of God that I survived, while one after another, friends and acquaintances either ended up dead in accidents or brought their lives to an end - and in most cases never hinting that something inside was tearing them apart.

I would try my hand at landscaping. Digging in the earth seemed a good place to start anew - a study in the root cause of physical expression, its cultivation, development and maturity. Who knows? Ecological observation might be the answer. They say when one is close to the earth, one can really get in touch with ones self. It was worth a try. This effort lasted about six months and although I enjoyed landscaping, the craving to entertain returned. I needed to sing but could I do my shows without drinking alcohol? That was the question. The thought occurred to me, that my friends, Jimmy Flynn and Peter Stonie had made a roaring success of their career on the other side of Canada and it was there I should also try my hand at entertaining.

WE EXPECTED YOU

The landscaping tools packed away, I headed down the Trans Canada highway towards Halifax, four thousand miles to the East. I was on my way to making a success of my singing career, or so I thought. It was not the best time of the year to be traveling across Canada. The onset of winter crept across the land. It proved pretty rough driving but the old truck, which had been purchased for the landscaping effort proved its worth on the long journey. Old Trojan puttered on and on, day in and day out until we arrived in Nipigon, a small town in northern Ontario. It was about two a. m. when I pulled into an empty parking lot of a service station. I was tired. I bundled myself into my sleeping bag and quickly fell asleep. Around six a.m. I was awakened by a fist hammering on the window and the beam of a flashlight shining into my face. It was a female officer of the Ontario Provincial Police. She politely asked me to show her my I. D. (identification), which I did. I was thanked for my cooperation and bid adieu.

I found it difficult to get back to sleep and decided to move on in the direction of Halifax. It was about thirty below zero outside the protection of my truck and only slightly warmer inside. It was time to turn over the engine, heat the cab and head down the highway. However, it was not to be. The engine turned but would not start. Later, the engine's timing chain was discovered broken. I had to remain in Nipigon until a new timing chain was brought in from Thunder Bay and that would take a few days. Little did I know, that I would be staying in Nipigon for the good part of three months. It was not coincidence - it was preordained.

The service station manager suggested that I stay at the Nipigon Inn until the truck was fixed. There were three hotels in Nipigon, but it was specifically the Nipigon Inn he suggested I book into. It was about ten a. m. when I entered the lobby of the hotel. A very pleasant lady who was co-owner of the establishment greeted me and in a moment I was checked in. Later, at breakfast, I had the opportunity of chatting with this lady, Jan, and her partner, Vern, and what they revealed to me left me in a state of wonderment and mild shock.

It was related to me that I was expected at the hotel and, for that matter, I was right on time. I asked how such a happening could be possible and it was explained to me that a well-known psychic in Thunder Bay had given a reading to her. The reading stated that an Irishman, a musician, was traveling from western Canada and would be staying for some time with them. The Irishman's name was John. I had no doubt I fit the description.

In a rather odd way I felt very comfortable among these good people whom I was predestined to meet. I was offered a job entertaining at the hotel and settled in to life in the town of Nipigon. It was here I would meet the writer - philosopher Orrest. Orrest and I spent many a night into the wee hours of the morning discussing those things that concern all of mankind. I truly believe we arrived at a goodly amount of answers but somehow they have slipped into oblivion. It was here also I met Larry, an avid fisherman who introduced me to fishing the Nipigon river.

It was about twenty below zero as we walked down to the banks of the river, not more than a mile from the town proper. Larry had come to this spot on the river many times. It was one of his favorite fishing places. I had to get the line cast as quickly as possible because the sub zero weather rapidly froze my hand. It was difficult operating the fishing reel with big woolen mitts attached to my hands but it was something I had to get used to. It was well worth the effort. It was not long before Larry had a nice fighting plump rainbow on his line. He played the fish perfectly. It was a beautiful catch, leaving me impressed at the skill of the fisherman and the excellent quality fish the river yielded.

I would spend many a day during my stay in Nipigon by the river's bank. I felt good here, comfortable with life. It was by the waters I would reflect upon the question of life and my purpose in the scheme of things. Nevertheless, I still had no idea why I was destined to spend time in Nipigon. Perhaps it was one of those quirks of fate that led me here. January arrived and other than a regular procession of hangovers, nothing unusual had taken place in regards to the psychic prediction of my arrival. Then a strange occurrence happened. Around two a. m., one Friday morning as I sat alone in the beer parlor, my eyes were drawn to an elderly man carrying a bucket and mop to the far corner of the large room in which I sat. He seemed unhurried, quite contented doing his chores. I had never seen him before. I wondered who he was.

The early morning traffic had fallen to silence as I became deathly aware of the stillness within the room where I sat. I became rather uneasy at the presence of the elderly man but not afraid. I called to him, asking who he was. There was no reply. I called again, raising my voice a little louder. Still, there was no reply. I then arose from my seat and walked towards him and as I did he simply vanished. It had been a few days since I had had a drink. I thought it a good idea to have one immediately. Orrst and Vern who had been away for a few minutes tending some pressing business returned to remark how ghostly I looked and indeed, did ask me if I had seen a ghost to which I replied in the affirmative.

A LOST SOUL AT THE CONCENTRATION CAMP FAREWELL NIPIGON

Orrest had taken the trouble to psychoanalyze the message in the songs of the album "The Sea Runs Red," which I had presented to him some weeks after my arrival in Nipigon. I had never heard of anyone psychoanalyzing a song or music for that matter. It was indeed, a very new thing to me. Orrest was no slouch in the department of intellectual smarts. He was a university graduate. Beyond that, I new little about his educational background other than he had a command of the English language that would make any professor of literature rage with envy. This opinion of mine is not without foundation because truly, I had, on an exhausting number of occasions, requested Orrest to simplify his spoken word so that I could understand our discussion.

I was shocked to learn from his analysis of my music that I was running from something I could not put my finger on. He told me that I was not comfortable with who I was and that I was searching for an answer to what I was all about but did not know how to solve my dilemma. I was a little annoyed at such findings about my personality and like the true "hero of the quest", stuffed such ramblings into the dungeons of my mind. It was not a wise thing for me to do.

The time had come for me to move on to Halifax, Nova Scotia. It was a fine night of merrymaking in the pub, one last bash before I headed down the highway. At three a.m., I put my head to the pillow. A short time later I was awakened. It was Frank, my Polish friend whom I had shared many a good conversation with and whom I had become very fond of. He asked me if I would drop over to his place and share a little time with him and his wife before I moved on. I was pretty drunk but felt complimented by the request and joined Frank and his good wife. Although I was drunk, I recall everything of our conversation that evening. What was revealed to me was to profoundly affect me. Perhaps this was the true reason I was destined to spend some time in this small northern Ontario town of Nipigon.

As is Polish tradition, the table was set with the finest of meat dishes, an assortment of breads, pickles, spices and fine drink. Although I had consumed a good quantity of spirits, I felt strangely sober through the hours I shared with Frank and his good wife. Conversation shifted from the usual lighthearted sharing to a song or two and then to a topic that would remain with me. Frank and his wife had been prisoners at the infamous Auschwitcz Nazi concentration camp during the war. It was here Frank met his wife and here they would witness the evil of the Nazi monster, the horrible works of Satan's hand.

Frank went on to tell me about cannibalism and the total dehumanization of the person. I was told of the tortures, the killings and the unspeakable cruelty by the Nazi cur. I was told about the moment he was condemned to death, when he was placed with ten other prisoners in an execution chamber and made to watch his friends writhe on the end of meat hooks which suspended them by their jaws until they writhed no more. Then it was his turn. In that moment before his impending death, Frank turned to the Nazi officer who directed the horrible executions. Screaming at the officer, he said, "You may kill every one of us here but there is a God and for your evil you will face Him. There is nothing that will miss the Eye of The Almighty, nothing! You will be made to stand before the great God and you will stand alone to answer. Hitler and his armies will not be able to help you." The Nazi grew pale, turned to his death squad and ordered them to leave the chamber.

I often wondered how I would have been affected by such a horrifying experience. I thank my Creator I was spared the Nazi evils inflicted upon humanity.

Frank and his wife spent the best part of the war years in the hell of Auschwitz. That they survived was a miracle. I felt I had truly met two remarkable people. The bitterness of those horrible years had not stripped them of their love and belief in the higher principles of humanity. It was a privilege to have met them. I would not see Frank or his wife again. I never forgot that night which now seems so long ago. Too be sure I never will.

It was about two o' clock in the afternoon when I started old Trojan's engine. I was ready to move on. The engine purred like a kitten as I pulled out from the hotel. I was on my way. Then as quickly as the engine had started, it also stopped. Try as I might, I could not get the engine to fire. I felt uncomfortable because I had traveled only four or five yards and was stuck in the middle of an intersection. I was pretty hungover from the night before and I really did not want anyone coming near me just in case I might cause them to pass out from high-octane breath. The traffic was beginning to build up in all directions and my uneasiness with it. Then, as luck would have it, a squad of Ontario police officers came to my rescue.

Nipigon was one of those towns used by the police department for the training of recruits. You get to know much of what goes on in a small town whether you want to or not. It's just that way. So needless to say, the police knew who I was and probably a whole lot more. Arnie, a young officer who always seemed to find a kind word and a smile for any given situation, was the first on the scene. In a loud, jovial voice, he hollered, "That's what you get for trying to sneak away without saying good-bye," and finished with a loud bellow of laughter. "Come on boys" he called out to his comrades. "John is trying to sneak out of town, so I guess we better help him keep it a secret." There were no less than five officers pushing Trojan's big bulk down the main drag. It was an interesting spectacle to say the least. Soon, the engine started and this time she continued. I thanked Arnie and the rest of the officers. I was on my way to Halifax.

A DRUNKEN FIASCO

It was a long, unnerving trip to the Maritime province of Nova Scotia. The roads were slippery and treacherous. I reached Halifax a few days' later, my nerves flayed a little. I received a wonderful welcome from Jimmy and his wife Sylvia and had the pleasure of meeting my folk-singing partner Peter yet again, but from that moment onward, things changed for the worse. I was drinking very heavily and found it more and more difficult to stop. I was a guest of my good friends and the good friend part was rapidly diminishing due to my inability to behave in a normal fashion other than being drunk and in the way. My good friends and hosts never hinted at the latter but I knew inwardly I was making a mess of things and I hated myself for it. Try as I might, I could not shake the liquid demon and truly, I felt a ragged remnant of a human.

Jimmy was kind enough to find a gig for me at the Mark four motel in Moncton, New Brunswick. I thanked him and his wife for their hospitality and moved back onto the highway heading west to New Brunswick. I had let my friends down badly and I felt ashamed but even worse than the shame was the crippling realization that I could not stop the constant insane urge - the need for another drink of alcohol. Although I gave a decent attempt to give a good show at the club in Moncton, I was truly losing my touch with reality. Through it all, Hank, a professional entertainer and the owner of the motel treated me decently. He seemed to understand what I was going through and did not hint at my lonesome burden. He was indeed one of the best. "Here you are Irish," Hank said as he handed me the money. "A few hundred bucks... should get you back to Vancouver. I think things will be a bit better for you on your home ground. If you come by again, don't be shy about dropping in to see me. You did a pretty decent show under the circumstances." And that was it! I was on my way.

Winter still had its grip on the land as I headed back west. I was pretty sick and downright miserable as old Trojan rumbled back across the prairies.

The afternoon was whipping up a bit of a rage as the snows swept across the Alberta highway. A mile ahead lay the town of Brooks. I was hungry, cold and tired. Wheeling off the highway, I headed uptown to the Telstar Hotel and booked in for the evening. "You look like you had a bit of a rough ride, sir," said the lady behind the desk.

"Yes mam, I just drove out from Halifax," I answered.

"That is a bit of a long trip. What were you doing out there," the lady asked curiously.

"Doing a bit of singing in the bars back there," I answered half heartedly.

"A singer, well I'll be darned. Mister, have I got a deal for you. The room is free and you get paid sixty dollars a night. How about it?" The lady said as though she might lose her job if I didn't say yes. So I said yes.

"I hear you're Irish! "Do you happen to know Dublin In The Green or The Black Velvet Band?" The rancher said as he placed a pint of beer on top of my speaker.

"Never heard of them," I said hoping he would just go away and not mention either of those two songs again. But the big rancher did not go away and asked why I did not know the songs he had just mentioned - because I was Irish and I should know those two songs. "I'm sorry sir but I never got the chance to learn them, perhaps I can sing something else for you," I said hoping against hope he would leave me alone. But the rancher held course.

"The name's Ross... Ross Murray... the family has Irish roots. Wouldn't know the Ba, Ba song would you?"

"The Ba, Ba song?" I replied somewhat disconcertedly.

"Yep, the Ba, Ba song," Ross repeated in somber tones.

"No sir, I can't say I do know the Ba, Ba song. Has it something to do with lamb stew or woolen socks?" I said, laughing at my silly interpretation of the Ba, Ba song.

"That is very funny Irish. O.K. I get it... reckon I'll just leave you alone and let you do your thing," he said as he made to move away.

"Just joking Ross... come back here and give us the first few words of the song and maybe we'll get through it together," I encouraged him as I sipped the magical contents of the mug of beer he had offered me.

"I can't sing a darn note, Mr. Irish but I sure will give it a try," Ross said as he stepped upon the stage.

"O.K. my friend," I said. "What key shall we do it in?"

"What key? What do you mean what key," the big fellow said, showing surprise that there was another category of keys other than the ones that opened doors.

"Yes Ross, what key? We have to sing in a certain key... a certain pitch so to speak... here let's try this key," I said as I strummed the C chord on my guitar.

"Sounds good to me, Irish," the rancher said seemingly amused at the process of singing.

"Right, Ross, now that we have established the key we are going to sing in... please do kick the song off and add as many trimmings to your rendition as possible. Adding trimmings to a song marks the difference between the pros and the amateurs," I said to the man who looked like he was not made for the stage life.

"What do ya mean 'trimmings'," the new born singer said with a quizzical about him.

"To sing with a little or much expression Ross. You know? To put a little or a lot of life into the job. To apply a little or a lot of character to the moment... that's what I mean by the trimmings."

"Where the hell did you ever come up with that load of superfluities," the big fellow shot back. And I left it at that because I had not the slightest idea what superfluities were.

"O.K. Ross, here we go... the key of C... and ladies and gentlemen... For heavens sake don't call them names, their my friends," the Ba, Ba singer said as he lit the stage with his broad smile and threw out the first few words of the Song.

> *To the tables down at Murray's to the place where Louis dwells;*
> *To the dear old Templar Bar we love so well*
> *See the Whiffenpoof assemble, with their glasses raised on high*
> *And the magic of their singing cast a spell.*
>
> *We are poor little lambs who have lost our way*
> *Ba... Ba... Ba.*

And on the singer went, mesmerizing his friends and travelers alike with the golden tones of a rich baritone voice – a singer's gift.

As the beer began to mellow my tensed mind, the rancher with some of his friends joined me at the bar.

I want you to meet some of my buddies, Irish," Ross said as his friends gathered around me at the bar. "This is Dillbo the head rigger out in God knows where… Pat on your right, and Glenn on the farther right… and on your left, the beautiful Jessica," he said as he nodded to the bar lady for a new round of drinks. And true enough, Jessica was beautiful but I did not elaborate on her deliciousness.

"Jessica is not with any of us guys so maybe you want to get to know her, Irish," the rancher said cagily.

And on hearing the freedom news, I turned to Jessica. "Is Ross usually as outgoing as he is tonight?" I asked the woman who was now beginning to feel at ease within the group of men.

"Yes, Irish, he is that and a whole lot more but in general he is one of the best," the lovely one said with a hint of sincerity. I liked how she complimented her friend as she slipped into question mode. "Is your name really Irish," she asked, an enticing smile warming her face.

"In a sense, Jessica but only because I come from the Land of Erin – the ancient name for Ireland. My given name is John but my wife decided she liked Sean better so now I am know to my friends as Sean and that is the name I would like you to call me because I like you and I would like you to be my friend." And Jessica became my friend – my very close friend.

Ever been out on an oil rig," Dillbo said as I prepared to board the stage for the second set of the evening.

"No Dillbo," I answered. "I haven't, but it is something I would like to try one day."

"How about tomorrow morning? I'll take you out there and show you what oil rigging is all about," Dillbo said, seemingly delighting in the challenge. Nevertheless, I was up for the job and I was going to prove I could stand with the best of hard working men.

"You got a deal, Dillbo," I said bravely. "What time in the morning are we talking about?"

"Me and the boys will pick you up at five a.m. right on the button," he said with a smile that is indicative of winning something mighty worthwhile. And as Dillbo smiled, I made my way to the stage to sing my second set of songs only this set was to be garnished with all the trimmings of romantic songs to be bestowed upon the beautiful Jessica.

The end of the night came almost suddenly. The singing and gaiety of the evening over, the oil men went their way, and the lovely Jessica came to me and took me in her arms. "Be careful out there Irish, I don't want anything to happen to you. Promise me that you will take care of yourself because it can be very dangerous work," she said as she hugged a little tighter.

"I'll be O.K. Jessica... I guess I should learn to keep my big mouth shut but I'm committed," I said, as dignified as a drunken person could be.

"Then be a little committed to me and come back in one piece... I'll like to see you tomorrow night, okay?" Jessica said, as she kissed me good night. Had I known what was in store for me I would most certainly have not left the comfort of my bed

The banging on the door of my cabin was right on time. My head thundered and my body rubbered around the floor looking for my clothes which were most unsuitable for the upcoming trial. It was more than a trial! It was the most stupid undertaking I had ever agreed to in my entire lifetime. Out the door and into the cutting wind of forty below – no coffee, no breakfast, no proper clothing – just a bloody awful hangover and a spell of frozen hell awaiting me. It was a great time to die.

And the winds sang their awful bloody songs of the freezing northland as I wondered how I could worm my way out of doing whatever I was supposed to do. "Just stay alive," my inner voice urged. "Think and step carefully and while you're at it, you may as well say a whole whack of prayers because you are going to need God in your life more so than you ever did up to this moment," the inner voice said, almost with a touch of cold sarcasm. And I grudgingly accepted. My manhood demanded that I not be a wimp, that I stop complaining and get on with it. But really, being a real man out here in the condition I was in and not looking forward to doing something with hooking up drilling pipes to a machine that bore each hookup into the earth at a speed faster than I could think, bore the realization into my head that this blasted job was the equal to being a choker man and under these conditions! A few million times the worse.

Just what happened to the savvy of John McDonald? Perhaps he did not have any to begin with and as I made my way up onto the high platform, which seemed only to jeer at me every step of the way, I could only relate to myself as the idiot of the century and such thinking was justified. "Here you are Irish," the voice of Dillbo shot through the wind. "Try these overalls on...

they're a bit oily but you'll be a lot warmer in them." And Dillbo was right. The overalls were a bit oily, so much so that I could not feel the cloth of the garment. It took a while with the struggle to break through the frozen oil-cloth overalls and I thanked the good lord that I was on the platform because the cloth was so stiff, they would not have bent at the knees as I struggled up the steel wrung stairs from ground zero – the big awkward boots, gloves and hardhat that followed were in the same vein of inelegance but I was here and I was going to work.

The generated lights from the power plant seemed oddly out of place on this frozen, snow swept landscape – a bubble of light against the backdrop of the prairie darkness. It was a strange and eerie place out here in the light of the darkness on the broad flatlands of Canada and strangely my mind slipped away to the peacefulness of the little garden in Dublin – an escape from the moment of frozen hell I was experiencing. The drill pipes went down, down, down through the depths of the earth in search of that stuff that pollutes every corner of our world and I envied those people who lived in the filth of the pollutants because they were far better off than me and my new found oil rig buddies.

Darkness moved to light and on into darkness again, ending the trial of a lifetime. I did not recognize myself when I looked into the mirror that evening. Streaks of black, greasy, crude oil pasted my face, arms and hair. Oil that not even the most efficient chemical removers could do in – and I had to present myself to the patrons of the hotel later in the evening, to take a guitar lovingly in my arms and sing my folk songs to the boys and my love song to Jessica.

And what a bloody sight I was. Hair matted down one side of my head while the rest stood in clumps of varying sizes over my scalp. My eyebrows and eyelids were no better off and the wood on the neck of my guitar took a liking to the oil caked on to my hands and stuck to it like a thirsty man would to a cold beer. I was in some mess but I was here and I would see the show through. I was indeed the quintessential black and white minstrel – that not even the great Al Jolson could outshine.

"Dear suffering Lord, is that you beneath that heaping of oil, Irish, the rancher laughed as he sputtered his mouthful of beer over the floor. "Very funny Ross . . .very funny indeed," I replied as I laughed heartily at the stupidity of my situation but a loving hug from Jessica relieved my anxiety when she told me she was happy to see me back and if I plan to go oiling the prairies again, I should at least be more rested and prepared for the undertaking. Jessica made sense and I was going to listen to her from now on.

"Did a fine job out there," said Dillbo as he sat by our table later in the evening. "For a guy that never worked the oil rigs before… am sure bloody proud of you. To be truthful, I thought you were a bit of a city boy but you sure proved me wrong. A ten hour shift… not even a coffee to go on… damned good show. The drinks are on me tonight Irish ... damned proud to have you out there… next time, I'll treat you proper," the Alberta oil man said, as he pressed a double shot of whiskey into my hand. Then he laughed loudly at the mess I was in saying there was no profit in the days work because I got all the damned oil over me leaving none for the company. And so it was, my days of being an oil rigger came to an end and I was not one bit sorry.

I would leave the town of Brooks, hungover and sick but much richer for the experiences I had gathered there. Ross Murray and Jessica would in time become my close and loyal friends, ever ready when the days came that I had to call on them when I was down, out and broke. A fond farewell with a kiss and a hug from the beautiful Jessica, a stout wave to the boys and it was back on the road again.

GREENER PASTURES

The greening of the land welcomed me as I approached the west coast. Here, by the Pacific shores, flowers presented their colorful petals throughout the four seasons. It was a wonderful change from the constant veil of white my eyes had been subjected to for the past four months. I was glad the trip was over, not because of lack of opportunity but because I had failed. I had failed my wife and my friends, who had so graciously tried to help me. I felt empty. The only thing to relieve the emptiness was more drink and that I couldn't get enough of. My wife was finding it more and more difficult to put up with the antics brought about by my drinking and soon it was agreed that we separate.

It was a sad Sunday morning when I pulled my old truck out of our driveway and headed down the highway towards the Interior towns of Coalmont and Tullameen, approximately four hundred kilometers southwest of Vancouver – the high country where my friends Irene and Carl dwelled.

THERE'S GOLD IN THEM THAR CREEKS

In the high country above the historical town of Princeton, Coalmont basked in nature's incredible beauty. This land through which the waters of the Similkemeen River flowed, had no equal in its resplendence. It was to this country that the gold miners came in the nineteen hundreds seeking their fortunes. The rivers had been generous in their yields of gold and platinum and many had struck it rich. Others were not so lucky. It was not far in the future when I too would play a losing hand to the river of platinum and gold. But up here in this pine tree country, my friends Irene and Carl dwelled. They had moved away from the bustle of the city. Here, I felt a little safe.

The usual sign hung in the door window of the Coalmont Hotel - "No guns or knives allowed." The ominous sign seemed very much out of place for this small peaceful town. No doubt it was one of those things dating back to a time when there was a lot of gold panning and sluicing activity along the river. The old hotel was built back in 1912. It still had that feel of the past about it. The feeling never changed when I entered through the doors - that feeling of familiarity with the past. Perhaps I had been here in a past life. Perhaps I had been shot up on Lawless Creek stealing someone's gold or defending my own. There was a presence here in this old building but it was a good one. There was a history here also, brutal, brave and trying. It was a place where the best and the worst had passed through in the quest for the "holy grail." Some had found it, others perished in their bid.

I wasn't at all surprised to see Bert. He had been around Port Moody for some years. Got to know him at the "Last Spike" lounge when I entertained there. Like others, he had found something inviting and comfortable in the high country. It was a late Sunday afternoon when I felt my tensed body and mind unwind to the effects of the booze. A few songs sung to the strumming of my Martin guitar, led to more beer, more songs and more company. I was indeed at home away from home. Before the evening had ended, I was offered a job singing in the hotel on a regular basis. This arrangement proved agreeable to both the innkeeper and myself. I was to be paid in quantities of beer, the odd bit of grub and a room to hang my feet in. My days were my own to do as I wished. I had made it big time and here in this little town that possessed a very large heart, I would meet some of the world's greatest adventurers and seekers.

Big Bob was just that, he was very big. He had arrived in town with his buddy, Jeep, a few days after my arrival. Jim, the window man, came in from

Alberta, a week or so later. A new and very interesting chapter was about to get under way in the lives of us newcomers. Big Bob had secured himself a gold claim up beyond Lawless Creek and it seemed fitting to Big Bob, since we were all lost seekers, the claim should be shared and worked between all five.

The heavy waters of spring run-off had eased to a trickle making it easy to pan the creek. We set up camp in an old clearing that had been logged many years before. We got working the creek bed. It was not long before smatterings of gold dust appeared in our pans, giving rise to great dreams and schemes. What to do with our bonanza was discussed at great length and lengthened even further when discussed over mugs of beer. We were, for sure, an odd assortment of humanity. Evenings saw me sing for my liquid supper at the hotel and not infrequently, I was accompanied by my gold prospecting friends. Life was at its best here, free from all the rigidity, laws, rules and regulations of societal living. We were, at last, unaccountable to the things we detested.

Sheila and Michael had arrived from somewhere and settled in among us. It was not important where people came from in this little town. It was important only that they did come here. And so, Sheila and Michael became a part of our well-knit group. Michael got a job as cook at the hotel and Sheila waitressed. Our clan was on the rise. It was not long before our gathering had grown to that magic number most suited for the makings of a championship baseball team. It was the height of summer. Coalmont was host to a baseball tournament. The town did not have a team to represent it in the tournament; this gave rise to the birth of the infamous baseball team, "The Coalmont Nuggeteers."

Our plan of defense and attack was discussed in great secrecy in the confines of the pub. This proved to be an excellent place to draw up the blueprint for victory. Our imagination worked overtime and before long we had a plan, a damned good plan. It was such a good plan that its success brought about unbounded shock even among the participants of our team. The games got under way at two o' clock one Saturday afternoon in the good and hot month of July. We, the Nuggeteers, were one of the teams first up to play. The game lasted an hour or so. We retired from the field the victors. We were all, to a woman and man, in shock. We had beaten a fairly good team that had been expected to at least reach the finals. We had good reason to be in a state of disbelief. We had formed our team in a matter of hours in the pub before the tournament and truly, as the saying goes, we were feeling no pain when we took to the field.

Copious amounts of beer were consumed to celebrate the rise of the newly formed Coalmont Nuggeteers and its first victory. At this point in the team's history, (which could of course be counted in hours) someone already had drawn up plans to apply to the American Baseball Commission for entry into the Major leagues. Some of us thought that may be pushing it a little but all agreed that it was worth a try. Sheila and Michael were really on the ball as they made sure our table was never without liquid magic. Life was at its finest and it was going to get much, much better.

Big Mike had come up from the miners to play in the second game for us and this was indeed a great stroke of luck. Big Mike was a huge man. He was tall, muscular and he was a baseball player. He had just come up from the miners because that is where he worked - in the mines somewhere on the outskirts of Princeton. The baseball field was located next to the Hotel and this was a most suitable arrangement for the team. Here, we could relax, drink beer while we laid plans to defeat the opposition and conveniently take to the field at game time.

I must admit I had never played a game of baseball in my life. In fact, I detested the game. I'm not sure why - just one of those things. The time had come for the second game to begin. We reluctantly spilled out of the bar onto the field to take up our positions. We had lost the toss - our opponents would go to bat first. We spread out across the field the best we could, each individual following his or her plan of action. This procedure seemed sensible because there was not a soul other than big Mike who knew what he was doing. Some sat on the field, one or two fell asleep and some began singing to themselves. We looked like anything but a baseball team. I was concerned. I felt we had a better chance of striking the "mother load" up on the claim than we had of winning the game. I do not know if the rest of the team thought the same as I did. If they did, they were sure keeping it to themselves.

The game had just gotten under way when a nasty bowser ran onto the field and bit one of our players on the arse. This caused great consternation among our well-knit squad. We responded to this bowser's attack with indignant protests of the most, foul kind. Hazel called out at the top of her lungs, "You dirty dog, how dare you bite our man on the behind." It was a rather nice way Hazel put it, because she was such a darling girl and did not betray her code of self-respect by uttering the wordy crudities of life. Robbie, who was a veteran in the gold panning and sniping business, responded to the

THE SECOND PURPOSE

dirty dog's attack with an attack of his own.

In the cab of his old truck, there was his faithful companion, Atilla. Atilla was a massive German shepherd and also very obedient. Robbie was a man who never allowed himself to be rushed. He informed the umpire that he was going to bring his dog to the scene of the vicious attack and have his Atilla chase the culprit bowser away. All he asked of the umpire was, that he delay the game a few minutes while he organized his strategy. The umpire agreed. In the meantime, Ebbeneezer, our man who had his behind torn apart, was taken to the hotel to have his wounds disinfected, sterilized and manicured.

When Robbie returned to the field with mighty Atilla and believe me, Atilla was mighty, he immediately set about to make things safe from attacks by dirty dogs. The culprit dog was still being very bold, so Robbie gave the order for Atilla to go after it and do the same thing to it, as it had done to our man. Even Hazel was much pleased with this decision. Atilla wasted no time in cornering the troublemaker but unfortunately he knew something about the situation we didn't. The dog that bit our man was a female and she was in heat, so off went Atilla and bowser happily together.

Eventually, the game got under way. Our pitcher was absolutely brilliant. I had never seen anything like the consistency of accurate pitching I observed that day from Madalene. Every ball she pitched was right on to the end of the opposition's batter's bat! Balls were flying left, right and center across the field. Fortunately, for us, most of those balls were directed into our gloves. The score remained tied as the game went into extra innings.

The patrons from the hotel had come to lend us support and we began to take great pride in the fact that we were a team of contention. As the first shades of evening approached, both teams remained stubborn. The opposition now had their turn at the bat. It was crucial to keep them off the board or at the very least hold them to a minimal score. However, that was easier said than done. It was obvious now that the game was up for grabs but its tone developed into one of great seriousness.

Madalene was again her consistent self, dropping most pitches on to their hitters bats but fortunately for us, their hitters were just as consistently gracious by walloping most balls into the gloves of our outfielders. But that kind of luck was just too good to last for us.

Their next batter to the plate struck the ball so damned hard that all heads turned to the sky to see the ball fly far and away. I figured the game to be over and lost. I hated to lose and this game was no exception. Then, from a distance, big Mike, who had taken off to retrieve the ball, was calling desperately to the umpire to come to where he was. In due course, the umpire came back and informed the opposition that only one run could be given because the ball had landed between two dogs that were making little puppies making it impossible for our man to reach in between the love making dogs and obtain the ball.

Robbie now knew where his Atilla was and we knew that big Atilla might have saved the game for us. It was now our turn at the bat and again it came down to the mighty Mike at the bat and their pitcher. We were now in full twilight. The advantage was with our opponents because it was almost impossible to see the ball that was being pitched to the batter. But somehow, big Mike made good his contact with the bat when the ball was pitched to him. It was a brilliant hit. By the time the ball came back we had scored three runs. It was too much for our opponents to overcome.

We retired once again to the Coalmont Hotel to congratulate ourselves over mugs of frothy beer. Atilla, was the main topic of the evening and orders were put in on the batch of puppies that were expected to be produced in the near future. A song was called for and soon the old barroom was resounding to the old familiar tunes. It was a good day. Tomorrow would see the Nuggeteers go to bat once again.

It was two o' clock in the afternoon when the game got under way. The number of spectators had grown noticeably larger. Nobody had given us much of a chance to win one game, let alone reach the semi-final but we were proving them wrong. We were in great form, riding high on our unexpected success. Nevertheless, the opposition got off to a good start. They belted a goodly number of balls far out of sight. Atilla was sadly missed. The score was very favorable but unfortunately, not for the Nuggeteers. The game had been underway for less than half an hour and we were fifteen runs to the minus. Something had to be done.

The man who sold hot dogs and popcorn from his little food truck was none other than the bold Jake Peppercorn. He seemed to realize and not without proof, that his Nuggeteers were in deep trouble, as much trouble as potatoes are in when dumped into the deep-fry-cauldron. We were getting fried. Jake developed a strategy of distance interference. When the opposition came to bat, Jake spoke in unknown languages over his speaker system, causing great irritation to all in the territory. However, his plan showed fruition because it was noticed that when Jake spoke in tongues, the opposition failed to chalk up a score when at bat. We were proud of our sausage man.

THE SECOND PURPOSE

There was hope for us on the horizon. While Jake lacerated the land with languages unknown, somehow, bottles of beer had found their way onto the field. It was an extraordinary development in the field of baseball. Our gloves seemed to litter the playing field and this of course had a grand purpose. The glove, as it happened, was large enough to cover a beer bottle, at least, the best part of it. In this respect, the partaking of beer on the playing field was successfully hidden from the umpire's eyes. The Nuggeteers blood sugar level was on the rise and so was our playing form.

With the continuing unknown language interference and the rise in our team's blood sugar level, the game began to take on ominous tones for the opposition. It was now just a matter of time before the enemy was destroyed. Slowly but surely, we chalked up the runs. It is necessary at this point of the game to give honorable mention to the indomitable Bert who was instrumental in the great comeback.

Bert was the only Nugetteer on the field who wore a hat. It seemed that Bert on this particular day, was in full touch with his sixth and beyond senses. It was almost as if he knew in which direction the ball was going to be hit. In the shade of the brim of his hat, it was observed that Bert scratched the left side of his nose, followed with a slight tip of his hat, then spoke softly to himself before he made his move. I had no idea what he was muttering to himself but from his follow up actions to this private conversation, it could be easily discerned it had nothing to do shearing sheep. He was always on the move before the ball was struck and always in the right direction. Bert was at his best.

The sausage man changed from speaking in tongues to singing in tongues as Bert made world class moves upon the field. Such amazing talents brought masterful results. The score drew even. Robbie, the gold sniper, was at his best also. He said things to our adversaries that mothers should not hear and sometimes Daddies.

The teams entered the ninth inning tied. The opposition was at bat in the bottom of the ninth and we were ready. The game was reaching fever pitch. Madalene was her usual consistent self, dropping every ball on the tip of the batters' bat as though she were tossing a potato into a pot of boiling water. Their people were hitting pretty good for this late in the game and we began to grow a little worried. Try as he might, the sausage man was not having the same negative effect upon the opposition as he had earlier. Bert was truly holding us in the game and we only just got out of the bottom of the ninth without a score against us. The teams were still tied.

Within minutes two of our men were retired after we came up to bat in the top of the tenth inning. It was now my turn at the plate.

She was quite a beautiful, the opposition's pitcher. I could understand why our men were having trouble hitting the ball. I too, became a victim to her seductive spell as she tossed me something or other. It was big Bob, who told me to snap out of it and get my mind back on the game. The opposition had indeed a most wondrous weapon working well for them and it was time the beauty's seductive run was brought to an end. I made up my mind to hit the next ball beautiful brown eyes tossed at me with the full weight of that pick and shovel swing I had developed in trench excavating on construction sites in the years of before. The time had come to unleash that pent up power.

I stared down the sexy look of the beautiful one as she lobbed in the last of the three balls. It was now or never. The bat was set back across my shoulder. It was in firing position and I was in full control of the trigger. The only thing that concerned me was, that I had to hit the ball high in the air, to avoid hitting the beautiful pitcher. The ball was on the way. I could see it as clear as a thirsty man may see a cold beer a few inches from of his eyes. I was ready for it.

The bat came from across my shoulder as all the power my frame could muster drove the weapon of delivery towards the ball. It was a sight to behold. Never in the history of baseball did a missile pierce the air in such flawless flight as it went up, up and away. All eyes were on the object that traversed the sky - a phenomenal display of power and accuracy. Even the beautiful one was impressed, in fact, she could not take her eyes from me for quite some time. Silence fell across the field and in that moment of hushed astonishment, Robbie spoke softly as not to break the magic of the moment and said he would retrieve the bat.

The game remained tied as the teams entered into the thirteenth inning. Our people got off to a good start. We had two men on at first and second bases. Things were looking good for us but they had looked good before and we had come out the other side of good. However, things were looking less good for the opposition. If they went down to a bunch of oddballs that had put their team together the day before in the bar, a team without uniforms, a mish mash of wanderers who had to borrow bats, balls, gloves and anything else we required to play with, it would be very hard to live down. We had nothing to lose but they had their pride and it was slipping. Then the unmentionable happened.

One of their players, whether it was out of frustration or because he was simply a jerk, shouted across the field, that they were playing a bunch of overweight boozers and it was time for them to annihilate us. It was not a nice thing to say.

The same kind of silence hung across the field as when my bat helicoptered through the sky. A deep sense of hurt stabbed at the hearts of each of our players. Nobody said a thing but you could see we were all thinking on the same train of thought. The bastard that uttered the insult had cost his team the game and it was made known to him that he should avoid the bar at all costs after the game. His words had a gut felt sting to them. Judgment was made upon us as how we looked and not who we actually were. I had been guilty of this kind of judgment many times and now, I knew what it was like to be judged blindly, just because we were a team who liked our beer. In my case however, it was different. I knew I was in trouble with the bottle but I did not need to be reminded on a baseball field by someone who could well have had the same problem I was dealing with.

Nevertheless, our bats were swinging with great gusto and two of our men managed to get to first and second base. It was now Hazel's turn to bat. It was not known if Hazel had ever swung a bat in her life. It was just one of those questions men did not ask women - at least in our case. We could see our dear sweetheart was a little nervous by the way she momentarily held the bat at that end where the ball is struck. However, she did catch herself in the act of mishandling the instrument and made immediate correction to the situation. Beautiful brown eyes did not have the same hypnotizing effect on our Hazel, as the goddess did on us men folk and this was indicated by the rather cold stare Hazel imparted towards her. The pitcher was down to her last pitch. We held our breath. The pitch was in. It was a low ball… too low. Hazel was still alive at bat. The pitch came in again. It was again too low but Hazel took a swing at it anyway. It was not a good thing to do - or so we thought.

It was a weak hit - one of those balls that just go ambling harmlessly across the field, an easy pickup for the defense. However, this was not the case. The ball seemed to have a mind of its own, wandering where it liked as it hit clump and bump, avoiding the open gloves of the fielders. By the time it was trapped, Hazel had reached first base safely, moving the other runners to second and third - the bases were loaded. It was now Bert's turn to bat.

The man who had called our team a load of overweight boozers would call us boozers no more. Our Bert made the connection, hitting a grand slam. It was a great moment for us but the game was not over yet. We were ahead by four runs. We had to keep it that way. We were now into the bottom of the thirteenth inning, both teams feeling a good touch of heat fatigue. Madalene had improved dramatically with her pitching and she too was putting in an amazing and spirited effort to bring her team home to victory. She had eliminated the first two batters. It was now up to their last batter to save his team. Robbie, who was not shy about imparting words of the unsettling nature to one who had caused him disturbance, approached the opposition's batter.

"So you're the "son of a bitch" who called us an overweight bunch of boozers, aren't ya, ya shit head." The poor batter had that 'I wish I weren't here' look about him. One could see that he was rather uncomfortable about what was communicated to him. However, it was about to get a whole lot worse for him.

Atilla, who was resting on the sideline from his exhausting acts of lovemaking from the day before, seemed to understand that his master was somewhat annoyed at the batter. Madalene was ready. The batter was as ready as he could be. He was leaning forward slightly, bat up high and angled across his right shoulder. The ball was on its way. It was not the best of Madalene's pitches and the batter had it labeled. As the batter prepared to strike the ball, Atilla poked his nose into that place that is so private to men. The umpire disallowed the play and Atilla was restrained from doing naughty things to batters. Again the play was set to go. The ball was pitched. The batter hammered it. Our hearts sank. The ball was on its way out of the park but so was our man, Big Mike the miner.

Over clump, dent, briar and hedge he followed the rocketing ball, never taking his eye off it. On, on he went, legs moving as a cheetah's might. The ball was on its way down from the far reaches of the sky. Big Mike was jockeying for position. He was beneath it. All he had to do was put his hand up and catch it. Then we noticed it.

Big Mike had lost his glove in the run of the clumps and dents. Our hearts sank into abject misery. The ball came down, down, down into the hands of Big Mike but it did not stay there. It bounced up, up, up and for a moment we thought he'd lost his presence of mind. It was quiet clear to us that he had attained a degree of expertise in the art of juggling as the ball bounced from his hands to his chin, to his nose- side ways, back ways and behind ways. The suspense was unbearable, as much so for the opposition as it was for us. It was obvious the impact against the bare flesh of Big Mike's hand had stung him pretty badly, making it painful and difficult for him to hold the ball. The last part of this most remarkable athletic display was to see Big Mike fall backwards into a clump of bushes while the ball was in the air. Then, from the bush, a hand was seen to reach up towards the sky and clasp the ball on the way down and there it stayed fully secured. We had won.

A long, exciting and arduous day lay ahead of the team. The final game was slated to be played at eight o clock and because of the mounting pressures that tend to accompany heroic success, copious amounts of beer were consumed to relieve ourselves of such unwanted mental tensions, and to add to our rising pride, one of our supporters dug deep in his pocket to buy the team baseball caps. It was a wonderful gesture but with the caps came ominous tidings.

The final game began on schedule. We took to the field as champions should - adjusting our hats, scratching our hair and wiping our brows with the backside of our forearms. That's how the professionals did it and we were pros - at least in our minds.

The game moved at rather speedy pace right into the ninth inning. Once again we were tied. Once again we could smell victory. Our opposition was formidable. They were good, really good. We knew we had gotten more than a few lucky breaks. But we did not complain.

If we were going to win this game, we needed more than Atilla's interference to see us through. Our team was now beyond fatigue. We were near the threshold of exhaustion when the final play came in. Madalene pitched the ball. The batter from the Merrit team made his hit. It was good. Our fielder was caught doing those things professional players do with their baseball caps and the ball went sailing by. It was unbelievable but that was how the game ended. The team from Merrit won the tournament and deservedly so. We celebrated our loss and their victory.

While we were into our cuffs of beer drinking, someone suggested that Coalmont enter a team in the upcoming raft race on the Similkemeen river. It was decided by our baseball team that Bert and I represent Coalmont in the river raft race. There were, however, hurdles to overcome. We had no raft, no life jackets, no paddles and the most serious hurdle - no experience in the sport of river rafting. That was about to change.

Big Bob and his buddy Jeep knew someone up in the Merrit country who knew someone, who in turn knew someone who had a very big rubber raft. It was decided that someone be sent to the good town of Merrit to find that someone who had the raft. That someone was located and the raft appeared outside the Coalmont Hotel the night before the raft race. The raft was indeed something to behold. It was a big, flat, sad looking thing in desperate need of repair.

The hotel office was commandeered as the fix the raft headquarters. Telephone calls went out to those who might be able to assist us in the recreating of a raft that would float. It was not long before help arrived. Pretty soon the Major holes and gashes were patched, the raft loaded on a truck and taken to the gas station at Tullemeen to be pumped with air. It was around midnight when we arrived back at the hotel with our inflated raft. We were now ready to take on the best in the business of raft racing. Our plan of strategy was discussed well into the wee hours of the morning over mugs of beer. Come hell or high water, Bert and I were going to give it our best.

At seven forty five a.m. that fateful Saturday morning of the great race, Bert and I made our way down from the precipitous road that seemed to hang a thousand feet up in a twisting horizontal position above the canyon of the Similkemeen River. Down the gravely trail we carried our rubber master of the river to that spot by the water's edge where the many competitors were gathered. Judging the competition, Bert and I did not think too much off our chances of winning the race. Still, we would give it our best. Lack of sleep and a night of heavy drinking had left both Bert and me in a semi-live state and if it were not for our friend, Whispering Tony from Tullemeen, we may not have made it into the raft to partake in the race.

Whispering Tony was a man who liked to whisper his conversation. He whispered so inaudibly low that one really needed a hearing aid in order to attend his utterings, which usually alluded to nothing more than a "hello." However, Whispering Tony was a little more on the ball than I had thought. The good fellow had had the foresight to see that Bert and I would be in need of that morning drink that was so crucial for getting the mind and body to respond to the demands of the day.

From the inside pocket of his buckskin jacket, W T. produced a bottle of liquid magic that did the trick for us. Bert, out of the goodness of his heart, insisted that I try the contents of the magic bottle. I do not know if he was being considerate or if I was a guinea pig. However, without much adieu, I took a swallow. Well, I tell you! It was so damned tasty I found it difficult to extract the bottle from my gullet. Bert saw to it that I did. We polished the bottle off in no time flat and in no time flat we were stone drunk.

So there we were, drunk as lords, sitting in a field of daisies by the river lost to all sense of time and meaning. Whispering Tony reminded us constantly why we were sitting in a field of daises and it was not to pick flowers to present to the Queen of the Coalmont Parade but to get off our arses, run down the hill as fast as we could, climb into the raft when we got to the water's edge and head downriver as a competitors in a raft race. These words W.T. uttered and not in his usually inaudible manner but with some measure of strength and concern.

"I hear ya, W.T.," I mumbled. "When the rifle is fired, just point me in the right direction, okay!" I said. Bert, at this point, was in no better shape than I was and asked the good W.T. for a little help when the competition began. W.T. said he'd be happy to help and added that we looked in fine shape and that he had great confidence in us.

As I lay there in the field of daisies, I noticed there were two rivers that weren't there before I drank of W. Ts liquid cure-all. I asked Bert and W.T. which of the rivers we would be using for the raft race and to my surprise I was met with ear splitting silence. Then, eventually, Bert spoke. "There's only one river, John."

"Where do you see two rivers?" asked W.T.

"Down at the bottom of the hill and there seems to be thousands of rafts floating in them," I answered.

"Suffering duck," said W.T., "the best thing to do is to put a patch over one eye and blot one of the rivers out." And so a patch, in the form of a red bandanna, was tied across my head covering my left eye. It worked. I could now see only one river and hundreds of rafts instead of thousands.

A rifle appeared in someone's hands. This was the first serious hint that the race was for real. In a most relaxed way, Bert and I made our plan of strategy. We were to stay ahead of the other runners at all costs as we raced down the hill to take charge of our rafts, which lay in the shallow water at the river's edge. As soon as we entered the raft, we were to head straight across to the other side of the river where the water was deeper and swifter. This way, the fast water would carry us free of the shallows in the river. It was a good plan.

At last, the time had come. The rifleman called out over a megaphone for all the competitors to assemble at the starting line. Bert and I took our place. The rifle fired. The race was on.

Bert somehow slipped when the line broke for the rafts but was quick enough in his thinking to fall in front of a competitor, bringing the man down with him. I was doing pretty well in the running until I ran into a furrow. This sudden sensation, like that of stepping on a downward step of a ladder that isn't there, is not good for the equilibrium. The gravitational pull was too much for my foggy state of mind and onwards and downwards I went until the ground came up to wipe my nose.

I had never known what it was like to look or feel like a pancake but now I did. I was literally and physically flat out. Still, my instincts were working and they were telling me not to be a lazy bastard but to get up, be a man and get on with it. This, I tried to do immediately but Bert, who was now making up for lost time, came running down behind me and planted the heel of his cowboy boot square into my face as I was trying to get up. We were not getting off to the start we had planned. If we managed to get to the river without killing ourselves, it would be a miracle.

Bert took time to apologize and help me to my feet and then he took off like a bat out of hell in the direction of the raft. I was now running hard behind him, calling to him to have the oars ready when I got to the raft. However, what greeted my eyes in the next few seconds was quite amazing.

Bert had reached the bank a good few meters ahead of me and took a flying leap from the bank to the raft. It was something to behold watching this man spring from the bank, feet first into the raft and then spring head first out of it into the river. This, I could not bear to be serious about and began to split my sides with laughter as I tried to catch up. I was still laughing when I got to the bank and made my jump and just like Bert, in I went and out again, hitting Bert as he tried to re-enter the raft. Now we were both in the river splitting our sides laughing, not a raft in sight other than ours, and on the banks of the river - W.T. telling us he still had confidence in us.

The unexpected dip in the cold mountain water seemed to do us both a lot of good. I began to snap out of my dizziness and Bert looked like he was in command of his faculties. Out and across the river into the deeper water on the far side we ventured. We knew what we had to do. Down the river we paddled like blazes, fighting to keep the raft clear of the jagged rocks and shallows. We had moved downriver about a mile before we caught up to some of the stragglers. This sighting injected a little hope into an otherwise deflated situation. At this point, Bert thought of an ingenious strategy - timing the paddle strokes. He roared back to me that it would pay big time to synchronize our paddle strokes on the count of "one - two." That way, we would achieve maximum paddling power. I liked the suggestion. It had a touch of militarism to it and if we were going to win, it would help enormously thinking the army was behind us on this effort.

Whatever was in the mix W.T. had given to us earlier was beginning to take hold. We paddled like desperate men. It was almost as though the safety of the world depended upon us winning the race. As we ran the current, eddies, and the rapids, we hollered to each other, encouraging ourselves every paddle of the way. About a mile downriver from the starting point, we caught up to the champions for the past three years running. As we tried to pass them, they tried to block us but the demons were in us and we pushed past them.

About a mile ahead loomed the finish line - the Princeton / Tullemeen bridge and it looked as if Bert and I were going to make it. Yes sir, it looked like we were going to win the raft race and bring the honors of victory back to Coalmont and Tullemeen! We were elated. Then the unbelievable happened. The water was lapping over the rafts side. We were beginning to take on water. It became obvious that the repair work had become unglued and we were sinking.

It seemed a shame to lose the race after all the extra effort that had gone into securing the raft. After the initial sinking feeling, it was decided that we both jump overboard and push the raft the rest of the way to the finish line. We had no other choice. At the count of three, Bert and I hopped overboard and promptly disappeared beneath the rush of the deep waters. When we surfaced, the raft had gone ahead of us quite a ways and curses were in vogue as we scrambled into shallower water. It was obvious now that we were not going to win the race nor even finish it for that matter. It was a bitter blow to us. Then, as we thought all was over, we noticed the raft had caught on a rock in the shallows and without thinking, Bert and I raced on down the river to retrieve it. All was not lost.

It was quite shallow along this part of the river, making it easy to run along its bed. We wasted no time in releasing the raft and pushed and pulled every inch of the way to the finish line. The rafts coming up behind us had run into the same problem in the shallows, thus allowing us to stay ahead of them. We crossed the finish line as the victors in the large raft category. We had done it.

WEDDING ON LONESOME MOUNTAIN AND THE WILD WOMEN OF SOCCER

Sheila and Mike who found employment upon arrival at the Coalmont hotel in the early part of the summer, decided to get married. The crew at the Coalmont felt it a wonderful idea. Big Bob suggested that he marry them up on the gold claim. The rest of us wondered what he meant by "he" marrying them up on the claim. To our merry surprise, he informed us that he was a legal minister of the church and was invested with the authority to marry people who wanted to get married but not the authority to marry those who did not want to get married. This we thought to be a very good thing indeed. The date was set - the place: Lonesome Mountain. Lonesome Mountain existed only as a pseudonym because the real name of the mountain was too hard to remember and too hard to pronounce. Lonesome Mountain was going to come alive, very much alive.

Our convoy was a rather odd assortment of vehicles as the tattered, motorized pieces of steel moved slowly out of Coalmont that late August Sunday afternoon, up the long winding trail to the mountain. This unusual assemblage gave hints of resembling one of those lost tribes of biblical times. Still, we were a well-knit group of gypsy like people given to the spirit of the event.

The clearing on the top of the mountain was a left over scar from earlier logging operations, a good example of horrific clear-cut logging practices. The scar gave an ugly twist to this pristine country and even though heavy drinking had blunted my senses, it did not ease my sadness towards the maimed landscape created by the asinine logging practices of government and business alike. Still, this day was a special day and attention must be given to the bride and groom to be. No time to be dwelling on the morose. No sir! There was much merrymaking to be made.

The sun was still high in the sky as we set about preparing the landscape to accommodate the sacred event in honor of the bride and groom. Before the ceremony took place, Mike and his wife to be were introduced to the fine art of gold panning. If the couple struck gold, they were to have a long and happy marriage with the blessing of many children. It was a sight to behold, as Sheila and Mike entered the frigid waters of the high mountains. Mike was given a pick and Sheila the gold pan. Soon, the glint of the fabled metal reflected in the light of the sun. Mike and Sheila had struck it rich. A great cheer arose from the crowd who had gathered along the bank of the creek - the celebrations had begun.

Robbie, the gold sniper (sniper: one who paces through the streams and creeks investigating the seams and cracks in the rocks in hopes of spotting trapped gold nuggets) sat on the stump of a tree paging through wads of newspaper. This was odd behavior for Robbie, because we knew him not as a man of literary interest. Then, when all papers seemed to have been investigated, he abruptly squashed and rolled them into one big round ball then bound it with string. When he seemed satisfied with his creation, he invited one and all to play a game of soccer football - the women against the men.

The usual search ensued for the pieces to make the goalposts and directives were given by one and all, to one and all as to how the game should be played. Every person, man and woman, one hundred in all, took to the field. Some played the game in cowboy boots, some in logging boots, others in high heels, still others in sandals; there were those who carried with them their handbags and there were the purists - insisting the game must be played in bare feet.

Well, there we were, on top of the world, a most ungentle group of humanity, belting and beating the hell out of each other on an uneven field of gravel, rocks and roots. The women seemed to fare the best. They just kicked their opponents instead of the ball and if that lack of soccer etiquette did not obtain favorable results, scratching, biting and screaming ensured it did. To be sure, it was not unusual for the men folk to receive a wallop across the face with a handbag and have every shred of clothing ripped from their person. The nature of these women, to be sure, was one of not losing.

I never really witnessed a contest so brutally fought. It was wonderful to be playing the old game of my childhood once again but I was not impressed with the barbaric assault the ladies made upon the men folk. I, who had a great measure of experience in the field of soccer, suffered miserably as I tried to finesse the ball with superb quality footwork, only to have a high heel stabbed into the top of my foot. It was not a nice experience. I thought it prudent to leave the field at once and become a spectator. It was a wise decision. The men folk, one by one, hobbled and limped from the field of soccer gladiators, some with bleeding noses, scratched faces, black eyes garnished with deep purple hues, to surrender to the more gentle pastime of nursing themselves.

It was clear the ladies intended to win the game, which they did by a very wide margin. The coveted prize - a bar of chocolate garnished with flakes of pure fresh gold obtained from the creek that very day. Congratulations being over and done, the victors set about repairing the assortment of injuries inflicted upon the vanquished. It was nice to have the women folk on our side once again.

Evening moved towards twilight - the precious moment of the ceremony. Then something happened that was not good under these circumstances. I fell into a deep sleep. I had consumed far too much wine. Falling asleep under these circumstances was not good because I was the one appointed to sing the wedding song. I had somehow found a nice nesting place behind an old outhouse that was left behind from those days of clear-cut logging. Deep was my sleep indeed. I awoke to the sound of running water. I could distinctly hear its gentle, rippling wash. It seemed like I was in a dream of mystical delight, basking in the wonder of nature. Above, in the firmament, the stars glinted their dance of the heavens as the northern lights rippled across the sky. All was peace and tranquility.

Somewhere in the distance of my mind the sound of voices rent the air, faint at first, then more clearly. "Come on John, its time to wake up, the wedding is about to take place," implored the voice of Hazel - then the sound of rippling water once again. Its sound grew louder and louder, so loud I began to feel its very essence. And feel it I did, because my good friends had carried me from that cozy place behind the outhouse where I was in a most gracious, drunken slumber and placed me in the frigid, pristine waters of Lonesome Mountain.

Apologies were made for this inhumane treatment suffered by my person but it was made clear to me that it was very necessary because in a few moments, the couple to be betrothed were to exchange vows. It was my profound and sacred duty to present myself in a manner of dignified composure at the Alter of love to sing the selected song.

Against the black of the night, a campfire flickered its fiery waves, giving a mystical radiance to the solemn starlit sky. Quietness descended across the camp. The soft, gentle summer breeze hummed its pleasure as the rippling of the stream lent its magical sound to the sweetness of the moment.

Shivering, saturated and dripping, I was led gently by the hand of Hazel from the creek bed to the candlelit table of love as I complained as discretely as possible about my unnecessary baptism. Big Bob looked splendid in his handmade buckskin outfit. Standing with Bible in hand, he began the ceremony. Not a whisper was heard except for the dull thud of a body hitting the ground. It was unfortunately my body. The proceedings were held up momentarily while my body was picked up and held up against the side of an old truck. Robbie held firmly to my left shoulder and Bert did likewise to my right. Sharron had the honor of placing the guitar in my hands and its strap across my shoulder. I was in business. Sharron stayed with me through my ordeal, as I kept asking her to remind me of the song I was to sing. She promised me she would.

The flickering of the campfire served only to draw my intoxicated mind into those dreamlike realms. There I was, physically supported by three of my closest friends as the essence of my being rambled through those places of the universe, far removed from the solemnity of the occasion. Big Jim the miner decided to help me from my detachedness. He fetched a large bag of crushed ice from the cooler and placed around my neck and true to form I called him a dirty swine for doing a most uncomplimentary thing to my person. However, it did help my mind return to the scene of the wedding ceremony on Lonesome Mountain. Sweet Sharron comforted me over the nasty behavior of the big miner and I welcomed her caring words.

Through all of the extracurricular behavior, the ceremony moved with the grace and dignity, to that of a swan, gliding through the waters of its tranquil sanctuary. Resplendent was the bride in her home fashioned dress of delights - the barman resolute in his Sunday cowboy attire. The gold rings reflected the magic of the fire's dance as the marriage was sanctified. Mike and Sheila were now man and wife. Sharron, at this point, reminded me that the song to be sung was none other than the "Rose." I thanked her. However, I still could not remember how the words of the song began. I had to get Sharron's attention once more.

"I'll ask you one question, if you don't mind Sharron?" I said to her as the shadow of my head swayed from side to side across the foreground of the campfire. And Sharron replied. "What is the question Johnny, my boy?" As her lovely smile lit up the night more magically and more beautifully than the morning sun could give delight to a bleak landscape. "Please tell me Sharron," I whispered as softly as any drunk could. "How does the song start?"

The night moved on to the sound of song and merriment. I had recovered a good measure from the earlier sleeping effects of booze. I was not sure if recuperation was due to my being placed in the cold running creek as I slept or attributed to the effects of John Barleycorn. A large circle was formed around the campfire and each of us took a turn in singing a song or telling a story. Even Bert, who possessed a voice much more unfavorable than my father's, belted out an old cowboy favorite, "Don't Fence Me In" and was given a tumultuous round of applause. Big Bob's hut was made into a honeymoon suite for the newly Weds. All was wonderfully well on Lonesome Mountain.

The songbirds were singing their praises to the morning's glory as my eyes gazed towards the last star before the approaching light. It was a nice way to leave the world for a while.

I awoke to the unpleasantness of the sun's intense heat. It was about noon. Vehicles were beginning to move on down the mountain towards Tullemeen and Coalmont. Fond farewells were exchanged as the wedding reception on Lonesome Mountain came to an end. The gold digging boys held back while the guests made for their homes. We broke a cap on another bottle, delaying the dissipation of the magic we experienced on the mountaintop. However, there was no time to tarry. Sharron informed us of a storm moving in. It was time to leave. I'm glad we listened to Sharron. The storm did break, causing havoc on the dirt road. Lightening bounced across the sky and the thunder split the heavens in a rare show of unimaginable power. The vehicle did more sliding down the trail than wheeling but Sharron got us safely to the hotel and out of trouble.

In the evening, Sharron and her friends moved across the back roads to Merrit, her hometown, leaving us miners and wanderers to providence. As the glasses of beer were ordered, I began to think about traveling a new trail. Although a man could not have more freedom anywhere than this part of the country afforded him, something inside, that gnawing at the heart, the answer I was searching for was not by the gold creeks. I was, after all, in the heart of the wilderness but it gave not a hint of my purpose. What could it possibly be? Where could I find it? Kilroy may have been wrong. What was this thing that drove me onwards with seemingly no purpose attached to it? Could it possible be the camaraderie, the free spirited interaction with the land and the people that had taken place over the past few months? If it was, I did not recognize it? Was it not the Master, Jesus that said; be like children once again and you shall find purpose and happiness in your hearts. Yes, indeed, the Master said so, but I was too blind to see and feel the true essence of life without booze. That time of pleasant, sober feeling and true laughter was far away - but I would try to reach it!

SAILOR TO THE RESCUE AND THE DIRTY DANCERS

Singing for beer does not put money in a man's pocket. It was time to call my good friend, Jack Gibson the sailor.

A couple of days passed before Jack arrived in the high country; it was good to see him. I had sobered up somewhat during the wait but that respite ended as a great boozing session began once again. A week later saw Jack and me bid adieu to our friends at Coalmont and head out over the back trails to the town of Merrit where my friend Sharron lived. Jack and I were making pretty good time in the old truck until it developed a radiator leak. Things were not looking good for us. We had to get water but where? We were stuck on the back road to Merrit, a road rarely used by vehicles. Jack suggested that we get out of the truck and throw stones into the dark. Jack was a smart man, high on the thinking scale but for the life of me, I had no idea why he wanted us to throw stones into the dark.

A cigarette lighter was flicked to give light to find stones along the trail. A goodly amount was collected. "Now," said Jack, "you throw your stones out over the left side of the trail and I will throw mine to the right."

"Why on earth are we throwing stones into the darkness?" I asked, betraying a little irritability in my voice.

"Oh, because if there is water out there we can go get some," he said. I thought him mad but decided to go along with the plan. Into the night we threw stones and more stones. Nothing of a water sound was heard. It was time to call this mad activity quits. And then it happened.

Out there in the blackness of night somewhere, a stone had found its mark. *Flopppp*, the sound we were straining our ears for interrupted the silence of the night. We had struck it rich! Jack, being excellent in the art of giving directions to others, placed the gasoline can in one of my hands, a cup in the other and sent me out to God knows where in search of water.

It seemed silly but necessary to be stumbling over rocks, clumps of grass and any other object nature had devised to hinder in my search in the blackness of the unknown. I had moved through the night, a goodly distance from the position of our truck. I could easily discern this, because Jack's voice was sounding farther and farther away from me. It was obvious Jack was able to throw a stone a far, far, greater distance than I could. I figured he had spent some time playing baseball and he no doubt was a pitcher. This bothered me somewhat because some of those baseball guys had no trouble in making a ball disappear while still on its travel through the sky. Still, out I ventured, farther and farther into the unknown and at last, there was a hint by Mother Nature that water was near.

It wasn't a pleasant hint because suddenly, the earth came to visit around my waist. I had walked into a mud hole. I could hear Jack's voice faintly calling from the far distance. He was wondering if I had found any water. I wanted to go back and choke him for sending me out into trails unknown but now I truly knew the meaning of being "a stick- in-the-mud". I had to dig myself out before I went to visit the land down-under. Extracting myself from the mud hole was not an easy chore. I was fortunate in that I carried a large gas container. I placed the airtight container on top of the mud, using it as a leverage point and pushed myself up by the forearms, thereby extracting myself from a rather unpleasant situation. I tried the best I could to circumnavigate whatever I was circumnavigating, hoping I was inching myself ever closer to the place where we had earlier heard the sound of *flopppp*.

Out there somewhere ahead of me was water but where I had no idea. Cloud cover prevented the moon from shedding a light on my situation and striking matches to guide me through the night was absolutely asinine. I was stumped! Then, a movement, the sound of a fish breaking the water's surface, followed by the call of the loon! I was close.

Approximately an hour had passed, since I ventured forth into the unknown. I had the goods Jack sent me for. As the water poured into the radiator, with it went tiny clumps of grass, weeds, mud, pebbles and a host of organisms that had been minding their own business out in the mud flats but now found themselves circulating in the cooling system of an old truck. Life was just not fair to some.

An hour later, I was with my Merrit friends dancing up a storm at the Valnicola Hotel. This would be my last visit to Merrit for a very long time. My friend Sharron, fortunately, was there to greet me as I wandered in, in my mud-covered frame - bits of the wilderness clinging to my clothes and me smelling like a dirty sofa. Still, she was happy to see me. Jack fell in love with her, as any man would, because there was about this lovely woman - a magic, that I am sure is found only among the delightful. After a while, it became noticeable that I could not maneuver on the dance floor as well as when I had first arrived. In time, I discovered what the problem was.

The mud had congealed and then hardened. I was beginning to resemble the dried mud flats of the Serengeti Desert - all cracked up. Pretty soon, however, I went through a complete metamorphosis as I shed my muddy burden upon the dance floor, relieving myself of the responsibility of future gardening. It was a fine night but as with most nights like this one, I would suffer its comeback. I loved my friends. Indeed, I loved my wife but there was something I loved far more and hated equally so - alcohol. It was killing me. It was killing me inside and out but the will to live overruled the morose and depressive bouts that followed. It was good to feel good when I was drunk. It was a rare occasion. The feeling gave me something to go on, something to look forward to. I just did not know what it was.

I would bid Sharron and my friends in Merrit adieu the following morning as Jack and I headed west to Vancouver Island. It would be some time before I would return to these fair lands of the beautiful Nicola Valley. In his death, David had created a journey for me - a journey I would undertake to discover "things" of life, a land and its people, the richness and loveliness of the Nicola Valley, for it was indeed as beautiful as its melodious name. It was out there by the Nicola Lake, below the hill where David, my singing friend from Scotland had ended his life, that I sat by the water's banks and penned the lines of "David's Song"

When my soul feels weary, I stand by the shores
Of the wild windy waters of the lake I adore,
As I gaze out in wonder, out over the deep,
Its here I find comfort, its here I find peace.
There's peace in this valley, surrounded by beauty,
There's hope and there's dreams and the passing of care.
Its wild and its free in this heavenly valley,
That's kissed by the breath of the pure mountain air.

Where the eagle soars above the high mountain
Where the wild flowers bloom in the meadows of spring,
Where friends stand beside you and help you when needed
And the evening surrenders in quietness and still
Yes, there's peace in this valley, surrounded by beauty,
There's hope and there's dreams and the passing of care,
Its wild and its free in this heavenly valley
That's kissed by the breadth of the pure mountain air.

NANAIMO BOUND AND BLACKBEARD'S PUB

There was a hint of autumn in the fresh morning air as Jack and I headed out along highway 42, towards Spences Bridge. From Spences Bridge, we drove through the spectacular Fraser Canyon, known for its breathtaking scenery and its rich history. It was in this canyon that gold was discovered in the nineteen hundreds. It was here that deadly battles were fought between Indians and whites. It was here that many Chinese people lost their lives to the roaring waters of the mighty Fraser as the workers tore away at the rock to lay level the ground for the coming of the transcontinental railway. It was in this canyon that many lives were lost to the snow slides, mudslides and the endless accidents during tunnel blasting in order to push a road through to the West. This was mountainous country in the real sense of the word. These mountains had extracted a high price in human lives before they stubbornly gave way, inch by inch, until at last the road was pushed through to the rich and fertile lands of the Fraser valley, completing the connection of the highway and railroads from the Maritimes to the Pacific Coast.

On we motored through the towns and tunnels - Boston Bar, China Bar, Hell's Gate - infamous for the day in history when scores of Chinese railroad workers had suspended themselves from ropes and dangling precariously above the turbulent waters of the Fraser river had grasped long haul ropes and pulled a stern wheeler through the thundering waters of the narrows of Hell's Gate, so she could continue on her way to the interior city of Kamloops. It was a memorable feat indeed and a very proud moment for a people who were so brutally subjected to racial prejudice. On we moved towards the town of Hope, nestled at the foot of the Coast Mountains - a footstep away from the Fraser Valley and one hundred miles from the city of Vancouver. This land was indeed diverse, lovely in the extreme and very, very rich, in its not so old history.

It was late afternoon when we reached the ferry terminal at Horsehoe Bay. It felt good to breathe the fresh, salty air of the Pacific Ocean as the ferry, The Queen of Nanaimo, bore us across the waters to the city of her namesake. Jack's sister lived there. She invited me to stay at her home. There I would recoup my senses and get in touch with the feeling of sobriety once again. Day by agonizing day, I began to return to the person I really was. It was nice to be back in my skin again. It was now time to find a gig, get back to playing music on a serious level and cut the crap out. The intentions were good but hard as I tried, my boozing journey was far from over and it would be here in this city of Nanaimo, I would come to know the depths of the great sickness alcoholism even more.

Eventually I secured a gig at Blackbeard's, a pub in the basement of the Malaspina Hotel. The pay was good. I had also secured a room at the hotel. I was set. I could now live high on the hog; the best of foods, singing in the evening and doing what I liked through the day. Life had taken a sudden turn for the better. Impoverished one day, the lifestyle of a millionaire the next. I thanked Jack's sister for her hospitality and moved into a plush room on the top floor overlooking the harbor of Nanaimo. From my window, the old colonial fort stood atop the cliffs of the harbor - a forlorn sentinel, faithfully waiting and watching as though it expected the sea to carry back from the past, familiar faces that sailed away into the mists beyond its shores. And beyond the fort, the islands of Protection and Gabriola and beyond these islands, the inside passage of the Pacific - a silvery, glinting carpet stretching across to the foot of the snow-crested Coastal Mountains of the mainland. There could not, in all creation, be a more pleasing setting to the eye. It was indeed, awe-inspiring and lovely beyond description.

Singing at Blackbeard's was a favorable experience and to show my appreciation to the good management and crew, I got about to writing a commercial for the namesake of the bar.

Chorus
Good old Blackbeard, a pirate through and through,
He's many a wife on a fine cold night and many that weren't his too
He'd sail the salt sea over with his motley looking crew
And he did all right in a high seas fight and he loved clam chowder Too.

So began my introduction to the singing world in the city of Nanaimo, Vancouver Island. Blackbeard's song was used on the local radio as a commercial. Nanaimo was good to me. I was beginning to stash away a few dollars in a bank account and even splurged on a new twelve-string guitar. Things were looking up.

It was an unusually quiet evening at Blackbeard's as I sung a few old folksongs in the bar, a pleasant change from the boisterousness the evenings usually brought. I had just completed singing Blackbeard's Ballad, when a man resembling Blackbeard the pirate approached me. "Howya doin buddy? Names Ali. Sure love your singing… come and join our table for a few minutes and I'll grab you a drink, " the big man who looked like a modern day pirate said. "Thanks my friend but I rarely drink – perhaps another time . . ." But before I finished, the pirate took control of the conversation. "The girl friend, she just loves to hear dem der ballads your singing and she would be mighty disappointed if you did not join us for a drink… how about it buddy… just for one… okay?" the bearded one said, his hands extended forward as thought he were starving and begging for a crust of bread. I faltered and then succumbed to the lure of the silent killer. It was a big mistake, a very big mistake indeed. It was clear to me that I must resolve to mean "no" when I say "no" because my very life swung in the balance by omitting that very little word from my vocabulary.

Suddenly, the small success I had in establishing myself as a folksinger in a new city, a new place was gone. My circle of drinking buddies widened. Mornings found me nursing my head in one of the early morning watering holes. Still, I would try to pace myself so I could at least put in an appearance at Blackbeard's. There was a lot of fun in that old pub but I wasn't part of it. At any time when one is suffering from a hangover, it is very difficult to function as a human being let alone do a job. Trying to sing and pretending I'm having a ball for four or five hours an evening under such circumstances is insanity at its best.

Even so, there were evenings when I was feeling half alive, so I was able to do half a show - half a human being doing half a show - the perfect equation. I hung in at Blackbeard's for six months but the hotel went into receivership, the doors closed - I was on my way. It was time for me to find myself a new gig.

The crew at the Brass Key, a private club in Nanaimo took me to heart. Once again I was settled in, singing to my hearts content. It was here, in this small lounge that I would enjoy some of the best nights of entertaining. It was here that the night of the INCO rebellion back in '68 was recalled to memory, that night in Thompson when I had first arrived in Canada, that night when the butter stuck to the ceiling, seats and chairs were tossed through the windows, buildings torn apart and security men were beaten, all came back in an instant. The Brass Key lounge seemed a strange place for such a reminder to happen but it did and with good reason.

Sixteen years had passed since that fateful night. Beside me at the long bar in the Brass Key sat a burly man, sipping a beer. His name was Doug Mac Cee. A conversation began between us and soon we touched on the subject of Thompson and the infamous night of '68. Doug was a veteran cop with the RCMP and had been stationed in Thompson as an undercover agent to report on those unusual happenings that made politicians and multinationals nervous. It was an interesting conversation. I would get to know Doug a lot better, so well in fact, that I would find myself employed as a salesman for his company. In the months ahead, I would embark on a career of selling those things that people watch, causing them to turn into couch potatoes.

In time, the conversation drifted from the business in Thompson to that of Dough's property which needed to be landscaped - an opportunity I jumped at.

AMONG THE GODS OF THUNDER

Turbulence built in the clouds as I worked the garden that Wednesday afternoon. Doug and his family were away for the day. A thunderstorm approached. It hit hard and fast. As the rains poured, lightening struck and the thunder split the heavens, I retreated to the safety and comfort of Doug's house.

I had read a little about astral traveling. I did not fully understand its concept - something to do with the soul releasing itself from one's body. It sounded fascinating, a subject of much interest to many but in my case relegated to the realms of curiosity. However, that was about to change.

From the window, I watched as the ships plied the stormy waters of the straits of Georgia, bouncing, heaving, and rolling on old Neptune's gloomy face. I sipped on a nice hot cup of coffee as I watched the energies of the universe unfold. Beside me lay a Bible. It was rare for me to pay attention to this Holy Book. Out of curiosity, I began to leaf through its pages. I was not looking for any particular passage; in fact, I was not looking for anything the Bible might have to offer. It just happened to be close by. The thunder grew louder and the lightening seemed to burn the very face of the earth and beyond into the far reaches of the sky. The rains lashed unmercifully as the clouds churned to the thunder's symphony, wondrous and mystique - its power and immensity beyond description. Then, suddenly, I was among the clouds. I had entered into the very essence of nature.

My spirit seemed to be encapsulated in a bubble, tumbling along through the turbulence of the sky. I was a part of everything in creation and everything in creation was part of me; yet, I was unique and individual. I was the energy within the cloud, the raindrop, the lightening bolt - it was all me and I was all it - we were indeed one. My spirit moved with all that is. There were no barriers. I simply passed through the heavens and earth. As my spirit moved with the energies, my hands leafed through the Book of the New Testament. I sipped on my coffee and experienced the sensations of both worlds, separated but connected. To be sure such an experience is beyond description. I was booze free. In fact, I felt quiet healthy since it had been some time since I had had a drink. Beyond certainty, I knew in the heart of my existence, I did not want to return to this world - and when my spirit returned from the powers of the heavens, I was very sad. I was very sad indeed.

When the storm moved on I was left to wonder at what had just happened to me. I had been momentarily a part of the make up of the Universal energies - perhaps I always was but just to blind to see and feel it. The power of the great God had touched me; that I knew for certain.

Later, I traveled with Doug to Victoria, the capitol of B C, to attend a business convention. It was a pleasant evening, the meeting successful. Business matters attended to, I retired to the hotel room to settle in for the evening. Later, Doug arrived. We chatted for a while and then Doug retired to an adjacent room. It was his practice to give thanks in prayer to the Great Creator before retiring, a custom I had put on hold a long time ago. The sun was burning across the sky as it too was retiring from the world and as it slowly sank below the horizon, I felt myself drift out of my body, out towards the sun. There was no unpleasant sensation. It was beautiful beyond description.

I was just drifting through the Universe, free from all physical sensation. I was indeed truly alive. The colors were exquisitely vibrant. I was a part of the color. It was part of me. I was part of everything. It was part of me. I was free from guilt, shame and judgment - all the trappings of human enslavement - to be sure I was free. No maps, no fear. I was one with all and again, I did not wish to return - but I did. Again, I felt the sensations of both worlds, connected but apart. I felt the Hand of God, the Power of God, the Sweetness of God, the Essence of God as I floated above and beyond and yet, I knew this was a simple fraction of the Eternal Glory, the Eternal Beauty, the Majesty and Delight of the Freedoms and the Blessings of the Heavens - and there, for you and me, a place, in the Heart of God.

I asked the Powers that be, to leave me to travel free from my body, free from the world I fought hard to survive in, free from myself and my inability to find and live by the truth; free from the madness of my make-up. But it was not to be. Again I returned to the physical world and watched as the sun dipped below the horizon. I did not know what was happening to me but I was not afraid. I slept well that night. Early morning saw Doug and me head back to Nanaimo. I told him what had happened. He was silent for a while, then, told me that it was the Power of the Holy Ghost that had touched me. With respect to my Creator, I did not feel that this was the case, yet, I wondered, why these out of the body experiences were happening to me only when I was around or in Doug's company. For a man who had sat across from me in the cafeteria of the INCO camp sixteen years previous in the mining Town of Thompson Manitoba as angry employees tore the place asunder, venting their anger of unfair treatment towards them by the Company, held something of a nature I could not put my finger on. Perhaps I never would.

While Doug was scouring the business world for opportunities, I bided my time at the Brass Key, singing and entertaining to my heart's content. Things were going well for me and I was making a good wage. Life was good, full and satisfying - until one day.

WALKING UPON THE WATERS

"Let's hit the waves," said the tug boater, Jack, whom I had not seen for a month or so. He had borrowed a speedboat from his lady friend Donna besides me, he invited two of our buddies, Dave Vestment and Criss Dingwell to travel with us for a few days on Old Salty's waves. I liked the idea.

"Its sure nice of Donna to lend you the craft Jack. How come she's not riding with us?" I asked him.

"She's a normal person John – not given to the mad adventure roll, know what I mean? There's got to be some responsible people in the world to run things – cant leave that type of stuff to lads like us – the world is in a bad enough mess as it is. Yes siree, Lady Donna is the best, John boy - a man couldn't wish for a better woman," Jack said as he turned the key of the craft to fire the engine. I agreed. I had met lady Donna on a number of occasions and I was mighty impressed with the gentle, loving nature of the woman and, in time, I would come to know this good person as a close friend and confidant.

The sun was sinking in its fiery folds as the Sangster eased out from Nanaimo harbor. On board were the usual staples necessary for a successful trip - beer, whiskey, vodka, Jack Daniels, wine in case some mermaids came aboard and a little food and a lot of fishing gear. The milky hues of the sleeping waters' gave rise to nature's resplendent setting as Jack opened the throttle, churning a wake to the stern. The glory of the moment demanded that I partake of the good things supplied by the distillers and to forget all about the pains of the past that it had caused me. And so I did. It was time to celebrate, to give thanks to the great God for the wonderful world he had created for me.

The first swig of whiskey did the job, the second even more so. The world grew more tranquil by the moment. I was not a whiskey drinker. I was a beer drinker. It never occurred to me that I should not drink whisky like I drank beer. It was too late. Its effect was almost instantaneous. The sky appeared to blend with the water and soon I could not distinguish between either one. I was now one with all and all was one with me. The bold sailor piloted his craft towards the Island of Texeada in full control of his faculties while Criss and Dave sang the sea shanty "What Shall We Do With The Drunken Sailor. The setting for an extraordinary trip could not be more complete. Our little craft was graced with the Sangster / Singers duo, ranting their songs of the sea to the tranquil face of Old Neptune as the vastness of the glazed waters beckoned to our importance while I glugged on a bottle of whiskey – my gaze drawn to the silver furrow of the boat's wake.

The engine's sharp pitch eased almost to that of a soft summers breeze as the effect of the whiskey upon my mind took on spiritual elements. The mystical qualities of the crafts wake – its opalescent umbilical cord – fading into the horizon – as I prepared to emulate the Master, Jesus. The waters' were right there. Why not walk upon them. All I had to do was to step on the top of the world of fishes and walk, just like the Master did in those Biblical times so long ago. Alone in my secret world of illusion I determined to imitate the Master. This undertaking would not require the assistance of a life jacket nor should I inform Jack or the singing duet of my intentions because this was a personal and sacred quest. Stepping from the speeding craft to the boys singing the song of the Drunken Sailor would add the perfect touch of dramatic dementia to the undertaking. The singers should be left alone and the captain should not be bothered.

The time had come for me to depart from the boats confines. A bottle in my hand, a foot on the gunwale and one long look at the sterns wake and I was on my way - just a teeny weenie step into the world of "oneness". And in that world I entered, I knew naught but blackness and quiet. Such blackness and quiet that I did not even know I was there.

From the wilderness, a voice called. "Steak and fish! Come and get it, steak and fish!" My eyes pierced the star-filled night. Was I dead? Was I alive? I did not know. The voice called again, "Steak and fish - come and get it." The stars flickered above the dancing streams of the aurora; then there was nothing. The stars had disappeared - the great blackness saturating my spirit into oblivion – my non existence complete.

Then from the morning sky a light that burnt deep into my eyes. I was alive but did not know if it was in death or life. Close by my ear I heard the gentle lap of water, then a voice of distant familiarity. "Time to wake up, John," the voice said. "Its bin three days and nights since you've bin in the land of the dead. Come on ol' buddy, time to come into the world." I discerned that it was Criss's voice but where I was and what had taken place over the past three days, I did not know. I felt sick, very, very sick. I wanted to go back to sleep; in fact I wanted to die. But the good Lord had other plans. I was going to live, going to suffer and suffer I did. I had no idea what had happened to me, how I had gotten into the state I was in and no recollection of the trip. I was indeed in a real mess. As I lay beneath my sleeping bag, an uncapped beer was handed to me. I knew I had to drink it in order to get feeling better. I did.

As the evening approached, twelve beers had taken the sting out of my sickness but I was on the way to getting drunk again. I cursed myself for getting into this state but at the same time felt helpless in avoiding the lure of the bottle. I was unhappy, perhaps the most unhappy man in the world. Guilt soon tore at my mind, as did remorse, shame and self-pity. But what to do I did not know. I needed help. But who could help? Had I the courage to ask for it? These and many more nagging questions flooded my mind. If this was being a real man, I wanted no part of it. I was a hard worker and when I decided to see a project through - it got done. But where did that strength go? Where did the ability to live responsibly and decently go? Where did the real laughter go? Where did my self-respect vanish?

I knew what it was like to walk in the valley of death and I knew what it was like to fear evil. It was around me, pulling, tugging and tearing me apart. I could not touch it but it could touch me. I could not see it but it could see me. I could feel it though, and it was destroying me. I knew I was a far better person than what I was becoming but this evil had me in its grip and slowly but surely dragging me along its road of death. And I could only ask time and again - how did this awful thing happen to me?

I had to find a way to fight back, to gain control of my life. I was beaten and afraid, a child truly crying in the wilderness and a bloody bleak one at that. All sense of dignity, self respect and pride had vanished from my make-up. I was alive but in truth I had died a long time ago. I had to go back and find the man that once was.

Three weeks had passed since the Pacific drunk. I was beginning to feel something like human. It was not to last long. Party after party followed and soon the bottle had complete mastery over me. Each morning as I awoke, my hand reached out from my bed across the floor in search of the bottle I had placed there by my bed the night before I had "crashed out." If I was out of booze, I had to make the torturous trip to one of the early morning bars, shaking like a vibrating conveyor belt as I tried to get the first beer down.

This ritual became my morning pastime. How I managed to entertain and stay alive is beyond my understanding. Someone must have felt it worthwhile to keep me alive - but who? Was it the ones gone before me who walked with me and prayed for my deliverance? Was it the constant prayers of my mother asking God to take care of her lost son? Was it the good Lord Himself who protected me from the madness that had gripped me? I did not know.

I walked like a cursed thing, alone, a mongrel lost to eternity, through the streets of Nanaimo. I may have looked human but all decency had deserted me. My soul, too, seemed to have flown; tired of the walls I had built to prevent it from expressing its essence. A body walking, pacing through the depths of hell - I had gone insane and I knew it. I became very frightened at the thought that I might not be able to retreat from the insanity that gripped my mind. The pain of silence was very real. It was the silence of the lost. On the sidewalk ahead of me rambled a little cocker spaniel dog, seemingly contented with his lot in life. That was the contentment I wanted. I would have gladly traded places with the little bowser. In fact, I envied the cute little fellow as he plodded merrily on his way, unaware that this poor human wanted to share in his contented space of mind.

REACHING OUT

There came a man one day to my abode. He had heard about my plight through the grapevine. He was an older man, wiser from his own battles with the bottle. He understood the madness that had reduced me to less than nothing. Through his advice and guidance, I entered a twelve-step program, thus beginning the fight back to the man that once was. Time and again I would falter, fall and cry to the heavens but the road back to sanity was being rebuilt, slowly, sometimes very slowly but it was being built with the help of the world's greatest engineers - those who had had suffered as I had and had paved the roads back to their sanity and kept them open for the others - the ones to follow.

The time had come to face the demons that tore at my soul. I had been shown a way out of the miseries I had endured for so long. The light was once again upon my path. I had been a slave far too long to a poison that had taken more lives than all wars combined. Alcoholism knew no boundaries; its devastation in human terms limitless, and those who fell victim to its lure were unfortunate indeed. Its grip upon me at last had been loosened but this silent murderer would lay in wait, perpetually impatient for the opportunity to strike at me again.

Doug Mac Cee opened a home entertainment center in the vine paradise of Canada, Kelowna, BC. It was time to take a break from the entertaining, get away from the drinking scene and try my hand at selling things people watch and listen to. The summer of '84 was blistering. Being of the fair race, I had a hard time with hot weather and, coupled with my displeasure of the weather, I also did not like my job. I did not like selling things to people. It made me uncomfortable. I was now faced with the dilemma that I may fall victim to booze if I returned to the field of entertainment and I possessed too heavy a guilt complex to develop a career in sales. What to do, I did not know but whatever I did, it was not going to be selling. I confronted Doug about my state of mind and it was decided that I leave the business of selling and give entertainment a try once more. I was on my way.

REFUGE IN THE FOREST

The winter of '84 was one of the most bitter Revelstoke had experienced for years. I secured a gig at the King Edward Hotel that would see me through for some months. Although I was back entertaining, I was really at loose ends. I was stuck between a rock and a hard place. I wanted out of the bar business once and for all but what to do I did not know. Winter slipped into spring, then the blistering summer.

It was a busy night at the King Edward Lounge, the usual weekend energy spending itself and I was singing to the life of it all. As the night wore on, I chanced to fall into the company of bushmen who were bent on having a good time. Somehow the conversation got around to logging, not an unusual happening among bush men. However, these men did something quite different than the usual logging practices and what they did appealed to my senses. A shake-blocker was something I had never heard of before. I was of the opinion that it was some kind of a block that one shook the hell out of and that was the sum total of my opinion. However, in time, it was explained what the true nature of being a shake-blocker entailed.

Pablo De Pocco was a man who liked his booze but no matter the amount of booze he consumed, he always imparted information with the knowledge and ease of a veteran bush man. What Pablo had to say about the life of a shake-blocker interested me. It had all the air and ring to it that was ideal for a wanderer like me. Away from it all so to speak, out in the mountains. I put my guitar away and off to the bush I went with Pablo and his crew to set up camp, prepare for the shake-blocker's experience and be eaten alive by every filthy insect that flew on wings. For the next seven years, I would spend my life shake-blocking in the Rocky Mountains.

"It is really hard to explain what a shake-blocker is all about," said Pablo as we traveled along the old Big Bend highway toward the Downey claim. Pablo and his crew had been working the claim for some months and were doing real well. "This is the way it is John," said Pablo. "We go after the big cedar trees but only the ones that are dead standing and the ones that have fallen in the storms. When we locate a cedar, we cut it into two-foot lengths. We may cut as many as fifty lengths from one tree. When this part of the operation is complete we stand the rounds up just like you would a barrel and remove the bark from it. Then we chop the round like you would cut into a pizza or an apple pie. Now you have maybe four or eight pieces of triangular shaped wood all two feet in length. From these pieces of wood which we refer to as blocks, we chop out the knots, making the block knot free. It is then sent, with a few thousand other blocks to the mill and there made into shakes or "roof slates," a term you may be more familiar with." Pablo explained it very well.

The coming months were to see me struggle immeasurably - I was in terrible physical shape. But I stuck with it and as much as I hated the blasted bugs, lightening strikes, bear raids, trees falling back on me and a host of other unpredictables, I began to develop a taste for the forest work. I learned my trade well and it was a life style that absolutely suited me. I was at last free. No one to answer to, except the forest service if I did not stick to the rules and regulations and at times I was made answer to them for my transgressions. Eventually, Pablo and his crew quit and took off to other places. I decided to remain out on the Downey claim to keep working it. Alone in the forest was a different ball game altogether. There was no room for a mistake. If I made one, it could well be the last.

The town of Revelstoke was built around the 1870's on the banks of the mighty Columbia River to accommodate the expansion of the transcontinental railway. Forty miles north of Revelstoke, lies one of the most beautiful spots in the world, simply known as Downey. Here, at the turn of the twentieth century, came a man who purchased a piece of land nestling at the foot of the great mountains along the shore of the majestic Columbia. He opened a coffee shop and gas station to cater to the travelers of the Big Bend Highway. The supplier of the gasoline was the Esso Company. Thus, he became known as Esso Ed. Indeed, my Esso calendar pictures on the walls of my schoolrooms from the past had come alive.

Ed had passed on some years before my arrival in the country and his estate was passed on to his next of kin, people whom I would come to know and grow very fond of. I was fortunate to come to know the Monk family because it was to these good people I would seek aid from when things went wrong for me and such occasions were a little more than I cared for.

The tree stood close to a hundred and fifty feet tall. There was not one green branch growing from its rusty trunk, indicating it was a dead standing tree. These were the trees the shake-blockers were allowed to salvage, plus the trees that had been blown over in a storm. The October winds were biting fiercely as I placed the wedge into the cut I had made across the back of the tree, the undercut in the leaning side already completed. I drove in the wedge easily and carefully until it gripped solidly. Now I could put more wallop into the swing of the back of the axe driving the wedge home to topple the tree.

The afternoon was quickly growing towards the early winter twilight. I had little more than an hour of daylight to operate in. A light film of frost covered my axe handle, as it did the wedge I had just placed in the cut. Raising the axe to shoulder height, I focused my swing on the back of the bright yellow wedge.

I do not know how long I had been out but when I came to, I had one massive bump on my forehead and my head screamed for a sedative. The back of the axe had glanced off the wedge causing the wedge to fly backwards out of the cut. It had happened in the twinkling of an eye and had hit me square center on the forehead, knocking me back a good fifteen feet into a ditch. It was now full twilight as I walked the trail down to the river where my raft lay moored. Across the Columbia, the light of Esso Ed's reflected against the growing darkness. The waters of the river moved placidly through the valley of the great mountains as the old twin two-stroke puttered towards the far shore. I was thankful for the calmness of the evening. As I secured the raft and made my way towards the safety of the cabin's light I felt as though the last vestiges of life were withdrawing from my body.

"My God, John, you look so ghastly pale, and the cut on your forehead!

What on earth happened to you?" Margaret asked as she brewed up some coffee. I was among good people, these people who had inherited this splendid setting.

"I was not paying proper attention to my work, Margaret," I replied. As I sat and pondered my state of affairs, Margaret fetched me a few aspirin to help improve the feeling of my headspace. This incident was the beginning of a series of events that would truly test my mettle and the follow-up was not long in coming.

The snows were hitting hard as I headed out along the Big Bend on a late November morning. The red indicator light on the truck panel flashed its warning. I had no idea what it might be - I just ignored it and kept going. It was late morning when I turned off the highway down the trail where the raft was moored. Then it happened. The truck's engine stalled! Luckily, the grade of the trail was steep enough for the truck to roll on down to where my raft lay and there I parked it. I figured I would fix it when I came back in the evening but for now, I had a day's work to put in. The old two-stroke fired with ease as I moved out across the water to the far side of the Columbia. I had an uncomfortable feeling about my truck but I tried to put that business to the back of my mind.

Upon reaching the far side of the Columbia, I moored the raft, started the snowmobile and moved on up the trail to my work area. The wind blew with cold venom across the snow-cloaked landscape, singing its forlorn song to all within its domain. The tall trees resembled legions of frozen sentinels sullenly awaiting the first hints of spring. The land was indeed cold, forbidding and brutally harsh and the sound of the quieted engine of my snowmobile gave rise to such ominous feelings. The engine quit and try as I might, I could not restart it. I decided to walk the rest of the way to my place of work.

The great cedar stood mightily tall and handsomely round. A tree like this would give a fine yield of prime wood. Things had not been going too well of late in the finance department and in order to keep my head above water, I had to get a good haul of wood to the mill. The tree I was about to bring down would help alleviate that problem.

I studied the lean of the tree. It was difficult to discern which way it was leaning since it appeared to have grown vertically to perfection. I put in the undercut on the side of the tree I thought had a slight lean to it and then proceeded to put in the back cut. I had made a mistake, a bad one. I had not duly taken into consideration the side of the tree that possessed the heavier branches. In a moment, the tree leaned back on the blade of my saw pinching it firmly. Hard as I tried, I could not free it. The winds blew a little stronger, its buffeting causing the tree to lean back even further on the blade of the saw and towards my own position. It was becoming a very dangerous situation. The constant buffeting by the wind weakened the tree even more and the more it leaned back the more it pressed down on the blade of the saw.

It happened suddenly, without warning. A powerful gust of wind whipped through the tree line, snapping the giant at the cut, sending it falling towards me. It was not a nice experience being stuck in deep snow, weighted down in winter clothing and looking at a tree that was intent on crushing the life out of me. I had one second to act. It wasn't enough time. The tree was on its way to do me in and, I thought, this was the tree the lumberjacks said that had my name on it.

That ominous saying is not without foundation. Lumberjacks say that the longer a man remains working the forest, the closer he gets to the tree with his name on it - the tree that is going to kill him. I was a dead man and I knew it. I had no time to be afraid as I awaited the hit. My mind had gone numb, leaving me without feeling as I awaited death. It did not come.

A display of nuts and bolts, springs, bits of plastic and steel lay across the ruffled, snow clad ground - my chainsaw had seen better days. The giant cedar, at the last moment twisted on its stump, spinning itself away from my path. It was hard to believe I was still in the land of the living, but I was. I even took it upon myself to pinch my flesh a goodly number of times just to make sure I was alive. In the silence of the aftermath, the pounding of my heart was heard loud and clear. For a while, I was fascinated listening to the strong, regular pounding of the engine that kept me alive. I was absolutely enthralled by the great life-force that beat within me. I had never really given much thought to the miraculous system before, but here I was, in the middle of the great Canadian wilderness, marveling at my heart's walloping. Yes! I was still alive and the engine that was keeping me that way seemed to be the only one working that day for all the others had packed it in.

I did not have a back up saw to complete my work - my day in the bush was done. I left this scene of great disconsolation and walked down to the edge of the Columbia where the raft lay moored. Although I was thankful to be alive, I felt thoroughly dejected. I was really giving this bush life a try for all I was worth but I simply wasn't getting ahead. Little did I know it was going to get a lot worse!

The raft's engine fired easily. I moved her out into the strong current of the

Columbia's waters, heading steadily towards the far shore. It would be just a few minutes before I was ashore and I could check out what the problem with my truck might be. But once again other plans were made for me. The old two-stroke engine sputtered, fluttered, muttered and shut up for good. I was now captain of a float-away raft, heading down the mighty Columbia. The winds sang their bitter praises in a most jeering fashion as they pushed me into God knows where. I thought, four engines all kaput - just what the hell is going on?

I had to get off the river before the freezing elements did me in. Downriver a few miles, lay Esso Ed's. I had to find some way to get as close to the far shore as possible and I had to do it soon. On the deck of the raft lay a wood wedge. It was all I had to work with but it was enough. I was able to force the wedge between two of the deck planks prying one of them loose. Although my hands had the comfort of good winter mitts, my fingers gradually grew numb. However, I had a plank and now I could try to steer the raft out of the main current in towards the bank. I was lucky - it worked.

I secured the raft to a tree along the bank, scrambled up the hill and out onto the road. From there, I made my way down to Esso Ed's and to safety. "You look like you had a rough day John," said Don as I sipped on a hot mug of coffee.

"You ain't kidding," I replied. "Think you could drop me up to my truck, I got some fixing to do on her," I asked Don.

"Sure thing," Don replied. I figured I would not need Don's help with the truck, so I did not ask him to stick around while I sought the problem. It was a mistake. The truck's oil pan had sprung a leak and the engine had seized. My truck was solidly out of commission, as was my snowmobile, my chainsaw and my raft. My shake-blocking operation was effectively terminated.

In the late of evening, I managed to hitch a ride back to Revelstoke. It was a night of "poor me" as I paced the floor of my room thoroughly dispirited. It was a dismal scene within these walls and as I contemplated my miserable situation, a knock came upon the door. "Are you John McDonald?" a young lady asked me.

"I am, Madame, I am indeed John McDonald but quite frankly, I wish I were somebody else right now," I answered.

"Oh really! That's too bad isn't it," she said with a hint of sarcasm. "I have something for you, sir," she said with the same hint of detachment towards me. As soon as I heard the word sir, I immediately felt uncomfortable. Something was amiss and I instinctively knew it.

"Oh, dear lady," said I to her with about the same portion of sarcasm as she bestowed upon me, "and what might a lovely lady like you have for a man you find worthy of calling sir."

"Why sir, your divorce papers of course - you are now legally and fully divorced," she said as she firmly pressed the papers into the palm of my hand and bid me adieu.

Oh my Lord, how alone I felt. A final departure from someone I loved, someone the bottle had taken from me, and now the pain of the memories driven like a bolt of cold steel into the center of my heart. The desperation of such a moment I hope never to experience again. Everything I loved in the world was gone. I seemed to be frozen in space and time, my mind numb, my body without feeling. I wanted to so desperately cry but the tears would not come. I was as lost as one could be. I wondered who I was, where I had come from and what I was doing in this world. I just knew I wanted to go somewhere but where? My heart cried as any heart would and the numbness of the moment brought only deep sighs of resignation - resignation from what? I did not know.

A LIGHT FROM HEAVEN

Through the frosted window of my trailer I gazed into the bluster of an icy world as the clatter of a distant train broke the silence of the night. Out there, the world was alive but I was not a part of it. I felt I was part of nothing – an entity shunned by all that is in the heavens and the earth. As my eyes gazed into the world outside, my senses were awakened to a beautiful spiritual presence within my humble surroundings. I was not afraid. I was fully aware of its power and sacredness. A light in the form of a globe then appeared before me, touched me by the heart and communicated to me. I knew at that moment I did not have to believe in a Creator any more. I knew beyond doubt a power far greater than this world existed. I knew! I knew! I knew!

A voice communicated to me that everything was going to be okay. It knew everything about me since the beginning of my creation. I could feel the power of the heavens and its expression of love and understanding. I knew I had a purpose in this world. I knew everybody had a purpose in this world. We were not alone and never would be. The great pain in my heart vanished and the feeling of oneness with the world of the unseen instilled peace in my heart - a peace I had never known. And the voice said, "Everything will be all right.

Do not worry, everything is going to be all right."

I went for a stroll that night, wandering around the town lost in the wonder of what had just happened to me.

"I hear you are having a spell of bad luck," called a voice in the darkness of the parking lot. I turned to see the concerned face of Ron Tench, a fellow shake-blocker walk towards me.

"Yes Ron," I answered. "Things are pretty dull right now but I guess they will get better. They always seem to... one way or another."

"You bet they get better and sometimes a whole lot faster than we figure they might," the tough shake-blocker said, leaving me to wonder at what he meant, my gaze being pulled by the glistening of the ice covered parking lot. "I got a saw for you my friend and I got a truck for you and I got a boat for you and I got a skidoo for you and you can have the whole darned lot," this man with a great heart and a smile lighting my darkened pathway said. I just stood there frozen in time just like the ice, and my thoughts were not far behind the freezing. "Come on my friend," said Ron as he tapped me on the shoulder. Let's go back to the apartment... Claire has made a wonderful turkey supper and it looks like you could do with good meal. And I met Claire, who charmingly invited me to feel at home in their place of easy contentment and I thought of the light once again as I sat at the table of these two good people. And that was how it was going to be allright. Just as the pure light said to me. Just like that! And I knew that the coming together of things was not a coincidence and somehow I also knew that Ron Tench knew it not to be a coincidence either as the evening slipped into night and then into light.

"Today Mr. John," said Ron. We are going to meet Ron Hall of the Cascade Cedar Company. And off we went to meet with the great, big, friendly, burly giant of a man called Ron Hall. "Our friend needs a thousand bucks or so to get himself organized Ron, can you do it?" Asked the tough shake-blocker. The nodding of the head and the great big smile of Ron Hall indicated I was not going to be refused. It was a good feeling leaving the Cascade yard that morning. These two good men saw to it that I was going to make it as a shake-blocker and I did.

It was to Cascade's mill that most of my wood was sold. Through the years of bitter struggle, trying to survive through the many daily difficulties of bush life, both of these men were always there for me. When I needed a cash flow, or tools of the trade, these good men made sure I had it. If I needed a road broken through to a claim, they saw it was done. They were good men, honest and damned hard workers. It was through the trust of these good men that I owed my survival as a shake-blocker - the only type of work I ever truly liked. All other ways of making a living that I had tried my hand at (and there were many) paled in comparison to the insane, adventurous world of the shake-blocker. In this world, I was alive - truly alive in the insanity, the dangers, the daily struggles in the heart of the great Canadian wilderness - the place, we shake-blockers call God's country.

As I prepared my plans for the next day's activities on the shake-block claim, my mind wandered to a time when I had loaned an individual a few hundred dollars. It was money I could not afford to lend but trusted the person enough that I would get it back from him within a few days. I never saw my money again but more than the money, it was a sense of friendship betrayal and I was now feeling angry about the dishonesty of the person. I caught myself in an ugly state of mind and immediately admonished myself for entertaining such thoughts - then from a far distance.

It seemed like I was staring into the far reaches of eternity, not through my eyes but through the back of my head. The sensation and experience was similar to the out of body experiences. I was fully aware that I was in the room of my trailer, just standing there, looking at my paperwork while my mind's eye gazed into the far depths of space. I was much like two people having two completely different experiences simultaneously. I was totally at peace as I watched a glittering spark come out of the blackness of eternity - closer, ever closer and then, into the back of my head, illuminating the darkness of my mind. I was told again that everything was going to be all right. My mind and body knew only absolute peace and tranquility - something from the realms of the divine had again touched my soul.

Such goodness of feeling lingered with me for a long time, eventually giving way to my undisciplined patterns. Back at work on the Downey claim, things had been going quite well as the year of '85 moved into history but that wellness was about to be bludgeoned.

FIRE ON THE COLUMBIA

I had just completed rafting a load of wood across the Columbia for delivery to the mill when I was approached by a shake-blocker who operated a claim further north on the river. "Damned miserable weather," he said, as he stood at the edge of the water, watching me unload the raft. "Got a call from a friend of mine in Vancouver who owns that raft you're using - wants me to take care of it for him."

"Who's your friend in Vancouver?" I asked. Oh, he's bin around this country for a good many years but eventually burned out at the shake-blocking bit and hit off to the city," he replied. "Told me to take care of the raft - that I could put it to use for myself," he further explained. I wasn't good at the game of deceit but this guy was. I never questioned him further and allowed the most valuable asset of the operation slip from my hands. I learned later that the guy who had wormed the raft from me could spin a lie as solemnly as a preacher delivering a eulogy. I had been taken pretty well.

When I had first arrived at the Downey claim, Pablo had been using the raft to ferry the odd load of wood across the river to sell at the mill. He had found the raft moored along the river. It had been apparently moored for the best part of a year, wasting its value. Pablo had decided to "borrow" it and thus put it to use in the transport of the "odd load." The money he made from the sale of the "odd load" of wood kept him going until he was ready to fly the Major bulk of wood out of the forest by helicopter. The raft had been invaluable. Now that it was gone, it had to be replaced. A friend of a friend knew a friend who had a ten-foot boat and a sixteen-foot canoe. I was in business once again. I had managed to retain the engine from the raft as it was the property of Pablo, passed along to me. However, deception must pay for its transgression and so it was, the man who wormed the raft from me was no exception.

The evening entered its darker state as I secured my snowshoes to my feet and prepared to move down the trail to where the boat was moored after my day's work. A little coffee remained in my thermos. I decided to rest awhile and enjoy the warm coffee before moving on. Lost in my thoughts, gazing down on the majestic Columbia as it wound its way towards the great Pacific, I chanced to notice a glow - a fire's glow, seemingly drifting down the broad river. The scene unfolding far below my mountain domain imparted a touch of surrealism. Rising high above the Columbia, the great, snow clad mountains rose sharply, reaching to the first stars of evening. Suddenly, the winds blew an ominous gust, turning the placid waters of the river into a rolling rage. It was not a place to be - out on the mighty Columbia in such weather conditions.

I withdrew my head deeper into the hood of my parka in an attempt to ward off the stabbing wind. Then, reaching for my binoculars, I focused them on the distant glow. It was my raft and it was on fire! On board were two men - one paddling for all he was worth and the other pulling desperately on the chord of the raft's engine. They were in trouble - the engine had quit. It was quite a scene unfolding before my eyes as I watched with a goodly amount of concern for the two men caught in the turbulence of the wild Columbia. If they did not make it to shore, the rising, rolling waves would smash the raft asunder. Oh Lord, how they paddled! There was no doubt their lives hung in nature's balance and their chances were not looking good.

A cold sweat began to ooze across my brow. The stage was most wondrous - the play deadly. Between the great mountains where the Grand River coursed, two men faced the cold call of death. My heart had moved up to nudge my mouth as I watched helplessly from the safety of the heights. It was just a matter of time before the ropes that held the raft together snapped apart. The raft was now fully ablaze and it seemed it had only moments left before it disintegrated. Then, on a sudden, the raging wind altered course, pushing the remnants of the raft towards the rocky shore. The surge of the water sent the fiery flotsam crashing up on the rocks and with it, the "ne'er do well" mariners.

It does not pay to get all "toked up" on marijuana on a raft in the middle of a wintry wild Columbia. Slyman Dunk and his buddy, Napenough, somehow managed to do the impossible on a river a half-mile wide - they got lost. That was the story that followed their disastrous rafting experience on the Columbia. I knew they were lost but I had a deep suspicion the "lostness" was between their ears. I was more than pissed off at the crazy bastards. Slyman Dunk had managed to worm the raft from me, a tool that was invaluable to my operation and wreck it beyond repair. I had much to learn about my sense of gullibility and trust in questionable characters.

"I'm sorry about the raft," said Dunk when I eventually caught up with him. "Got mighty bloody cold out there on the water, had to get a fire going to keep us from freezing. We had a few cedar blocks on board, decided to light them up but the whole damned raft caught fire because Napenough threw too much gasoline on the damned wood," he said.

"Well I guess your friend in Vancouver doesn't have to worry about his raft any more Dunk," I said coldly as I moved from his company forever. He had made things difficult for me, simply because I failed to read into his dubious mindset.

GHOST IN THE FOREST

Winter passed into spring. I had located a nice amount of wood deep in the Downey forest. It looked pretty promising. I needed some help on this one. Through the grapevine I heard Jo Danniels was a good shake-blocker. I searched out the man and in time found him swigging on a beer in the local bar in Revelstoke. "I hear you can make an axe fly at shake making, Mr. Danniels," I said. "Interested in working out on the Downey? I got a "fly-out," a hundred cords or so and I need a good man," I concluded.

"When do we start?" said Jo.

"I'm moving out at five a m in the morning. I'll drop around and pick you up, O.K.," I said.

"You bet! I'll be ready," he replied.

There was a spiteful bite to the wind as I fired up the truck in the quietness of early morning. Revelstoke was still in the grip of slumber as I drove across town to pick Jo up. It was five a.m. right on the button when my fist rapped the door of his old weathered, beaten apartment. I waited in expectation of an answer to the door but none came. I rapped it again, this time a little harder; still, no answer. I was beginning to grow a little impatient as my ears strained for any sound of movement from inside his apartment but there was none. One more time I thumped the door, sparing it no gentleness. That should do the trick, I said to myself as I waited expectantly for an answer; still, none came. I muttered a few expletives and decided to head out alone. It was an hour's travel to the boat crossing. Early spring offered little more daylight than winter to work in. It was important to be on the claim at first light.

The white caps were whipping up a bit of a rage on the Columbia. It didn't look good for a crossing. Still, I was here! I'd take the chance. I put my gear in the skiff, fired the engine and headed out onto the open river. It was rough as blazes. Good thing I had a skiff as well as a canoe - no way the canoe would make it across in weather like this. The winds are merciless on this part of the river, particularly early Spring. But this is what makes the life of a bush man interesting - the madness of it all. I liked it out here on the Downey claim. Too bad Jo wasn't with me.

I made it across the river but not without difficulty. As I headed on up the trail to the work area, I looked back across the river and was again thankful I had the skiff.

The first hints of light gave rise to the departure of darkness as I settled in by some old cedars. Here, I would spend the rest of the day cutting and splitting. The chill of the early morning lost its discomfort as I axed out a good number of shakeblocks before the sun broke across the mountains, giving the valley its first promise of spring Still, the mist was a little heavier than usual this morning, thick, slow-moving streams giving uneasiness to my mind. I had the unmistakable feeling I was being watched. I tried to put such thoughts from my mind as I prepared the chainsaw to fell a couple of old, gigantic cedars. It was risky falling these old trees. Had Jo being with me I would have felt a whole lot more comfortable tackling them.

The bush was silent except for the odd falling twig bouncing through branches and occasionally the twisted moan of interlocked trees rasping against each other. I was fully conscious of my surroundings, so much so that I could hear my heart pound out its beat. I sat a while on an old crusty log contemplating the lean of the cedars. It was important to get it right.

Rolling a cigarette and having a smoke became a bit of a ritual with me before the undercut went in and this morning was no different. A little more time, a little more respect for the great giants of the forest. The match struck, I drew in on the cigarette, inhaling deeply. Then it happened!

The form stood there, immovable in the shroud of morning mist. Instinctively my hand reached back for my axe, which lay on the ground behind me. My eyes stayed fixed on the form as a gripping fear moved through me. My heart raced, my head spun and then I was on my back struggling to get to my feet. I had missed reaching for the axe handle, and in my petrified state, I fell backwards. "Jesus Christ, its a ghost!" I kept saying over and over as all and everything I was part of moved in slow motion.

I was afraid to look again but I had to. My eyes welled with the fear of the unknown and this was the unknown. It was not my imagination acting up; it was a ghost! I was on a claim where no other human feet trod. This claim was like my own little country. Nobody lived here. Nobody could live here! I was alone; at least that's what I thought! I struggled to get to my feet but the dew-laden, mossy carpet beneath them kept giving way. For a moment, I thought perhaps I was seeing things. Perhaps it wasn't a ghost. It might simply be a form created by the heavy mist and I looked again towards the unknown. The form was still there but not immovable. It moved towards me ever so easily. I screamed inside and the fear ripped through my body as my spine tempered like steel. The flush of blood flooded my burning brow as I recoiled in desperation. There was, after all, another world. A world of spirits, ghosts, of other beings. I did not have to believe or disbelieve such things. I now knew them to be true.

Collecting my shattered thoughts, I pulled myself together the best I could. I was trembling but I was going to face this spirit no matter what. I stood on my feet, my axe in hand. I knew the axe could serve no useful purpose other than offering a little reassurance. I took a very deep breath and moved towards the spirit. Again it was still, silent. Then a burst of sunlight split the mist, revealing the form. Again I stood, still, lost in mixed confusion as the voice of the form spoke. "Pretty damned rough crossing in the canoe."

I stood, pale and speechless, then, as unsettled as the scene that had just unfolded, sat on the log and remained motionless for a good measure of time. "Sorry about not being up this morning but that damned alarm… been meaning to get a new one for the past few years," said Jo

"Yes," at last I uttered, "you should do something about your alarm clock Jo, before you cause me to have a heart attack… scared the hell out of me."

Still, I was amazed at his courage to cross the Columbia in a canoe. Something only mad or very brave men would attempt. Maybe he was both! Who knows? All I knew was, that this man was a good man and it was a pleasure to know someone with the raw guts he possessed.

IT'S NOT WISE TO JUMP ON A BEAR'S MEAL WHILE HE IS EATING IT

Chris, my friend from Nanaimo, who with our friend Dave was singing the song "The Drunken Sailor" as I attempted to walk upon the waters' in time's past had come up from the coast to see what I was up to. It's a good thing he did. He was a burly, fair-haired fellow with a strong hint of a prairie accent, possessed a great sense of humor, was easy with life and always wore smile.

"I'll have the coffee ready by the time you return and don't bother returning until if you find the prized wood," the man from the Pacific coast joked. I smiled as I moved out from camp in search of wooded treasure. The sun shed its merciless heat over the land as I ambled across a hillside towards a stand of giant cedars nesting above a long draw. Ahead of me, the undergrowth thickened, compelling me to employ the use of my machete to break a trail. As I drew closer to the draw, the towering red cedar giants gave rise to the promise of excellent salvageable wood.

The thick grassy terrain gradually descended towards a dying creek lazing its way through the draw. I swathed a pathway towards the creek, then followed its course uphill to an open plateau, lush with high grasses and sweeping, broad ferns. Here, the massive cedars towered and below them, great timbers of former days lay across the wild pastureland fading towards a new cycle of life. In the cooling breezes beneath the shades of the ancient trees, I pushed forward through the high grasses. Ahead, a gigantic fir tree lay horizontally blocking my path and forcing me to climb over its great mass to reach the far side.

A rank smell permeated the air and through its odor swarmed a myriad of horse flies. What caused such stench? I had no idea. I climbed quickly over the toppled tree to move beyond the smell. Upon reaching its top, the stink intensified and, not wishing to further subject my nostrils to such a foul odor, I hastened my departure from the treetop, dropping to the ground on the opposite side. It can be said at this time that the cautious procedure of "look before you leap" would have been in order but by then it was far, far too late.

As my feet contacted the ground, I felt something other than earth beneath them. Upon further investigation, I observed below my feet, the half-eaten remains of a dear and beside the remains, the one who killed it - a formidable black bear. There is no time for thinking in situations like this, at least not for me but the bear was thinking he should kill me for being very rude. I could see by the way he stood on his hind legs that murdering me had crossed his mind. As the great bear stretched into the heavens, I simultaneously stretched my machete towards the same place and screamed at the gluttonous swine. I screamed the great painful cry of primordial sacrificial death. It was a good scream. It bore results, but not favorable to me.

The bear decided to come down from the sky and move closer and that was almost impossible. The width of the deer's carcass was only two feet, give or take a half-inch – the bear standing by the spine and me by the belly. I was not in the best of situations. By now every hair on my body was standing to attention and my flesh, tempered like one gnarled steel knot. To die or not to die was not the question - I was going to die. Again, I threw my arms in the air, swirling my machete above my head, hoping I did not cut my thinking apparatus off. This dangerous execution bore some fruit. The big black bear backed up slightly. I repeated my machete-swinging trick once again and by golly he backed up a little further. I felt I might just have a little chance at surviving - a very, very little chance.

We stood facing each other, each waiting for the other to make the first move. It was me. Ever so slowly, I moved backwards to create a greater distance between us but I had forgotten about the tree I had jumped down from, rudely landing on the bear's meal. When I stepped back into it, I realized I could not retreat and my concentration was so intense on the gravity of my situation that I could not even think of a swear word to utter at the tree. Moving to my right, I eased my way into the tall grass, each moment expecting the bear to charge. Ever so slowly, the distance grew between man and beast. I was going to make it.

THE BRAZEN PORCUPINE

I felt it prudent not to try to return the way I had come so I moved farther across the plateau. Coming upon a fast running creek spanned by a downed gigantic cedar, I climbed upon it and began my crossing. As I made my way gingerly to the other side, I noticed a creature of the bush approaching from the opposite side. I had had it with the beasts of the forest for the day. I had a machete, I had the right of way and this critter was going to get off my tree or pay the price.

I stood my ground, firm and resolute. I was a member of the human clan and I had dominion over all creatures great and small as long as they were not the human type. It said so in the Bible! Here, I was in charge. Here, I was superior and the creature was my subject to do with as I pleased. The creek ran swiftly at center and this critter was going for a swim if it did not backup. He did not backup. It was now time to notify him that he stood in a human's way and if he did not go back or go swimming - its blood would flow. The steel of my machete glinted in the midday sun giving a touch of sparkling drama to the murderous plot. As the strange looking critter came closer, I observed it to be none other than the fabled porcupine - and the fabled porcupine was full of barbed quills that scribes did not write with. The bundle of quills that waddled its way towards me was indeed ugly and very, very bold. He had moved to within ten feet of my feet and slowing not one inch. The moment had come to deliver the mortal blow but I could neither find the will or the brutality within me to strike.

It was a cold creek I stepped into that dragged me across its boulders that day. I eventually reached the far side of the bank, fully refreshed. Looking back towards the culprit that had caused me such ill design, I watched as he climbed from the trunk of the tree and disappear into the brush not even affording me a glance. To the creature, I was simply something that was in his way. I was truly humiliated but we were all alive and well somewhere in the great Canadian wilderness.

As I made my way back to camp, I felt my body grow weak from exhaustion but I was thankful I was all right. This life of the bush was proving its worth. I had been badly frightened but I felt there was a great lesson in the encounters. What it was, I did not know but whatever it was - it was good. The fresh aroma of coffee lingered in the air as I relaxed at camp. "Did ye find the hidden treasure? " Chris asked with a touch of joviality. " Aye Chris, I found the hidden treasure. Would ye like to hear the bear facts about the find," I said as I lay my head against an old tree trunk. "Aye, I would if ye don't mind," Chris said. I paused awhile, then, relived the moments of before.

CHAINSAWS MAIM AND KILL

The late summer breeze brought a cool freshness to the mountains. The sun had been up an hour or so as Chris and I made our way up the side of a ridge to where a couple of old, dead giants stood. If they were solid it would be well worth the effort. From a point of safety, Chris watched as I toppled the first tree. The wood was of excellent quality. The tree came down in heavy undergrowth, which I had to clear to make a safe, clear working area. I began the routine procedure.

As far as I can remember, it was the first time I wore protective head and face gear working with a chainsaw. It was a good thing I did. I had heard about a chainsaw kicking back and I had seen the horrible damage it had done to some bush-men but I figured it would never happen to me. As I moved along the downed tree, cutting shrubbery clear, the tip of the saw touched an object. When the tip of a running chainsaw touches an object, such as a branch, it will cause the saw to "kickback" or to be sent with lightening speed back into the face of the person who is using it. No amount of physical strength will prevent it from kicking back, once the mistake is made. This action is responsible for countless deaths and injuries.

I saw it but far, far too late. In the twinkling of an eye, the saw had kicked back into my face, splitting it, simultaneously lifting me clear off the ground and knocking me uphill about ten feet as the chainsaw sailed through the air. A great darkness seemed to swallow me as I fought to hold on to consciousness. But the blackness was overpowering. I drifted off into the blackness, unafraid, as I felt my time had come and it was not so bad after all - there was nothing to be afraid of. Then, from the distance, I heard a voice call. It seemed to echo through the far depths of my mind and then it came closer. I could now hear the voice outside my body calling to me from above the hillside. It was Chris. "Are you all right?" I heard him call to me. I did not know! I was laying face down in the ground and as I raised my head, I saw the blood gush forth from the hanging flesh of my face. The chain of the saw had bitten into my face, smashing some teeth, cutting into my cheekbone and dislocating my jaw. But I was still alive - just barely.

"Come on ol' buddy, let's get you to the doc," Chris said as he helped me to my feet. He then asked me to cover my face with my shirt as it was not in its most handsome state. I did not thank him for such reassuring words. It seemed an endless drive to the hospital but Chris got me there. When I felt a little better, I began to wonder about a number of things. Why on earth had Chris shown up when he did - unexpectedly and unannounced? And I wondered why for the first time since I had started shake-blocking that I had worn a hard hat, face guard and earmuffs. Had I not been wearing them, I would have been killed instantly. The rip in my face stopped at the rim of the hard hat. Again, I had no doubt someone was watching over me.

RUBBER BOOTS, UNDERWEAR AND A GRIZZLY BEAR

Summer's end saw the shake-blocking dwindle out at the Downey. It was time to locate another claim. Just south of Downey, in the same valley, was an area known as Frisby. There was some good shake-block wood in this area and I quickly moved in on a claim. My claim was adjacent to some newcomers from Alberta who were relatively inexperienced at the business. I offered what assistance I could to the threesome, one of whom was no more than fifteen years old.

The day was somberly cool as I drove out of the bush to pick up supplies in Revelstoke. As I headed down the trail, I noticed about a half a mile ahead of me, someone in rubber boots and his underwear, running for all he was worth along the logging road. It was indeed the oddest thing I had ever seen in my life and even odder that the incident was happening in the far depths of the Canadian forest but when my eyes fell upon a great grizzly bear on the bank above the logging road, made it quiet clear why the boy was running – it was for his life.

I stepped on the gas, got him out of harms way and headed back towards the grizzly. Behind the seat of the truck lay my 303 rifle. I had not the need to use it before; perhaps today might be different. The scene of that fateful day, now long past as I moved along the trail of a Grizzly with Evan the Indian hunter, came back to memory. I was not as skilled as Evan. In fact, I was not skilled in the art of hunting at all. What would I do if the bear attacked? Would I panic, run or stand my ground? I did not know. I hoped inwardly I would not have to respond to any such questions that stabbed at my mind.

The boy had quenched his thirst with some orange juice I had in my thermos and made use of some extra work clothes I had in the cab. Within seconds I had moved the truck up the banks trail, on past the grizzly stopping at the boys camp. If the grizzly went into the camp, he would destroy everything within seconds; food, gasoline, oil, tinned goods, the destruction of the camp itself. Exiting the cab and grabbing my rifle, my eyes scanned the terrain for the form of the great bear and a moment later from a depression in the ground, I spotted the silvery fur of the massive animal move ever so slightly above the blooms of a clump of wildflowers. I waited, the rifle's magazine fully loaded.

From the relatively safe distance of about fifty yards, I waited for the bears approach, inwardly hoping that there would be no confrontation. As I trained my sights on the heart of the animal and prepared to fire if he approached, I became mesmerized by the placid behavior of the grizzly. The great creature seemed to sense it was not threatened and showed no signs of aggressive behavior towards us. In a moment, its huge, rippling, fur clad frame ascended from the ground's depression, then, the magnificent one ambled on up the hill and disappeared into the protective forest. It was a good day for all of us.

THE FISH RIVER COUNTRY

The summer of '87 moved into the mountain tapestry of autumn's ever changing carpet of colors. This season of ever unfolding blends of magical hues swept the land. The undergrowth of the forest surrendered its foliage to the incursion of the season's change and the high grasses transformed into clumps of lifeless straw. The bugs, too, go their way this lovely time of the year, leaving the land to the fresh cool breezes – winter's gentle symphonic prelude to the rages of its storms.

South of Revelstoke, Ron Hall had secured a shakeblock claim for me in that part of the land known as the Fish River country, an area as rugged and as beautiful as the Downey country. It was here gold prospectors came at the turn of the nineteenth century trying his luck in the water's of this wild and wondrous terrain. It was in this country that the words of sergeant Flannigan would come from the past to ring hard in my ears. "Never, ever forget how to fully secure the firing pin to the bolt of the rifle, boys. Your very life may depend on it!" Would come from the past to ring hard in my ears.

Nothing much but the wind moved at five a.m. as I slowly drove my old Ford beater off the ferry at Galena Bay. It was a good feeling moving into the Fish River country. Word had it that there was real good wood in this country and the terrain was easy to work. The headlights of the truck pierced the early morning blackness as I moved off the paved road and onto the old trails the pioneers had built back in those rough and tumble early days. I enjoyed traveling on the gravel trails - something special about being off the paved roads. It was a sense of old time liberty, way out in the outback, not a soul to have to explain things to - life at its finest.

The morning broke to the usual magic of nature as I prepared my chainsaw and other tools of the trade. Across the land lay huge cedar logs, victims of high winds and old age. My old faithful truck lay snuggled in against the low rising bank just above the road a hundred yards or so from where I was working. The terrain was somewhat rolling between the great mountains making it easy to work the land. I began work on a beautiful, large cedar, the chainsaw biting into the wood snuggly. A good measure of time passed without my having to sharpen the chain. This made for good shakeblock production, the tree producing first class quality shakeblocks. I had been going pretty well non-stop for a couple of hours and I was beginning to tire a little. It was time to take a break.

With the chainsaw turned off, the wilderness came alive. The fresh gentle bite of the early autumn breeze blew its death knell over the last vestiges of wilting foliage as the first layers of high mountain snow began its encroachment below the jagged peaks. I had about six weeks before the valley floors disappeared below winter's icy blanket; there was no time to waste getting the wood out before the coming snows closed the roads. However, although things were getting off to a mighty fine start in the Fish River country, nature had its surprises and I was beginning to get mighty tired of some of them.

I finished putting my coffee thermos away and began axing the great rounds of wood I had cut throughout the morning. My energy was good and it's a good thing it was because I was going to need every ounce I had, plus all I had in reserve. The axe was above my head ready to be hammered down and into the block of wood when I first noticed the movement. It was slight but enough to warrant further observation. I finished driving the head of deadly steel into the wood and glancing in the direction of the movement, I was given to the thought that I was in for an unpleasant morning. The massive black form moved with grace and ease but with an aura of mischief about it.

The beast moved slowly but surely towards me, his head lowered and shoulders hunched like that of a dog in the attack position. I knew he was not coming to wish me well in my difficult and dangerous profession and I must act immediately to thwart the murdering marauder's breakfast plan. I grabbed my chainsaw and instantly started it. I revved the engine to maximum and then I ran towards the great mass of furry blackness, the saw screaming in my hands. To my surprise, the bear did not budge. He just stood there as I approached. I was stupefied as what to do next because I thought that with the saw screaming its murderous unpleasantness, the bear would run off - but he didn't.

I hesitated momentarily, then, moved forward much more slowly but with grim determination. Still, the bear held its ground but I wasn't stopping. His eyes were locked onto me as I approached and such ugliness in eyes I had indeed never witnessed before. Dank, cold and satanic, the gaze of the beast stared me down. I kept going. My adrenaline flushed to a cold burn as my grip on the chainsaw handlebar tightened. The bear too, seemed resolute in his intentions, not giving an inch and I knew that in a moment, there was going to be an awful mess of flesh and blood and hopefully it was not going to be mine. I made my move. I charged - the saw held upward and forward of my shoulders. The bear rose onto its back paws, exposing his belly and chest and in that moment as I swung the screaming saw from across my shoulder, in an instant, the bear wheeled and dashed away to the safety of the thickets. I was thankful it had turned out that way - I was alive and the bear was gone.

My heart pounding, I returned to the business of chopping wood and tried to think of what had just happened was a normal part of the day's work but my imagination was not that good. I sat again for a while and tried a little deep breathing but all that exercise seemed to do was cause me to hyperventilate. I even recalled to mind, those recording tapes of nature's sounds - rippling streams, warbling birds and singing winds. Indeed, from where I sat, it was not difficult to imagine Mother Nature at her best. But the thoughts of an animal wanting to kill and chew me up before he happily went on his way to hibernate with my essence to nourish him, stirred a raging hate within – a flaming revulsion unsettling to my spirit.

The moments seemed to linger forever as I tried mentally to deal with such a violent intrusion into my life and just when I thought I had it figured out, the bear came back, his ill intent a lot more pronounced than in his previous introduction of foul design. The thief that wanted to steal my life from me through the most savage means, was moving across the flat, open terrain slowly and menacingly towards me. I grabbed the chainsaw and pulled the cord, but it failed to fire. With the coolness of one who was truly in full control of his mental faculties, I yanked the cord again but the saw would not respond. I yanked again with a little more vigor and this time, I got very bad results - the starting cord of the saw snapped, blowing listlessly in the cool morning breeze as it dangled from my hand. Then, with the insight of one who had fought many wars and lost, I hurled the uncooperative saw at the advancing bear.

It was a good shot. Nevertheless, I was greatly displeased because it stopped the bear in his tracks for about one second before he took up his interrupted breakfast walk once again.

My head was almost bursting with the pressure of adrenaline as the scene became one of the most personal I had ever experienced in my entire life. Beyond this patch of earth where my life lay threatened by this wild animal, nothing existed. My memory closed down and my focus was totally on the bear. The sounds of nature found only silence in my mind and my own defensive movements were just as silent. My body reacted as though it were without feeling, responding only to the primordial call of survival. Since death was imminent, I decided to do as much damage as I possibly could to my antagonist. Then, in a moment, the whole scene took on a different element, an element I had experienced before but not under such fearful circumstances.

It seemed I had moved out of my body and was floating above the ground watching a bear charge a man. All was happening at a very rapid rate - but oddly, in slow motion at the same time. The man was me. My right hand had gripped the axe and in an instant it was hurtling through the air. The hit was accurate and with force. It struck the oncoming bear across the snout and this time, it was not for a second it was halted but solidly in its tracks.

While the bear was wondering what had hit him, I was bolting across the terrain towards my truck, my spirit seemingly moving above me and with me.

"Where the hell is the rifle," I muttered, as I got closer to the truck. "Is it beneath the seat? Is it behind it? Do I even have the damned thing?" While my mind was figuring where the rifle might be, the thought occurred to me that I had lost the magazine some months ago. I also had only one round of ammunition and I was not sure where that was either. I was also aware that the rifle had not been used for a number of years and the barrel could be well clogged with rust or dirt. If I did find the bullet and load the rifle, the chances of the round exploding in the chamber and injuring my face, or at the very least, damaging my vision was very, very real. Still, I forged ahead and did what I must. It never occurred to me that I did not have to take this line of action but my mind had lost all aspects of rational.

Jumping into the cab of the truck, I searched out the weapon. I found it beneath the long singular seat. Grabbing it, I searched desperately for the round. I had no idea where it was. I searched beneath the seat, behind it, in my toolbox, on the dashboard but to no avail. Then I remembered it being in the small toolbox in the back of the truck. By now the bear had recovered from the wallop of the axe and was now circling the truck. Still, I had to take a chance and retrieve the small tool-box in the back of the truck. In an instant, without thinking, I was out the door, grabbed the box and hauled it inside the cab. A cold sweat rolled down my forehead and my hands trembled as my spirit floated above. At times, I did not know if I was in the cab, in the sky, or both places at once but what I was certain of was that the bear wanted to kill and eat me. It was my intention to prevent such a happening but first I had to assemble the weapon. It was going to prove a lot harder than I had imagined.

I was not in the frame of mind or in a convenient position to check out the barrel of the rifle to see that it was free of obstruction. The thought of the chamber exploding in my face because of a blocked rifle barrel made this whole situation even more nerve racking. The only convenient progress I made in assembling the rifle was the discovery of the rifle bolt sitting on the dash of the cab. I was in business. I pushed the bullet into the breach and placed the bolt in position to secure the round but the bolt would not cooperate. I swore high and low but swearing did not help one bit in my attempt to lock the bolt down. Here I was in a most vulnerable situation, in the middle of a fight with a big bad bear and nothing was going right. Old ugly face was wandering around my truck with a thick lip and a bleeding nose which he had gotten from the wallop of my mighty fine Swedish axe and he looked like he was not in a very forgiving mood. Neither was I.

I was getting more frustrated by the moment because I could not lock the bolt down, then, from somewhere in the far reaches of my mind, a voice said, think, think, think! And think I did. I thought back to the days when I was in the militia back home in Dublin. The rifle I now had was the same model I had used in military training, the standard 303 rifle. I recalled how sergeant Flannigan had emphasized the importance of the bolt and the firing pin. "Remember lads, the singular most important thing about your rifle is the firing mechanism, the precision fitting of the firing pin to the bolt... your life may depend on it one day."

The sergeant's words had stuck firmly in my mind and now I was, in desperation, recalling the technique he had shown me so long ago. Sergeant Flannigan had done his job well. I set the bolt. I had done it. I was ready. It was now time, hopefully, to kill the dirty marauder of the forest.

The bear was still circling the truck but for some reason had widened the circle. I recall the radius of the circle to be about twenty yards, enough for me to step from the truck, take aim and fire. By now, my whole body was beginning to tremble slightly but I did not give a damn. I stepped from the truck and walked towards the bear. If things went wrong, I could end up in a horrible mess. The tempo of the drama had not changed. Still, I seemed to move in slow motion and nothing of heaven, earth or hell existed in my mind other than my rage towards the bear. The creature now moved ever more erratically, then turned towards me.

Once again, I saw the dark lifeless look in the eyes of the creature. This bear was ugly and I suspected that this was the bear with a reputation for raiding work camps, trailers and tents. He was deemed extremely dangerous and it would only be a matter of time before he entered a shelter and killed someone, perhaps a child. His days were over.

The echo of the rifle fire tumbled across the valley - on and on, it rolled, thundering through the silence of this lovely wilderness and in the throes of death lay the form of a would be killer bear. In a moment, I was running full flight across the terrain to where my axe lay. Grasping it, I ran forward to the downed animal - my intention to drive the sharp edge of my axe into his skull, making sure he never rose again - but life and death have their surprises.

It happened in a moment. The axe came down towards the bear's head; in its drive, every ounce of strength I could muster. But with a speed I had witnessed only in the amazing agility of a cat, the bear was up, spinning its rage like that of a savage tornado. Then, my body was hurtling across the ground. I had been hit really hard but since I was in this until death did us apart, I didn't bother counting my aches and sprains. I still had the axe in my hand and scrambling to my feet, I prepared for an onslaught but it did not come. The bear had been seriously hit, yet did not realize he was supposed to be dead. The bullet had knocked him down and although he had the will and the strength to revive, I had no doubt that he was seriously wounded.

After he effectively introduced me to flying lessons, he took off to the safety of the underbrush but I was not having any hide and seek - I would find him and I would kill him. There was venom in my mind and soul that I never knew existed and it frightened me. It was an ugly thing to feel such madness course my veins but my mind was made up - I tracked the bear through the underbrush

My heart was pumping beyond a grave capacity as I moved ever so slowly along the trail of broken brush. My axe ever at the ready, the only sound disturbing the silence of the wilderness was the pounding of my heart. I knew I had wounded him seriously and yet my chance of being the victor did not give rise to a feeling of self-assurance. I was somewhat anxious that I could get killed but my fear of being afraid drove me forward. Something was happening here that brought proof of my ability in this world and that I had reason to live. It was not that I could kill a bear but that I suddenly found a value in my existence and I was prepared to defend it - this value called life.

Suddenly, I had realized I was blessed with so much and the force that gave life to my being was sacred. And I thought of the scholar, Kilroy. "It may be that you shall find the answer to life's meaning in the silence of the wilderness, Mr. John," said Thomas Kilroy in those long past days back in the hills of Kiltimage, Ireland. It all sounded so dramatic - so abstract, so heroic, so painfully wrought with acts of uselessness and futility but the poetic essence of the line, "finding meaning in the silence of the wilderness" was manifesting its worth, its power and its essence right here in every thing that was brutal. And I wondered if there really was something in the ritual of a blood sacrifice - a libation to the gods. Yes indeed I wondered! Still, a wounded bear is a very dangerous creature.

The singing of the birds and the bite of the early autumn's wind slowly stole through my senses as I moved across the swatted path through which the bear had retreated. Beyond about fifty yards, the broken brush trail abruptly ended. On both sides of the trail stood large clumps of loganberry bushes intermingled with high, broad ferns. Such a place could prove an excellent hideaway. Ever so cautiously, I moved closer to the place of danger, my mind racing in slow motion (an apparent paradox but true, nevertheless). I was within a few yards of where I thought the animal was hiding and it was here indeed that the bear lay mortally wounded in the underbrush. I could hear him breathing. Inch by inch, I moved slowly towards him, the axe handle gripped with deadly intent

Again it seemed that I was hovering above my body, a faithful spectator urging myself on - not to be afraid. The bear too, was trying to survive but it was not the time to be mulling over such sentiments 'ere the moment lose favor to the one who wielded the axe. Slowly, ever so slowly, my eyes searched through the browning ferns as I moved towards the wounded beast and as the ferns thinned to the inside of the loganberry bushes, there, beneath the autumn's rusting foliage, lay the massive bulk of the bear, his rich, dark sheen shrouding his finality. The animal was laboring its last moments of breath

Death came to the creature, not from an axe blow - the rifle shot had proved fatal. I was thankful to be alive. As I walked back to my old truck, I was aware that my mind and body were trying to normalize, to overcome the state of shock I was experiencing. I knew that I had undergone a profound experience, something that could only be measured and expressed in my inner core. The savagery that had just taken place created a fundamental awareness in me that no matter the circumstances life's meaning cannot be trivialized or wasted. That awareness was the feeling and essence of life, its depth, force and sacredness. Proof had been presented to me, that there is no greater power in the universe than life and the will to live. From this day forward, I would never question my existence.

Nevertheless, there was that elusive purpose. What was that all about? I had discovered one part of the question of life but there was that other part - its purpose. I felt like a starving man might feel, sitting at a feast table and not knowing what to do with all the treasures that could nourish him. In time, perhaps, the purpose may be made known. I walked back to the wood I had been chopping earlier and sat awhile in distant thought.

As the morning moved on, I thought it prudent to drive to town, purchase a rifle magazine, ammunition, and to find Jo Danniels and Jamie. I had the feeling that things were not going to get better. Other bears would come to feed on the one that lay dead and eventually take over his territory. There was trouble ahead and it would not be long in coming. It was only when I turned the key in the ignition that I realized I could have simply driven away to safety from the attacking bear. I wondered why such a wise thought never entered my head.

In the early afternoon, I was back in Revelstoke. I secured the necessary wares and located Jo Danniels and Jamie. I also hitched up a trailer, which I had purchased previously, stocked up on grub, then drove back to the Fish River country later that evening. Before darkness ascended, we had set up camp. All was well in the wilderness of the Fish River country as we three shake-blockers slept the sleep of honest kings. Then, from that far off dream state, so far off that one does not remember, I was called back to the world of wakefulness. As I became a little more conscious, I felt that I was in a giant rocking chair being swayed rather brutally by someone or something that had no respect for the sleeping. In moments, the rocking had intensified to the point where I thought the trailer was going to turn over on its side. In that hazy dreamlike state, I peered through the window of the trailer and in the glow of the last embers of the camp fire Jo had made after returning from Revelstoke, I observed a great big furry-faced creature looking in the window which I slept beside.

    The great big bear was very bold and seemed unafraid of anything or anyone. This boldness was made quite plain by the way he was pawing on the window and shoving his snout across it. By the time I had gotten my mind in thinking mode, Jo had the propane light going. In this wonderful moment of illumination, I observed, in detail, the interesting facial characteristics of furry friend number two. It was a dignified face of bold curiosity, garnished with those sweeping, distinguished markings peculiar to the family of the raccoon. However, this furry creature with the most notable and noble of facial features was not a raccoon. It was a very large black bear that wanted to introduce himself to the food in our trailer and throw the shake-blockers out. It was not the best of moments.

    I do not know if it was sheer madness or stupidity that gripped me but the thought occurred to me that I should belt the window with my fist and roar very loudly in the hopes of scaring the critter away. The stage was set. Jo had moved closer to the window with the propane lamp, giving an unmistakable view of the imminent danger, particularly to me, because I was still beneath my blankets and the bear was on the other side of a transparent veil of moonlit glass – only two inches away. With the help of Jo, I immediately went to work on scaring the hell out of the bear. I hammered on the window with my fist, shouting the necessary unmentionables but the bear only responded by shoving the right side of his face against the window as though to obtain a better view of the unfortunates inside. This indeed was not a good thing, of which I instantly informed Jo. He suggested that I belt the window a lot harder with my fist. I responded in the affirmative. It was not a good move. The windowpane broke and I mean it really broke. I was still tangled beneath my bedding when the very bold bear took the opportunity to shove his head in through the window with the intention of biting my head off. Things were not looking good for the shake-blockers in the Fish River country.

It was some sight to behold, the head of a real, live bear poking through a broken window, giving me that "what's happening man" look. I responded the best way I could. I gave him a clout with my fist on the nose, then, I rolled out of my bed, becoming more entangled in my sheets as I fell on the floor. It was as comical as it can get. The clout on the bear's nose seemed to do the trick as he removed his head and turned his attention to the wares that were stored at the back of the trailer. From our mountain home, we could see through the glassless window, in the last glow of the dying fire Jo had made late in the evening, the bear engaged in the most incredible juggling act we had ever seen. Out of spite, I'm sure, he grabbed our extra mattress, which was lying at the back of the trailer and tossed it up and down through the air as though it were a beach ball. Jo and I stood dumbfounded in the precarious safety of our little three man trailer, watching as this most bold and spirited bear of the Fish River country showed us how and why he should be in the circus business. We were much impressed with the new arrival in the Fish River country but we did not come here to scout for talented bears that juggled mattresses in the midnight glow of a dying fire. We were going to have trouble with him and it was time to bring the show to an end.

I really did not want to kill him but in this case, lives were in danger and those lives were Jo's Jamie's and mine. I had had enough dangerous action in the past twenty-four hours to last me a few life times and sadly, I decided to eliminate the bear. I prepared my rifle to do the dirty deed, only to find that I had left the ammunition and magazine at my apartment in town. I was mighty upset. My mattress was now in tatters along with my oilcans, gasoline cans, pots, cooler and my trailer had a broken window. When a bear decides to raid a camp, it is no different than an angry bull taking his frustrations out in a china shop. Everything is destroyed and so to must the bear be.

At about three a.m., I left camp and headed back to Revelstoke. It was about a two-hour drive from the Fish River country to the ferry. I would catch the five o clock ferry across the Arrow Lakes and drive on to Revelstoke. There I would coffee up, grab my ammunition and magazine and purchase the wares the bear had damaged. I knew the bear would not be there when I returned at daylight but I had no doubt he would be back when darkness fell.

It was around ten a.m. when I returned to camp. Jo and Jamie had been hard at work. The shakeblocks they were producing were excellent quality -

a promising yield for the market. Throughout the day, we kept our eyes peeled for rogue bear number two and surprisingly he was not sighted. Jamie figured he was feeding on his look-a-like and might not be back. He figured bear number two would have enough food donated by the one who dwelled in this land before him, to sustain him through his hibernating winter. Maybe Jamie was right, maybe he was wrong but whatever Jamie assumed about the bear, the one thing Jo and I could not understand about Jamie was why he was not aware of the presence of the midnight juggler. When asked, he simply answered that he had slept through the whole event. The question was left to Jo and I to wonder how deeply Jamie slept and I hoped that neither one of us ever reached that state unconsciousness - at least not in bear country.

The sun yawned its lasts strengths as the long shadows of the tall timbers stretched over the resting land. In the great heavens the first star of evening gave proof to the immensity of creation, while below its majesty and splendor a hunter sought his prey.

A fierce resolve burned within me; a resolve to end the pilfering of troublesome bears. Still, I was bothered by the business of killing animals. I found no sport or thrill in it but I had to make a living and I had a right to live. Philosophizing did little to help except for me to feel a wallop of guilt about the whole murderous affair. After all, the bear lived here before I came along, so why should he be bothered? Then I figured that he was the one that started all the trouble by rocking our trailer and beating up my mattress and storage containers. As much as I fooled with such thoughts, I knew I had made my mind up to kill him but I did not feel good about it. I even developed a fondness for this juggling bear because he really did have character and seemed more inquisitive than bloodthirsty. The big, cute, raccoon like mush he sported upon his neck began to create a sentimental crises within my shattered heart and a deep feeling of sadness overcame me.

The long timber shadows were soon lost to the first hints of twilight as I moved along a well worn trail of the forest dwellers. Stillness crept across the land as I carefully moved over the beaten path. Beyond the high, lifeless brush hummed the song of the river where the trail widened to a clearing. I crossed the open ground to the edge of the river and followed the trail along its bank. In the sky, the moon seemed to be keeping a watchful eye over me as I continued following the trail, which turned abruptly from the river leading almost directly back towards our camp, then blazed off in the direction of the landing where I had shot the troublesome bear. In the air the smell of the dead bears carcass carried on the breeze, giving warning that it may well be along this trail I shall find the juggler. Suddenly I was upon him, his form resting beneath an old, mangled cedar tree. Jamie was right about him feeding on bear number one, bolstering his weight to see him through five or six months hibernation. The wind blew towards me giving no betrayal of my scent. The sound of the river had silenced my approach - I raised my rifle.

The bolt was set, the safety clip undone, the head of the creature squared in my sights. Yet, I held my fire and I'm not sure why. Perhaps it was because the animal was defenseless. Perhaps it was because he was asleep. Perhaps it is only a coward who would take the life of a sleeping creature. Perhaps, perhaps, perhaps! Ever so cautiously, I backed up slowly along the trail from which I had come. It had been a good day. It was better left that way.

As I meandered back to the camp, the thought of killing for the "sport" of it hammered at my mind. I was relieved that I did not kill the creature that slept by the river and the thoughts of individuals killing animals for their 'braggarts den' - that place where the great and daring hunters display the heads of their victims, bothered me. What a great accomplishment by these brave individuals who hide in the forest and kill some unfortunate, unsuspecting animal with a high-powered rifle! To me, it was no different from the slaughter of "Little Red" back in my Emerald Isle so many years ago and right on par with the stupidity of the bloodthirsty upper-class of European society who gallop around on their mighty steeds with a pack of hounds leading the charge over hill and dale to trap and have torn to shreds by the dogs, a little fox. And then have the gall to return to their upper class watering holes, down flagons of sherry and congratulate each other on work well done. Yes indeed. It was one thing to hunt to survive - another to kill just for the "sport of it".

The northern lights danced a dance of heavenly delight as I made my way back to the trailer. Jamie and Jo had a good supper cooking across the campfire and as darkness came full strength to the land, we watched with awe as the lights of the aurora swept like immense flaming sheets beneath the splendors of the heavens and I wondered: Does Raccoon, the bear juggler, understand anything about that stuff that goes on up in the heavens? Yes, it was a good day for us all to live - I just hoped the juggler would keep away from our camp.

The wood harvested, the season came to an end without further incident. The snows had moved down to the valley floor and soon this lovely piece of paradise would rest from the infringement of the outside world until the greening of spring infused its life force through the land once again. It was time to close it down and begin another operation in the mountains where roads were kept open throughout winter. These were the roads built by the logging companies and in those mountains of bitter winters men and machinery are tested to the fullest.

A MAN WITH A VISION

She's as miserable as it gets for winter, John," said Darcy Crugal, a man I had not seen for some months. Darcy was one of those fellows, usually quiet in nature until someone mentioned, the Justice system, lawyers and politicians. That was the devils triumvirate as far as Darcy was concerned but even worse; if the word environment or ecology slipped out of someone's mouth in conversation, then, the anger towards those responsible for the plunder and rape of our forests, the poisoning of our rivers, lakes, and streams; of our farm lands, parks, and oceans were the focus of Darcy's scorn. And I was not treated any less than those that dared, even by mistake to unwittingly dig up a topic on any of the above. "Are you still working up in the Fish river country"? Darcy said, in his easy-go-anyway-waiting-to-attack style."

"No Darcy, I finished there last week. I'm on my way to the Gold River country. I hear there is some real good shake-wood there," I answered.

"Yes, I hear so too, but I believe the logging companies are pushing farther and farther back to get at the bigger wood and before you know it, the last of the old growth timber will be a thing of memory," Darcy said, his eyes slowly building to a cold glow. "It's a God damn shame what the bastards are doing to the forests, it really is, and it seems there is only a handful of dedicated people who are standing against the swine," Darcy cried to the Heavens as though it was time for the Great god to come down and put us all straight. I hadn't intended to get Darcy rolling on about the bad, the ugly, and the more ugly but a storm from his oral cavity was brewing to ferocious immensity and there was not a darned thing I could do about it. I liked the guy and although he got hot about the collar on certain issues, I did enjoy listening to him in small doses.

It wasn't as though Darcy spoke a load of garbage. In fact, it was anything but! It was just that he went on a bit about things. Even so, it was refreshing at times to listen to what he had to say, and what he had to say, contained a whole lot of truth. Darcy had spent a few years studying at the University, and his thing - was life! It was life and what life was all about. It was about nature, respect, ignorance, love and stupidity. It was about plunder, rape, pillage, greed and hypocrisy, it was people living with their heads stuck in the ground, in a deluded world, destroying itself moment by moment. A world ripping the very life out of the planet that sustains it, and beyond the rape, the poisoning of every blade of grass, every leaf, every drop of water, every living thing on the earth and in the ocean, there are the dandelions killers. "You know what a dandelion killer does to our environment, John," Darcy said, his eyes growing more alive than an early morning summer sun. "They poison the very ground they dwell upon. The horrible pesticides they spray or have sprayed upon their gardens poisons everything it touches, then, finds its way to the ocean and there contributes to poisoning everything within the ocean's domain. Believe me John, humanity can be as thick as shit at the best and the worst of times," Darcy said his head turning slowly from side to side and concluded with the statement. "Dandeloin killers! - If only they had half an idea of the damage they do our environment just so they can have their squeaky, clean green lawns." The man said how it was and I could not argue. I could, however; wonder how much I had contributed to the pollution, the garbage and the poisons of my environment. Was I one of those useless bastards that he so scornfully called those in government and, the others – the general snoring mass of humanity? Perhaps I was! I had some thinking to do. After all, I was told by the wise one's of my Church that I was born something less than clean, and here, on the corner of the Trans Canada highway and a country trail, Darcy was reinforcing the teaching's of Mother Church. I did not like what I was hearing but as far as the environment was concerned, perhaps I was just as irresponsible as the many others. It was really time to listen and take stock of the many ways I was contributing to the pollution and filth-making in our very beautiful world. It was natural to ignore the poisonous vapors from my truck when I turned the ignition. After all, I needed my truck to do my work – to get around – like everybody else, but then again, did I?

    The Catholic Church told me I was born in sin. I certainly was not! But that is what they led me to believe - that I was the product of a union between my parents and that union was indeed a sinful thing and therefore I was a sin. So I looked at the world's population and I said to myself. "John! There are six billion people on the planet and they're all sinful things because they were born in sin. So if all the earth's inhabitants were born in sin, then it is only reasonable to assume that all life was born in sin; the deer, the buffalo, the kittens; the rabbits, the snakes, the hippopotamus' and old Shep, the bowser. And what about the flowers? What about the trees? Do they not have a unique energy? A mind of their own!" That's the stuff Darcy threw at me – the real stuff about life. He never told me I was born in sin, leaving me to feel that I was some sort of dirty human rag but he loaded me with a measure of guilt about the whole unclean affair of our biosphere, and truly, what he had to say, was the simple sad truth and... Darcy was not finished bending my ear.

"Have you seen the decimation of the forests out on Vancouver Island; in fact to the whole whack of the ancient coastal forests that ran from Alaska to California, John?" Darcy said, the coals of his eyes beginning to dance a bit of a burn.

"No, can't say that I have, Darcy. What exactly is going on?"

"They raped the whole blessed thing for Crrisss sake, except for a very small percentage in British Columbia and the greedy bastards want to get there filthy hands on the last remaining stands of the priceless forest; to finish the rape of the most sacred and beautiful places. In those places, John, there is creation at its most perfect and yet, we are too blind to see and feel the healing energies of the universe - of God, if you will – bubbling in these retreats beyond preciousness. Are you with me so far, John, boy?" Darcy said, indicating by his tone that he was just getting under way with his treatise on "The Human Environmental Blood Suckers", and if I had something to do of importance or unimportance, I had better forget all about it until he had concluded.

"Darcy," I said, doing my best to sound knowledgeable about the whole dirty affair. "We can't just stop everything and make a new plan!"

Darcy's hands reached to the Heavens as though he had created them. "That's just it! That's exactly what we got to do and we can do it. We better bloody do it before we destroy everything that's decent, and the rate we are going at it does not leave a whole lot of time before we all drop dead from the poisons and filth we are creating. Just think of the poisons and filth you create when you turn the key of your truck, John boy" he said, knowing he was making me fully aware of my complicity to the shameful scene mankind created. I was at a loss for words and indeed I felt overwhelmed, but one thing I knew for sure, Darcy was telling the real truth, the real down to earth truth. And the thought occurred to me that although I disagreed totally with the Catholic Church telling me I was born in sin, I might agree with them if they had told me I was destined to be a sinner. And so I am indeed a part of a very big sin and like most of the world's population, I have my head stuck in the ground pretending life is just fine and we are really all very happy, and if there are a few problems, the person capable of fixing them shall arrive in our moment of need.

And as always, at such times of self analysis, the words of George came creeping to mind: "the white man must eventually turn to the way of the Indian to save themselves Mr. John." And again, I thought, the people we must turn to, to help us back to sanity - we tried so hard to exterminate. We are indeed mad and undeserving of the immensity of Gods Love.

"You see, John," Darcy continued, his voice rising, snapping me out of my mind's wanderings. "We are not as clean as we think we are. In less than a hundred years – since the beginning of history as we understand it, we have made our home disgustingly filthy. We have to do something," Darcy said, as though it was a job for the two of us to clean it up, but I simply remained quiet and did not interject in the one-way conversation. "Unfortunately," Darcy badgered on, "irresponsible greedy bastards and spineless governments see only figures - dollar figures. And while such destructive individuals hold power and license, it can be surely expected that the rape of the forests, indeed, of all natural resources will continue.

It is so ironic that these greedy short sighted governments and conglomerates, alike, cannot see that responsible farming of the forests would provide sustainable employment for great numbers of people, vastly more than are employed presently in that industry. It is heart breaking to view from the air the staggering areas of forests butchered; massive swats of mountains, valleys and flatlands devoid of their life force, as though a gigantic scythe had leveled all that dwelled there. No sir! No different than the terrible destruction of Nagasaki and Hiroshima. The Indian folk have always referred to the trees as standing people. Standing people with a soul, with feeling and with a mind. How else would they grow, survive and develop? They are like cities of people working each moment to make sure that you and I have clean air to breath. Without them, we would not exist. Without them, the vast majority of wildlife would be extinct. And yet, look what we do.

Look what we allow ignorant governments and their crony backers do to the world of exquisite beauty and boundless life; life that we humans need to sustain us; life that the planet needs if it is going to survive. And yet, because we cannot see the terrible cancers creeping across our world, the terrible sicknesses we bring upon ourselves because of the filth we create, we say:

"Ah, there's got to be someone that can do something about it." Well there is – and it is you. And, until you wake up and get your voice heard, the plundering and filth making will go on. I mean for Chrissss sake, the Beluga whale is officially classified as a living pollutant. It's environment is so poisoned it is deemed one hundred percent toxic. And what about all the other creatures in the ocean? What about them? Are they not just as toxic as the Beluga whale? Listen, John, boy! Governments are made up of people, no different than you and me. But some of them are extraordinarily stupid and have no right guiding a nation. But they do! Who puts them there? So if we can put people in power, surely we can demand that the rape of our forests and poisoning of our environment stop.

In the Scandinavian and other European countries, their methods of tree farming are astoundingly successful, and that is because the people and the governments have control over the natural products of their countries and not a few foreign companies creaming the crop as we have here in Canada. What goes on in Canada in regards to the handling of our forests is indeed an anathema beneath the heavens," Darcy concluded, as though he had been waiting forty years to get what he unloaded on me off his chest.

"What is it about the trees of the ancient forest that is attractive to those greedy bastards, as you call them Darcy?" I said in a rather subdued tone.

"It is because the timber of the ancient trees are valued for their density. As a tree grows older, its grain tightens to almost that of steel. Such density affords a beautiful, high, natural finish. That is why the tree is butchered – for its characteristic warmth and loveliness. What a bloody joke! The sons of bitches bleed the land of its very life force and they can't see it's their life and everybody else's they're bleeding. The earth is suffering unimaginable shock, scarred beyond recognition, left as ugly as the minds and money that did it to her. Not the loggers! No sir, not the loggers! These good people must make a living like the rest of us and indeed their sacrifice is great. It's too bad that they are so thoroughly caught up in the greedy web of the few," said Darcy, as his torrents of verbal anger diminished to a fast trickle. I was fully aware I had been taken captive, but I had to wait until I could politely find a way of excusing myself, and then make a run for it. Eventually, Darcy exhausted his pent-up frustration on the matters of nature, corruption and dandelion killers leaving me to make a dash to my mountain retreat. I guess I just wasn't ready to recognize the terrible truth.

INVASION OF THE MARTENS

The road to the Gold River was opened up to the graders in the winter of '87. I managed to acquire a claim beside the logging company that operated in that area. It was a lucky break for me. To be able to use an open winter road was a big plus in the life of a shake-blocker and I was going to make the best of it.

I had prepared the trailer, purchased the tools and hardware that were needed for the job, precooked enough food to last me for two weeks, then, set out for the Gold River country in a blinding snow storm, with my precooked meals on wheels and the necessary wares to make my little trailer a happy winter home. All went well until the absence of my propane tanks was discovered, forcing me to return to Revelstoke.

Late that same evening, I arrived back. It had been a little difficult driving in the heavy snow but Trojan, the old 4x4 proved her worth. I looked forward to heating up the trailer, making fresh coffee and treating myself to some of the pre-cooked food. Then, the surprise! I had precooked about seven trays of chicken, pork, beef, pots of stew and spaghetti. With this assortment, I had also brought vegetables, bread, fruit and a few packets of sushi, rice and a sack of potatoes.

It was difficult to discern at first glance but upon closer inspection, I noticed that all my precooked food had been eaten. The door had been locked, as were the windows and roof vent. It was puzzling, to say the least, where my food had gone. I was not amused. I was really hungry, cold and tired and I needed a bit of comfort but it seemed that I was not going to get it. I decided to cook some potatoes, make a pot of coffee and try to figure out what had happened to my precious grub.

The plate of mashed potatoes went down quite nicely, as did the coffee and then it was time to bed-down for the night. The propane heater installed in the trailer did not work so I left the stove on to keep the trailer warm. It would not serve as well as the heating unit but it would keep the temperature at around zero. I would sleep the sleep of honest kings, awake come morning and return to the town to restock the provisions. However, it was not to be. A nightmare was about to unfold in and around my little trailer in the middle of the Canadian winter in the middle of the great Canadian forest.

Not even the wind murmured on this bright, moonlit night. There was a hush throughout the snow-mantled forest and through this blanket of quietness an uneasy feeling of being observed pierced my restless mind. The blue glow of the propane jet below my bunk added hues of foreboding to my unsettled state. It was ever so peaceful - too peaceful. The winter's grip on the land was a month old, giving me a measure of comfort that all bears were now in hibernation. Still, there was something amiss. What was it that caused my food to go missing? How could it have happened? There was no mess! The trays were picked clean as though they were washed and dried after use. Just what could it be?

My rifle stood in a corner near the door, fully loaded and ready for action if need be. I tried to convince myself that all was well with the world but it was just to quiet - too damned quiet. Tiredness began to take hold of my troubled mind and soon I felt myself drifting to meet the spirits of the little sleep.

Sometime during the early morning, I awoke to what I perceived to be the sound of someone knocking at the trailer door. Then it was silent. I thought perhaps, I was hearing things and tried to re-enter the deep sleep that had earlier overcome me. Then, I heard it again. Who could it possibly be? I knew there were no trappers or hunters out in this neck of the woods and the only people who were in my proximity were my friends the Monk family at Esso Ed's on the Downey Resort. However, they were a good fifty miles away, so who could the visitor be? Anxiety slithered into my voice as I called out "Who's there." I expected a reply but none came. The knock sounded again, and again I asked, raising my voice. "Who's there?" Still there was no answer. I was beginning to get annoyed with the whole situation but knew I had to unwrap myself from the bedding and check things out.

Outside the trailer, the temperature had dipped below minus thirty degrees. Inside, the glow from the propane jet did little to generate heat under such extreme winter conditions. By the time I had squeezed into my clothing, my body was barely functional. From past experiences with such weather conditions, I figured it would take seven to ten minutes for my body heat trapped beneath my clothing to raise my temperature. In the meantime, I was fully engaged in a one-sided conversation with whomever or whatever was outside the door.

Silence, snow, cold and ghosts knocking at my humble trailer door, lent an authentic air of quiet insanity to the unfolding mystery of the wilderness. I reached for my rifle but my hands were so cold that when I grabbed the steel, my flesh fused to it. I breathed rapidly against the steel of the rifle and the flesh of the palm of my hand - the hot air from my breath helping release a sticky situation. I fumbled with the rifle, trying to prepare it for potential battle. Eventually, the weapon was at the ready. This time, however, I avoided the problem I had with the firing pin in the Fish River country. . .

I was now ready but ready for what? Behind my trailer door, I remained immovable but for the shiver and shudder dance my body insisted on performing. The silence seemed to grow beyond its boundaries, broken only by the thunderous roar of a snow slide echoing across the valley, then into disturbing silence again. Still huddled behind the door as though it were the safest place to be in the whole of the universe, I toyed with the idea of wandering outside to investigate the unknown. However, two reasons told me not to bother engaging in such a venture - one being the loss of the meager heat from my trailer as soon as I opened the door and the other – there really might be a ghost outside.

The thought occurred to me as I lay tucked behind my little trailer door with my rifle at the ready, that I possibly had graduated into the great realm of lunacy. While I was mulling over the depth of my sanity or insanity, the sound of knocking once again broke the silence. "Who dat der?" I shouted with dignified alarm, as though a slight change to my accent would encourage the intruder to volunteer identity. Then silence again. Fear's icy maulers began to choke the life out of me. Perspiring from head to toe while immovable in the freezing position gives proof to such a statement.

I ventured my ear a little closer to the inside of my door, straining it for any movement on the outside. All remained quiet. Then, on a sudden, the rap, rap, rap, broke the murdering silence but this time, from the end of my trailer where my bunk was situated. I was now becoming angry and confused - not a favorable quality of mind under such circumstances. Pulling my tattered mind together as best I could, I decided to fire a shot through the roof into the universe, in the hopes of scaring whatever it was that had come to do me in but eventually dropped the idea as it would only put a hole in my roof, causing the measly amount of heat to escape. Then, suddenly, again at the end window beneath my bunk, a movement blotted the reflection of the moon. To be sure it was not a wandering cloud.

Again the breaking of the moon's beam! What could it be? Then fleetingly, three little faces appeared looking at me through the end window, leaving me with the impression that I was the intruder and those who owned the little faces wanted me out. Then they were gone, just like that! I was having difficulty believing I was not asleep experiencing a horrible nightmare, but a pinch on my flesh gave proof to my state of wakefulness.

THE SECOND PURPOSE

Once again the sound of rap, rap, rap was heard - this time coming from the roof of my trailer. What could I do? I was not sure. Did the three faces float to the roof and tap it with their noses? Oh, dear! How I wanted to call out for my mammy but manhood demanded I do no such thing.

Mustering as much physical and verbal expression as I possibly could, I decided to make a fight of it from the safety of my trailer. Thumping, banging, kicking and beating the walls of my little trailer, accompanied by the appropriate expletives, the valley of the Gold River country echoed with my liberated expression. It was a show like no other show on earth - all my own creativity - all my own performance. I was truly alive and well in the land of "let loose." Then, as suddenly as I had lost "it," I regained "it." Again there was silence. The strange language I had heard upon the roof of my trailer had ceased, the rap sounds had stopped and my world returned to a measure of normalcy. Whoever they were, or whatever they were, they must have been alarmed by my performance and took off to safer places. It was time for me to return to sleep.

Removing the handle from the broom, I secured a knife to one end of it, making a crude but deadly spear. As I lay drifting to sleep, beside me lay a loaded rifle and a very long handled knife - my arsenal of defense, just in case the creatures returned.

How long I had been sleeping when I was awakened by the sound of what seemed to be a hundred dancers, all dancing out of time and all talking in the strange language I had heard hours earlier, I do not know. Almost directly above my bunk, the roof vent was being pried open. That was it! Whatever animals were on my roof, which seemed to be a few battalions, had managed to squeeze the vent open and help them selves to the food in John's Rocky Mountain restaurant. Which animal? I did not know but I was about to find out. Patiently I waited, spear at the ready for the first creature to pop his head through the opening. All my yelling and screaming had been ineffective in scaring them away and I began to think that they might do to me what they had done to my trays of high mountain pre-prepared cuisine. It was not a comforting feeling.

The blue glow emitted by the propane stove seemed to add a deep sense of stupidity to my very unusual situation as I lay in my bunk waiting for the onslaught. Patiently I waited, so very patiently, for the first face to appear through the frame of the vent. I did not have to wait long. There he was, a cheeky little mush of a marten - cousin to the ferret and weasel, poking his head through the vent into my domain. I had him in my sights. He was done for. Like a flash, I drove the lance forward with the intent of impaling the little bastard that had had the nerve to break into my domain with all his cheeky buddies lining up behind him. Then, also in a flash, the supporting bar of my bunk slipped from its notch and out I sailed over my blue flamed stove, narrowly avoiding impaling myself on my spear.

It was not a pleasant experience because I landed on my shoulder, hurting it severely. The rifle was the next to arrive, thumping me square across the face. It only added a great touch more of unpleasantness because it was set on a hair trigger. The valley echoed and reechoed to the rifle's roar as I lay flat on the floor, my dysfunctional completeness garnished with an odd assortment of weaponry. Slowly, I raised my head to peer out the window and there, bouncing across the frozen, snowy landscape, were the battalions of martens heading to the trees from which they had come. The smell of cordite permeated my humble space as the invaders disappeared into the wilderness. It was the last I saw of them. I was thankful.

The frozen land soon gave way to the singing of springtime. Since the mad night of the martens raid, things had moved pretty steadily for me. I was getting a good supply of wood out to the mill and even saving a dollar. The Gold River claim worked itself out and I managed to secure a claim at Martha Creek, a steep, mountainous piece of land at the three thousand foot level, fifteen miles north of Revelstoke. The seasons moved on without mishaps, as autumn's carpet of ever vibrant foliage swept the land from mountain top to the shores of the magnificent Columbia, giving rise to nature's eternal changes of exquisite beauty. Here, in the high mountain meadows by the pristine streams, I lay my chainsaw down and on the back of an old cigarette package, penned the words of the loveliness of it all.

> *Have you been to the mountains, have you seen the tall trees*
> *Have you been to the mountains, to rest by the stream.*
> *It's here you find richness, the fullness of life,*
> *Where the wings of an eagle span the sky in its flight*
>
> *Have you been to the mountains in a midsummer shower.*
> *Such fragrance and beauty of the wilderness flowers,*
> *The songbird's sweet music, cast unto the wind*
> *Have you been to the mountains to rest by the streams.*

THE SECOND PURPOSE

It's here you find richness and the fullness of life
Where the wings of an eagle span the sky in its flight
The songbird's sweet music cast unto the wind
Have you been to the mountains to rest by the streams

Have you been to the mountains when the autumn steels in,
Such color, such beauty soothing within, the winds ever whisper
Through rustling leaves, have you been to the mountains
To rest by the streams

Its here you find richness, the fullness of life
Where the wings of an eagle span the sky in its flight
The songbird's sweet music cast unto the wind
Please come to these mountains, come rest by the streams

The snow's fell steadily through the winter of '88 making it difficult to work the forest. It was at times like these that the snowmobile proved invaluable, breaking trail and seeing me through to the work site. But the forest was beginning to take its toll on me. It was wearing me down mentally and physically. Day in, day out, trudging through fresh snow in search of the prized wood was a tough occupation. It was a high price for freedom - to be away from the busy world of society. At times, the only respite from my mental anguish was my preoccupation with digging beneath ten or fifteen feet of snow to test out the log that rested beneath its icy blanket - a tree, hopefully, that was cedar. Under such winter conditions, hours of digging, more times than not, yielded disappointing results - life could be cruel for some and out here was no exception. This land did not yield its treasures easily. The wilderness demanded respect - and if it was not given - it extracted its price.

It was a long, savagely cold day as I moved across the side of the mountain on my snowshoes, testing each lifeless standing tree for its soundness - all of which proved disappointing. Sometimes, I would fell the tree just to be sure about its quality of wood but each time would see it crash into the snowdrifts, smashing into a thousand pieces - the wood, too thin and brittle to be useful.

Sitting in a drift of snow, mulling over the ins and outs of life while winter is spitting its dreadful rage, is a very uncomfortable experience. Winds singing their mad song through the trees' snow-clad-boughs seemed to taunt my smallness in its domain of cold power. Then to its manifolds of icy scorn, an inner rage cast its fury to the wind.

The chainsaw sailed through the snow-freckled air as the scream of a madman echoed across the valley. My axe drove through the frozen face of an old rotten pine, lying horizontally across the hillside. The rage built in all its fury as I yelled in a language beyond expressions of expletives - those grinding, grunting sounds lost a half million years ago to our ancestors' history. A ranting, raving Irishman, in the middle of a Canadian winter's forest, had finally lost it. Kicking, yelling, screaming - running through the drifts of snow, I hurled my madness at anything that stood in my path as pent-up frustration unleashed its fury - the sounds of insanity jeering back at me as they escaped in rolling echoes over the frozen Columbia River.

Then, as suddenly as the insanity had gripped me, it spent itself. There, lying in the blood-spattered virgin snow, a quietness gripped my being - a quietness like that which lay beneath the frozen land. I wondered what had happened. I wanted to cry more than anytime I could remember but tears refused to blur my vision. The taunting winds seemed to sense my hurt, leaving me to the silence of their kingdom - as I pondered who and what I was, while the blood dripped steadily from a gash in the side of my head. I could not recall how I had gashed my forehead - it didn't matter. It was time to get back to work

Across the banks of a frozen stream lay a snow covered, gigantic tree. If it was a cedar, it could prove profitable. I decided to clear the snow from the top of the tree to check its bark. After an hour's shoveling, I exposed the bark all along its length. It was indeed a massive cedar. Daylight began to fade. I had little time left to work before darkness descended. Standing on the tree, I quickly made a test cut in the center of its long span, to check the quality of the wood. The chainsaw spit rich chips of cedar wood from the cut as the blade sank to the midway point of the tree where it lay across the ice-covered creek. I was not disappointed. It was beautiful, solid and knot free. It was time to head home.

Early morning light gave proof to a night of intense snowfall. The red flagging ribbon I hung from a tree the previous day, indicated my work area. After three hours of snow clearing, a two hundred foot long cedar lay uncovered - extending over each side of the banks of the creek - an impressive find indeed. The underside of the tree, a sagging belly from the tree's immense weight, cleared the face of the creek by only two feet but enough for my saw to cut from underneath - a method used in tree cutting so the blocks, when cut and loosened by the wedges, would fall freely to the ground - eliminating physical handling. Standing on the frozen creek, I began to dissect the tree by making undercuts. These cuts were designed to go from the ground upwards to the center of the log at two-foot intervals - the length of a roof shake.

Accompanied by intermittent blasts of winter's swirling winds, the snow fell relentlessly. From a gnarled branch of a leafless oak, the irritating cawing of a lone crow only added to the mocking forlornness of winter's face. Cumbersome snowshoes slowed my every move as I pounded in the wedges to release the blocks. It was difficult going. However, slowly but surely, huge blocks of rich, red cedar wood yielded to the pressure of the wedge.

From the root end of the tree, I knocked out block after block, working across the creek towards the tree's center. As the blocks of wood fell to the ground, the upper part of the tree began to straighten, releasing the strain on its sagging belly. As the tree rose, I was able to crawl beneath its great body affording shelter from the constant falling snow. The five-foot diameter trunk of this giant afforded me a measure of shelter as I drove in the wedges from end to end, rather than on the side of the tree. But something felt not quiet right. What was it? I did not know. It was a strange, ominous feeling.

The woodblocks continued to yield and as the bark of the wood accumulated, I built a windbreak along the length of the tree, affording me shelter from the winds bitter bite. All was well in the land of snow and wood. I was now a couple of blocks from the center of the tree's spread across the frozen creek. The belly of the trunk had lifted completely, allowing me to move beneath it on my knees. Still, something nagged at my mind, something disturbing but I could not identify it. My mind was perhaps flushed with the excitement of a huge yield of prime wood, thus, lessening my keenness to the dangers of the forest. Around me, the groaning and twisting of the trees, broken only by the echo of the wedge being hammered into the wood, seemed to beckon my attention. I became fully aware that something was about to happen and yet, I had no idea what it could be.

Beneath the center of the tree I tapped the wedge slightly until it gripped. I then brought the axe back across my shoulder and swung it forward to drive it home and split out the block

It happened in the twinkling of an eye. As the axe swung forward, I instantly realized what it was that was nagging at my mind. I had forgotten about the test cut I had made in the top of the tree the evening before. The sharp snap from the center of the tree collapsed the giant down on me.

From the bank of the creek, I could only wonder how I was standing thirty-six feet away from where I was just seconds ago. I knew I should be looking at my crushed body beneath the weight of the great cedar but I wasn't. I was safe - the path of snow to where I stood, unbroken by the slightest interruption. Someone was here, standing beside me. Someone I could not see. Someone had lifted me from the jaws of certain death, but who? I had no idea. Was it the One who had come in the form of the bright light? Was it the One who traveled from the far reaches of the universe in the form of a spark? I did not know but I was certain that an angel or a guide was protecting me from danger. I paced the distance back to the tree in long strides. It was exactly twelve paces across the undisturbed, virgin snow - thirty-six feet. It was also uphill.

Winter moved into spring and far away in the land of China, the tanks rolled through the streets of Beijing, killing an untold number of students who were peacefully protesting the government's undemocratic mandate. The world was shocked by the savagery in which the authorities crushed the peaceful movement. That same spring, in the peacefulness of my mountain domain I penned the words "A Flower Grows in China" to honor those who defied a brutal regime - to sound the call for democracy.

> *The Beijing night was starlit, the moon hung in the sky*
> *People voiced their anger, freedom was their cry*
> *A nation held in bondage, a country in despair,*
> *Somewhere in the mountains a sweet scent filled the air*
>
> *A flower grows in China, the blood rose of the spring*
> *From its ancient highlands, the voice of freedom rings*
>
> *But tanks and war machines tried to crush their dreams.*
> *In Tiannemen Square, where the people dared for true democracy*
>
> *Still, a flower grows in China, the blood rose of the spring*
> *From its ancient highlands, the voice of freedom rings*
>
> *The night fell black and the rifle's crack pierced the springtime air*
> *Blood ran red from the dying and the dead throughout Tiannemen Square*
>
> *Still a flower grows in China, the blood rose of the spring*
> *From its ancient highland, the voice of freedom rings*

IT'S TIME TO GO HOME

Spring passed into summer and again from the heights overlooking the Columbia River, I watched as autumn crept across the land then give way to the rage of winter. I felt a sense of longing as the chopper dropped the longline to haul up the last sling of cedar blocks to be flown to the awaiting trucks. "That's it for this show," Randy, the pilot, called over the radio.

"Yes my friend, that is it," I answered.

"Okay, I'll be back to pick you up," Randy called back.

"This spot seems as good as any for you to fly in low, Randy and pick me up. Bit of a rolling slope here but when you come in, I'll grab the skid and haul myself up and into the cockpit, okay?" I called over the radio.

"Roger. Be careful to ease up as slowly as possible, John. The 'Huey' (name of the helicopter) is pretty sensitive to unexpected movement. Don't take much to turn them over if there is a sudden shift in weight," Randy warned me.

"Okay, Randy, see you when you get back," I concluded.

From where I stood among the great cedars, I could hear the chopper hover momentarily while dropping its load by the trucks, then banking sharply and roaring up the mountainside to pick me up and take me out. As the chopper hovered above me, descending ever so slowly, the winds created by the rotors caused the ice and snow blanketing the treetops to dislodge, burying me in its "mini avalanche." Not a pleasant experience but a good laugh for the pilot as he watched while I dug myself out. Then, inch-by-inch, the chopper's skid on the passenger side came within reach of my outstretched arms. This was an extremely dangerous maneuver because once I grabbed the skid, I could not communicate by radio with the pilot and he would not be able to see where I was. However, rather than call the plan off, the unspoken madness of great and daring men kicked into high gear. Intuition was the order of the moment on the windswept mountainside of Martha Creek.

My hands at last clamped onto the sleek, icy skid and slowly, ever so slowly, I pulled my heavily clad body up until my knees were resting on the skid, then, grasping the door handle, I undid the latch, opening it wide to the wind. Then, ever so carefully, I reached across to undo the strap of my snowshoes. That done, I placed them on the passenger seat and prepared to climb aboard - then it happened! The moment every bush pilot dreads, his worst nightmare realized.

The winds had been blowing lightly and steadily throughout the day but their moans were ever ominous. Here, above the hillside of Martha Creek as I prepared to enter the chopper, a blast of wind struck solidly, toppling the chopper slightly but enough to loosen my lax grip and send me falling to the ground. The sudden, uneven balance threw the chopper to its side and only the masterful skill of the pilot took it back under control. It was a hell of a scare. We abandoned the idea. Two hours later saw me emerge from the bush. It had been a good day. It had really been good day.

Six years had passed since I took to the forest - it was twenty-five years since I had seen my Emerald Isle.

"Hello, is that you Marien?" I asked over the phone.

"Yes this is Marien," then there was a slight pause.

"Is that you John?" my sister said.

"Yes, dear sister, this is indeed your brother John. Would you be kind enough to pick me up at Dublin Airport tomorrow - I'm coming home."

Then there was that short pause of curious silence on the other end followed by a joyous scream! "Ah, Janey Mc, (Janey Mc is a term of endearment curious only to Dubliners, I think) you're not joking are you John?" said Marien.

"No dearest sister, I am not joking. Please let the family know."

The November snow fell lightly as the coach pulled out from Revelstoke. I was on my way to Calgary Airport. I sat back in my seat, pondering the past years since I had come to this old, historical town to sing at the King Edward Hotel. A lot had happened here. It was a tough world out in the forest but I would not have had it any other way. I grew up a bit out there. Further to the east the bus pulled into the town of Golden, picking up some passengers. A young Chinese lady sat beside me. She was a student visiting Canada. We talked about the horrible events that had recently taken place in Beijing and the peace in the land we traveled through.

At the Calgary Airport, I took my guitar from it case and sang the song, "A Flower Grows In China" for my new-found friends, Ana and her traveling companions. She cried softly, as did her colleagues. I would never see them again but I would surely never forget them. The Boeing taxied down the tarmac, took to the sky and set its course - north by northeast, out towards Greenland and then South towards my little Island in the Atlantic.

"Anything from the duty free store?" the hostess asked. I thought for a moment and then decided it would be a good idea to take advantage of tax-free liquor and cigarettes.

"A carton of cigarettes and a large bottle of rye whiskey, please," I answered. It had been a long time since I had ordered liquor. The enemy that had almost destroyed me, once again lurked in my possession. I wondered, as I had often done in the years of before, where this amber companion would take me.

The green land seemed to rise through its veils of mist, reaching to embrace the silver ship as it descended from the sky. At the airport, my family awaited. I did not recognize them or they me. I wandered for sometime hoping to be found and true enough a light tap on my shoulder beckoned my attention. I turned to look into the pretty face of a young blond haired woman. "Excuse me, but are you John?"... and the smile told it all. Twenty yards away, a platoon of people gazed longingly at the blond girls reaction. Then all smiled, as did Marien's twin, Joseph, who now stood looking down at me from a goodly distance. Soon, I would lay fast asleep in the room of my childhood and beyond the sleeping - the awaiting of words, drawn from those safe places in the heart. The precious souls I had not known before my journey - new guardians from the heavens, sang, danced and laughed a welcome to a man they had never known - a stranger from afar. Faces of the ones I loved were but vaguely familiar but the unseen connection made its strength known in the laughter of our hearts, moments of endearment, giving more worth to the meaning of life than the jeweled strengths of empires.

The garden was as lively as ever, giving essence in the form of Savoy cabbages and those hardy plants that stand against winter. "Be the hokey, son, those pigeons play havoc with the cabbages," my father complained. "They fly over from the Holy Ghost Fathers (a local seminary) and plunder to their hearts content and what's more, they never seem satisfied," my father said with a sigh that indicated the acceptance of the thieving birds that flew in from the Holy Lands. "Ah, shur, no matter what I do, I can't seem to hold them back... a bunch of flying devils... that's what they are," Dad said, as he studied the land and its life with that peculiar look of distant attachment, betraying a soft affection for the garden that gave him so much comfort.

The hard years had taken their toll on my mother but her quiet sense of dignity and grace blossomed above the pains of long gone days - bitterness and hurt cast to the winds. Here, once again, by the little fireplace, sisters and brothers gathered - less unruly as in times past.

Mother's voice, honed to pure loveliness from the gathering years, quieted the bouncing banter as that familiar melody of childhood carried on the wings of evening.

O' the days of the Kerry dances, o' the ring of the piper's tune
O' for one of those hours of gladness, gone alas like our youth too soon.

When the boys began to gather, in the glen on a summer's night.
And the Kerry's pipers tuning made us long with wild delight.
O, to think of it, O, to dream of it, fills my heart with tears.

BLAITHIN (LITTLE FLOWER)

As the songs were put to silence and the evening surrendered its laughter, the darling child looked to her mother and whispered: if Uncle John is taking me to stay at Aunt Tereasa's while you are at work tomorrow, then tell him he must hold my hand as he walks me to the cottage.

The chilling winds swept from the Dublin Mountains as I crossed the foothills by midnight - at my side, my young niece, Blaithin (Little Flower). The Moon was full in the sky, its veils softening the darkness of the land.

"Do you really have to go back to Canada?" the child asked.

"Yes, I must go back for a while Blaithin, but I will come back again," I said, trying not to invite further questions.

"Why do you have to go so far away? " she said.

"Its difficult to answer your question, little one," I said.

"Why is it so difficult to answer, Uncle John?" the princess fired back smartly.

"Oh, why do you ask such difficult questions, Princess?" I responded.

"I see nothing difficult about the questions so why is it so difficult for you to answer them," she said with that innocent air of authority that left my heart singing with easy frustration.

"Because young lady, there is something I must do there," I answered forcefully.

"Then you can tell me what it is, can't you, Uncle John?" she said in her soft Dublin whisper.

I was stuck because I was not sure what I was going back for and I was not sure what I was looking for and how does one tell that to a child without feeling absolutely stupid and yet, I knew she was not going to let me worm my way out of her relentless barrage on the question - but I would try. "I must go back because I have lived in Canada for a long time and I do have friends there," I said.

"Well, you can live here for a long time and you have friends here, besides, I want you to stay, Uncle John," the princess said, as she began to control what was quickly becoming a one-way conversation.

I thought it best to bring the discussion to an end before the child found me a job and got me settled down.

"You know Blaithin, I have been searching for something for a long time and I have not found it yet but when I do, I will write to you and tell you all about it. That is our secret and it must not be shared with anyone and I do promise I will come back, okay," I said.

"Okay, Uncle John, I won't tell anyone," Little Flower, said. There was silence for a moment as we gazed into the star filled sky and truly I wondered what it was my heart was searching for. I did not really know! But within moments another part of life's puzzle would surrender its mystery to me. The princess spoke again. "Uncle John, is there really a man in the moon?"

"You know Blaithin, I really don't know but if there is, I do hope he is wearing a nice woolly coat to keep himself warm," I answered smiling.

The midnight wind sang its dirge across the sweeping foothills. The man that once was, took the princess in his arms and as he carried her towards the safety of the cottage light beyond, he experienced for the first time, the grace of caring for another and in those sacred places of the heart, he knew his life at last had found meaning and so too, did his journey - a journey that was far from finished. And as he bid goodnight to the princess and his sister, he thought once again about the amber liquid snuggled within the safety of his backpack. How appealing it was to his senses. The silent killer once again beckoned. Would the precious meaning to life he had just discovered fall victim to the liquid that had sent him to the depths of hell so many times? Had what he had seen and horrified him that day so long ago in the garden of his childhood, do to him what had been done to the plants he had so carefully nurtured? He knew not from whence they came. He knew only that the slugs did, leaving the life that sprung from the rich, fertile soil butchered and withering back into the earth.

Printed in the United States
1347300004B/109-117